Created and Directed by Hans Höfer

INSIGHT GUIDES
BELIZE

Edited by Tony Perrottet
Main photography by Darrell Jones and Tony Rath
Additional photography: James Strachan and Tony Perrottet

Editorial Director: Brian Bell

HOUGHTON MIFFLIN COMPANY

APA PUBLICATIONS

BELIZE

First Edition
© 1995 APA PUBLICATIONS (HK) LTD
All Rights Reserved
Printed in Singapore by Höfer Press Pte Ltd

Distributed in the United States by:	Distributed in Canada by:	Distributed in the UK & Ireland by:	Worldwide distribution enquiries:
Houghton Mifflin Company	**Thomas Allen & Son**	**GeoCenter International UK Ltd**	**Höfer Communications Pte Ltd**
222 Berkeley Street	390 Steelcase Road East	The Viables Center, Harrow Way	38 Joo Koon Road
Boston, Massachusetts 02116-3764	Markham, Ontario L3R 1G2	Basingstoke, Hampshire RG22 4BJ	Singapore 2262
ISBN: 0-395-71053-7	ISBN: 0-395-71053-7	ISBN: 9-62421-197-3	ISBN: 9-62421-197-3

ABOUT THIS BOOK

as an old Belizean proverb graphically states: "Ax me no question, I tell you no lies, if you ax me again, I spit in your eyes." A few short years ago, anyone suggesting a travel guide to Belize would have been wise to keep their eyes covered. Few people had heard of the place, partly because, before it gained independence from Britain in 1981, Belize had been known as British Honduras. Even amongst the cognoscenti, who could actually locate the country on a map, not many could find a compelling reason to visit it.

All that changed in the early 1990s, and Belize was "discovered" virtually overnight. But, although there has been a deluge of guidebooks to Belize, most have been superficial or have focused purely on wildlife. The time was ripe for the combination of incisive text and stunning photography that makes the 185-title *Insight Guides* series unique.

The Writing Team

The book's editor, **Tony Perrottet**, an Australian writer and photographer living in New York City, has based his career on exploring the world's forgotten fringes: having graduated in history at Sydney University, he was lured to South America by tales of relatives who worked on the sheep farms of Tierra del Fuego. Perrottet spent several years as a foreign correspondent in Buenos Aires before becoming Insight Guides' editor-in-chief for South and Central America. He also edited *Insight Guide: Iceland* and photographed *Insight Pocket Guide: St Petersburg*.

No sooner was *Insight Guide: Belize* assigned than Perrottet was packing his mosquito repellant and heading for the tropics. During a month-long quest for contributors, he hired a four-wheel drive to scour the rainforest and visit the recently-exposed ruins of Caracol, battled two six-inch scorpions that slipped into his thatched hut in the Maya Mountains, and learned how to imitate the mating shrieks of howler monkeys while on midnight canoe rides through the jungle. As well as editing *Insight Guide: Belize* and contributing many photographs, Perrottet wrote the history chapters and sections North to Altun Ha, Lamanai and San Ignacio.

Belizean journalist **Karla Heusner** became one of two major contributors to the book. The daughter of American expats, Heusner draws on a dual cultural heritage for a unique angle on the country. Several doomed attempts to live in Los Angeles led her back to her roots to run a local TV newsroom (covering everything from international drug busts to the death of Belize City's most beloved mule). Heusner has volunteered on archaeological projects, taught primary school (the classrooms resembling a miniature United Nations) and written for regional Caribbean magazines – all the time studying the gestures and expressions that Belizeans take for granted. Amongst other topics, she has written the chapters on Belizeans, Food, Music, the Northern Cayes and her much-maligned home, Belize City.

The second major contributor to *Insight Guide: Belize* is **Tony Rath**, a US-born marine biologist and environmentalist who now lives in Dangriga. Rath first visited Belize in the late 1970s while working for the Smithsonian Insitution. Within a few years, he had married a Belizean, Therese (who is also current president of the Belizean Audubon Society and the owner of Dangriga's

Perrottet *Heusner* *Rath*

Pelican Beach Resort). For this volume, Rath penned the crucial chapters on Belize's fascinating wildlife and marine ecology, as well as writing on Dangriga, Placencia and the Far South. Rath's contribution also strengthened the volume's visuals: while still working part-time as a consultant to conservation agencies in Belize, he has turned more to freelance photography, developing his own agency, Nature Light.

Writing on Creole is **Dr Colville Young**, a Belizean professor of linguistics also renowned for his creative writing and music (including a folk opera, Creole songs and the *Missa Caribena*, the first musical setting of the Mass by a Belizean).

The difficult chapters on remote Orange Walk District and Corozal were tackled by US-born **Carolyn M. Miller**. She first came to Belize in the mid-1980s with her husband (they had been married only a month), both on assignment to study the Mussel Creek drainage system. The couple remained as conservation workers sponsored by the Wildlife Conservation Society (their advocacy was largely responsible for the massive Chiquibul National Park being declared in 1991). Today the Millers live in Gallon Jug, where they are conducting research near Chan Chich Lodge.

The chapter on Ambergris Caye (San Pedro) was written by New Orleans-based writer **Errol Laborde** (whose interest in Belize has nothing to do with the Confederate soldiers' settlement there in the 1870s).

Archaeologist **Joshua Starr** was asked to write the chapters on the Ancient Maya and Caracol when the editor ran into him digging on site in the middle of the rainforest.

The chapter on Tikal, in Guatemala, is contributed by old Insight Guide hand **Lynn Meisch**, an expert on Pre-Hispanic cultures. Having written her Master's thesis on the Mayan epic the *Popul Vuh*, she was the ideal candidate for explaining one of Mesoamerica's most astonishing sites.

The Travel Tips section was put together by Australian **Lesley Thelander**. An artist by trade, Thelander spent many weeks in Belize visiting bizarre hotels and lost jungle lodges to give the most up-to-date recommendations for a visit. Additional information for this section was provided by **Joanna Clarkson** of Trips, a British tour operator.

To solidify the photographic core of the book, Miami-based **Darrell Jones** was sent on assignment to some of Belize's remotest corners. With his work published regularly in the leading travel magazines around the United States, Jones is a Belize veteran: this was his sixth visit to the country.

Also contributing valuable shots was **James Strachan**, a London-based photographer who turned his attention to the visual arts after a career in investment banking.

Special Thanks

Special thanks also go to **Suzanne Stephan** of the Belize Tourist Board in New York City for the assistance she provided in organizing the Insight team's trips to Belize. In Belize, several anecdotes about the country's piratical past were suggested by **Emery King**, a North American native who found himself in the country when he was shipwrecked on the Barrier Reef in the 1950s (he has lived here ever since, and is now Belize City's best known historian, raconteur and bon vivant).

The book was proofread and indexed by **Pam Barrett**.

| *Young* | *Miller* | *Laborde* | *Meisch* | *Jones* |

History

People & Culture

Activities

Places

Maps

TRAVEL TIPS

Compiled by Lesley Thelander

**For detailed information
see page 305**

WELCOME

If the world had any ends, [Belize] would certainly be one of them. It is not on the way from anywhere to anywhere else. It has no strategic value. It is all but uninhabited.

— Aldous Huxley, *Beyond the Mexique Bay* (1934)

Huxley's off-hand observation remains the most famous made by a foreign writer about Belize, if only because he was one of the few to ever visit what was at the time the most irrelevent corner of the British Empire (and even then, Belize remained a minor footnote to Huxley's more hallucinogenic visions of the region).

Indeed, Belize's sheer obscurity had been the country's defining trait for centuries: first settled by English and Scottish pirates in the 17th century, it soon became a secret haven for loggers and their African slaves who operated under the noses of the Spaniards. By the 19th century, British Honduras (the name Belize was only taken upon independence in 1981) had became the ultimate backwater, an English-speaking, largely black Creole outpost in Central America.

In an irony that Huxley might have appreciated, Belize's centuries of under-development have guaranteed the country's greatest resource: nature. Today, Belize is squarely on the map as one of the world's leading "eco-tourism" destinations. Contained within its borders are vaste swathes of untouched rainforest, endless savannah and mangrove coasts, all containing the greatest variety of animal habitats north of the Amazon basin; off-shore, Belize's coral reef is the most splendid in the Western hemisphere, second in size and grandeur only to Australia's Great Barrier Reef. Add to that the over 900 ancient Mayan ruins scattered around the country and you begin to see why Belize has enjoyed a sudden popularity.

Even so, Belize's most beguiling attraction remains its Old World eccentricity. It's a place where villages are named Double Head Cabbage, Go-To-Hell Camp, Pulltrouser Swamp and Bound To Shine. With a population of less than 200,000, Belize remains relaxed and intimate as a small country town; yet, while everyone seems to know everyone else, it is one of the most cosmopolitan places on earth – a mixture of black Creoles, Spanish-speaking Mestizos, Mayans, Indians, Syrians, Mennonites, Chinese and North Americans, all getting along in a far more amicable fashion than most of the country's Central American neighbors.

There's a whiff of Joseph Conrad about the place (in fact, Nicholas Roeg filmed *Heart of Darkness* in Belize City, with hardly any extra props needed). The languid tropical decay and eccentric characters recall a Somerset Maugham short story. The film version of *Mosquito Coast*, Paul Theroux's modern tale of self-imposed exile, was also shot in Belize. So what makes the film world so enthusiastic about this small country? This *Insight Guide* tells all.

Preceding pages: the Belizean rainforest; Creole gal; dawn over the Maya Mountains; wreck on Half Moon Caye; on the Reef; a cab-driver's bounty, Belize City. **Left**, amongst the cayes off Placencia.

THE ANCIENT MAYA

When the first Western adventurers redis-covered the ancient ruins of Mesoamerica in the 19th century, they were dazzled by the size and beauty of the temples that lay hidden in the rainforest. But they were at a loss when trying to unlock the big puzzle. Who built these memorials to brilliant past achieve-ment? The Lost Tribes of Israel? Aliens from space? Maybe the lost civilization of Atlantis?

Of course, the identity of the great builders was right in front of them: the cities were built by the ancestors of the living Maya. But the faces on the stone monuments, the stelae, were hidden behind puzzling decorations and costumes that confused the modern trave-lers. They mostly failed to link the ancient and modern Maya until the American diplo-mat-cum-archaeologist John L. Stephens sug-gested the connection in his classic *Incidents of Travel in Central America, Chiapas and Yucatán* (1841).

Notes of the cruellest enemy: Today, schol-ars have pieced together an understanding of the ancient Maya from an ironic source: the writings of the Spanish Friar Diego de Landa, one of the most despised figures in all of Mesoamerica.

De Landa, a Franciscan who was sent to the Yucatán from Spain to convert the Maya, committed barbarous attacks on Mayan cul-ture in the 16th century, the most famous being the auto-da-fé in 1562 at Mani, where he destroyed the last known hieroglyphic Mayan texts (although at least four have been discovered since). Upon his recall to Spain to face legal charges brought against him for his actions, he wrote *Relación de las Cosas de Yucatán*, in which he managed to write a virtual ethnography of the Yucatán Maya in his legal defense. The ancient cities of the Maya had been abandoned long before de Landa's arrival, but his detailed accounts of 16th-century Mayan life have proved, with archaeological confirmation, that it was very similar that of their more famous ances-tors, whose culture reached its apex from

around AD 250–900 (the Classic Period).

De Landa's work also led to the modern decipherment of the Mayan glyphs. As one scholar has noted, "ninety-nine percent of what we today know of the Mayas, we know as the result either of what Landa has told us, or have learned in the use and study of what he told." Only with the recent translation of Mayan hieroglyphs have archaeologists been able to take the next step and recreate ancient Mayan life from writings found on monu-ments, tombs and other places.

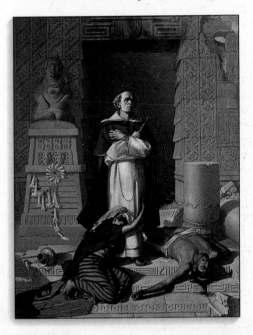

Unlike the Aztecs or Incas, the Mayan civilization was never unified and controlled by a single ruler. Instead, the region was controlled by competing cities, rather like Greek city states. Yet the whole region was unified through common cultural beliefs, technologies, languages, and trade.

The Mayan world view: At the core of ancient life was a belief that everything – animate and inanimate – had a place in a cosmic order, and that everything contained some form of spirit or power. This ideology con-tradicts the Western notion of separation between the natural and the supernatural or the unexplainable. The Maya considered

Preceding pages: restored Mayan frieze, Xunan-tunich. **Left,** carved Mayan statuette. **Right,** the Franciscan friars both attacked and defended the Maya, all in the name of the church.

time, stars, stones, trees, and various natural phenomena, to be alive and with power.

They believed they lived in a Middle World, beneath the 13 levels of the Upper World, and above the nine levels of the Lower World, or *Xibalba*. They believed in an after-life or a paradise, to which ruler, priests and those who die by sacrifice, suicide, in battle or in childbirth gained automatic entrance. And they believed in the destruction of an earlier world by flood.

A string of gods represented the same power held by all objects, but found in various forms: they appeared as different dates, days, colors and often had good and evil sides. Rituals and offerings to the gods in-

Human sacrifices: The ritual significance of blood was such that the Maya indulged in human sacrifice on a regular basis. Friar Diego de Landa, despite his cultural ignorance, gives a vivid account: "If [the victim's] heart was to be taken out, they conducted him with great display and concourse of people, painted him blue and wearing his miter, and placed him on the rounded sacrificial stone, after the priest and his officers had anointed the stone with blue and purified the temple to drive away the evil spirit. The *chacs* then seized the poor victim and swiftly laid him on his back across the stone, and the four took hold of his arms and legs, spread-

sured the continuance of the basic needs of life, health and sustenance. A complex procedure of sacrifices, fasting, feasting and incense burning was held on annual occasions, including New Year; and also used to induce rain, and for success in hunting, fishing, honey collecting and war.

The most powerful offering was blood – especially the blood of a king, who was considered a kind of god. The ruler would use an obsidian blade made from volcanic glass or a sting ray spine to pierce the penis, lip, tongue or earlobe and use the blood to anoint an idol. During the blood-letting, the king would hallucinate and visualize a fa-

ing them out. Then the *nacon* executioner came, with a flint knife in his hand, and with great skill made an incision between the ribs on the left side, below the nipple; then he plunged in his hand and like a ravenous tiger tore out the living heart, which he placed on a plate and gave to the priest; he then quickly went and anointed the faces of the idols with that fresh blood.

"At times they performed this sacrifice on the stone situated on the top step of the temple, and then they threw the dead body rolling down the steps, where it was taken by the attendants, was stripped completely of the skin save only on the hands and feet; then the priest, stripped, clothed himself with this skin and danced with the rest…"

In many rituals to meet with ancestors or other powers, the Maya would ingest special concoctions like *balche*, a mixture of fermented honey and bark from the balche tree. Special tobacco leaves were used to make cigars; some scholars speculate about the use of hallucinogenic mushrooms, peyote, water lilies, morning glory and glands from tropical toads (occasionally a quick ingestion by means of an enema). Incense was another mainstay at ceremonies – usually copal, which would be formed into small cakes.

Deciding the dates of many rituals was the elaborate Mayan calendar, based on precise

in history repeating itself every *katun* or 20-year period.

The Mayan timeline: It was during the Middle and Late Preclassic periods (roughly 800 BC to AD 250) that the Maya developed systems of agricultural terraces, raised fields and irrigation channels. The staple food was corn, or maize, which was controlled by its own god, Yum Kaax (also known as God E). Farmers would also allow wild trees and plants to grow – in cutting arable plots, the Maya were careful to not destroy the ecosystem and exhaust the topsoil.

The apex of Mayan culture was the Classic Period (roughly AD 250–900), when trade and the arts flourished. That was when the

astronomical observation. Their system of counting was vegidecimal – based on the number 20 – and they relied on two calendars which coincided every 52 years. The 260-day almanac was for ceremonial life, for birth dates, patron deities and perhaps for birth names. The 365-day calendar, *haab*, counted the solar year. The end of the 52-year Calendar Round was the end of a cycle, a powerful moment and a period of fasting, prayer and sacrifice. The Maya also believed

great cities were rebuilt into the great archaeological sites now in the jungles of Mesoamerica. The men of conquered cities possibly spent one month a year in work tribute to the victor, building *sacbeob*, the raised roads, or public architecture such as pyramids, temples and palaces. Otherwise, the local residents might do the construction themselves. The labor-intensive process of cutting, transporting (without pack animals or wagons) and placing the stones for the construction required a mind-boggling number of man-hours.

At some point in Mayan history, the rulers increased the number of human sacrifices –

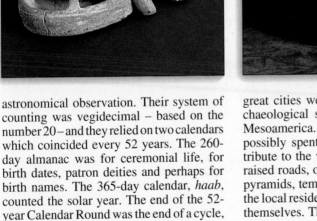

Left, artist's impression of the construction of a Mayan pyramid. **Above**, Lord of Lamanai. **Right**, the jade head found at Altun Ita.

possibly as natural resources diminished and the gods demanded extra blood in return for blessing. Prisoners were sought from neighborhood cities, so the confrontations snowballed. During the Early Postclassic Period (900–1200), Mayan culture collapsed quickly and mysteriously, and most of the great cities were abandoned. The causes of the apocalypse are still hotly debated by archaeologists, with everything from earthquakes, famine and disease thrown into the theorizing. However, a few cities – including Lamanai in modern-day Belize – survived until the arrival of the Spanish.

Everyday life in a Mayan city: At their height, the Mayan cities would have looked very woven sheet. The Mayan life cycle was carefully regulated. Upon a child's birth, the family and perhaps the shaman would look at the 260-day almanac to determine the destiny and character of the baby. The ancient Maya probably conducted something similar to the modern Mayan naming or *hetzmek* ceremony. Two godparents would carry the child and circle nine times around a table holding nine symbolic objects the child would use in adult life. The child would receive 3 or 4 names – a *paal kaba* or given name, the father's family name, the *naal kaba* or father's and mother's family names combined, and the *coco kaba* or nickname.

At age four or five, a small white bead was

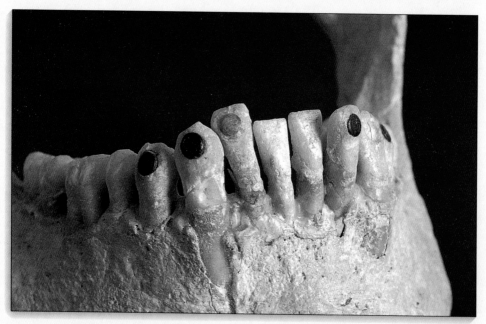

different from the skeletons one sees today. Imagine replacing the ocean of green rainforest with wide open areas of farms, roads and public plazas; the stone buildings were plastered and painted white or in various colors. Contrary to earlier belief, the cities were not solitary ritual centers for peace-loving priests, but were lively centers of commerce, art, bureaucracy, and power.

The average family lived in a thatched hut located on the outskirts of a city and a few miles from the family's maize field. The home might have an open front room for receiving guests and a closed back room for sleeping. Beds were made of reeds with a fastened to a boy's hair and a girl would have a red shell hung around her waist. These were to remain in place until a puberty ceremony when, before a public audience in a sponsor's house, priests would recite prayers and the youths would be anointed. After a gift exchange, the children could abandon the white beads and red shells.

The young unmarried men lived together and helped their fathers in farming, while the young women would be taught to be cooks, weavers, and housekeepers. Most adult men continued to work in agriculture, though other occupations were allowed – pottery, stone cutting, mining, salt- or shell- collecting and trading. The Maya used cacao and other natural items like red shells for money.

Matchmakers negotiated with parents and young couples to arrange marriages. The groom's family would give a dowry of dresses and other articles. The marriage ceremony was brief, followed by a small feast for the families and special guests. The son-in-law lived and worked for six or seven years with his in-laws. Apparently, divorce was simple: the Maya were monogamous, but the men eagerly left their wives for other mates.

In death, relatives would silently mourn by day and wail in sorrow at night. The family often buried the deceased inside or near their home, and unless the family was

would have dangled balls between their baby's eyes). All Mayan men had a bald spot burned into their pates. And some men would file their teeth to a point and inlay them with pyrite or jadeite.

Not all Mayan fashions were so dramatic. Common Maya men wore a loincloth, or *ex*, wrapped around the waist and often decorated with feathers, designs and faces. Covering their shoulders was a square cotton *pati*, decorated according to their position in society. Women wore a variation of the *huipil* still worn today in Mesoamerica – often white dresses or blouses with square cutouts for the head and holes for arms – along with a *booch*, a strip of material thrown over the

very large, they would soon abandon the house. More important people were either cremated or buried in elaborate vaulted tombs – often with food and currency like jadeite as well as idols and tools.

High fashion, Mayan style: The ancient Maya had some unique concepts of beauty. A good-looking Mayan aristocrat would have had his or her forehead well flattened (the parents would have bound their heads as children between a pair of wooden boards). He or she might be artificially cross-eyed (the parents

Left, ancient dental work. **Right**, a noble's skull, deformed for aesthetic purposes.

head that acted as a headdress and scarf. Both men and women wore double-thonged leather sandals that were bound to their ankles with rope; their black hair was worn long and often braided.

The upper classes wore more colorful costumes with intricate woven designs, animal skins and feathers (including the quetzal). Priests wore jaguar skins. High-ranking Maya wore a dazzling range of jewelry – bracelets, necklaces, earrings, nose rings, lip plugs and pendants made from jade, shell, teeth, claws, wood and stone. Every few days, men and women also anointed themselves with a red, sweet-smelling ointment. The men would often paint their bodies: unmarried young men black, warriors black and red, priests in blue (the color associated with sacrifice).

Ritual ball game: The intimate connection between daily life and the supernatural is shown by the role of a ball game played in every Mayan city. The game was also played to reenact parts of the creation myth, the *Popul Vuh*, in which the Ancestral Hero Twins trick and defeat the Lords of Death of *Xibalba* (the Underworld). In Mayan legend, the ball court was where the legendary Twins actively challenged and outwitted the gods.

The basic rules were simple enough. Two teams using only particular body parts – usually hips or knees – tried to send a rubber

language, the most common being Yucatec. In ancient times there were also many varieties, but only one form of written hieroglyphs, a standard used throughout the civilization.

A key source of glyphs are the stelae, tall needles of stone planted to resemble ceiba trees. They were commissioned to commemorate important anniversaries, bloodlettings, conquests and coronations. The messages solidified the power of the ruling lineage over their own people, and let visitors know whose land they were entering. It is uncertain how many people could actually read these messages, however. For the illiterate masses, the geometric and free form designs in pottery, clothing, stelae and archi-

ball through a hoop sticking out of a wall or atop a post in a playing field between two parallel buildings. The rules, team size and court size would vary by region and changed through time. One famous tradition held that upon shooting the ball through the hoop, the successful player could then claim the jewelry of the spectators unfortunate enough to witness the event. The game often held ritual significance when played by nobility or rulers, or with captives (who, when they lost, were sacrificed and sometimes bound up like a ball and rolled down pyramid steps).

Deciphering the Mayan writings: The Maya today speak nearly 30 variations of the Mayan

tecture may well have communicated the same propaganda.

Modern scholars have uncovered only a minuscule portion of ancient hieroglyphs (others are found on painted ceramics, rooms and tombs). Spaniards like Friar de Landa destroyed many scrolls, wooden carvings and outdoor stucco mouldings, while centuries of torrential rains have taken care of the rest. Even so, the remaining glyphs are a treasure chest of secrets, the key to slowly turning Mayan studies from speculation into actual history.

Left, and **right**, pieces of Mayan pottery.

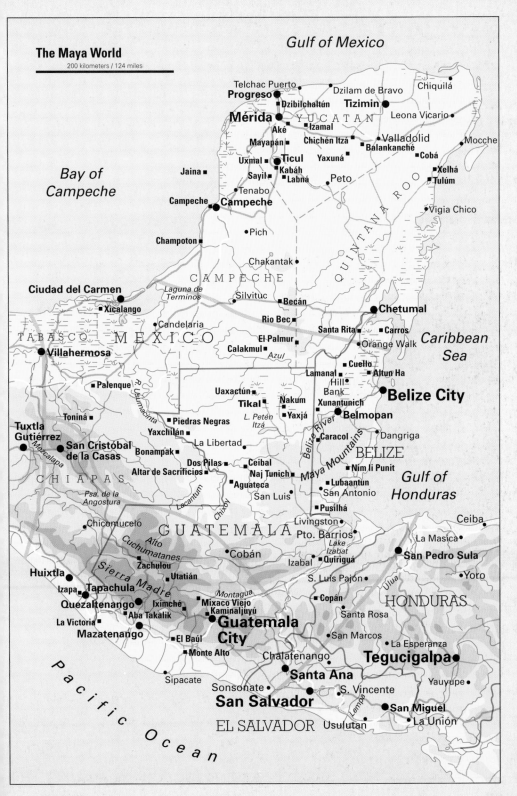

The Maya World

200 kilometers / 124 miles

Gulf of Mexico

Bay of
Campeche

Telchac Puerto
Progreso
Dzibilchaltún
Mérida
Aké
Mayapán
Uxmal
Jaina
Sayil
Kabáh
Ticul
Tenabo
Campeche
Campeche
Champoton
Pich
Chakantak

Dzilam de Bravo
Tizimin
Chiquilá
Leona Vicario
YUCATAN
Izamal
Chichén Itzá
Valladolid
Mocche
Balankanché
Yaxuná
Cobá
Xelhá
Labná
Peto
Tulúm
Vigia Chico

QUINTANA ROO

CAMPECHE

Ciudad del Carmen
Xicalango
Candelaria
TABASCO
Villahermosa
MEXICO

Laguna de
Terminos
Silvituc
Becán
Rio Bec
Santa Rita
El Palmur
Calakmul
Azul

Chetumal
Carros
Orange Walk
Cuello
Lamanal
Altun Ha
Hill
Bank

Caribbean
Sea

Palenque
Toniná
Tuxtla
Gutiérrez
San Cristóbal
de la Casas
Bonampak
CHIAPAS

Uaxactún
Tikal
Nakum
Piedras Negras
Yaxchilán
La Libertad
Dos Pilas
Altar de Sacrificios
Psa. de la
Angostura

Xunantunich
Yaxjá
L. Petén
Itzá
Caracol
Belize City
Belmopan
Dangriga
BELIZE

Gulf of
Honduras

Chicomucelo
Huixtla
Izapa
Tapachula
Quezaltenango
Aba Takalik
La Victoria
Mazatenango
Sipacate

Ceibal
Naj Tunich
Aguateca
San Luis
GUATEMALA
Cobán
Izabal
Zachulou
Utatián
Iximché
Mixaco Viejo
Kaminaljuyú
Guatemala
City
El Baúl
Monte Alto
Chalatenango

Ceiba
La Masica
San Pedro Sula
Yoto

Nim li Punit
Lubaantun
San Antonio
Pusilhá
Livingston
Pto. Barrios
Lake
Izabal
Quiriguá
S. Luis Pajón
Copán
Santa Rosa
San Marcos
La Esperanza
Tegucigalpa
HONDURAS
Yauyupe
San Miguel
La Unión

Santa Ana
San Salvador
S. Vincente
EL SALVADOR
Sonsonate
Usulutan

Pacific Ocean

In Belize City they sell a T-shirt proclaiming: "Where the Hell is Belize?" It has ever been thus. Well into the 17th century, when Spanish rule had been ruthlessly stamped on the rest of Central America, authorities were only barely conscious of the region that now goes by the name of Belize. Spanish explorers avoided its coral reefs, and few conquistadors or missionaries ventured south of the Yucatan. Those that did reported none of the cities of silver and gold that would excite a conqueror's imagination, only murky swamps and mosquito-filled forests.

Nor were the local Maya Indians friendly. Their first encounter with Spaniards set the tone for relations, when a handful of shipwrecked sailors landed in northern Belize in 1511. Five were sacrificed, their still-beating hearts torn from their bodies, and the rest were made slaves. Most Spaniards decided to seek their fortunes elsewhere.

As a result, Belize became the first refugee crossroads of Central America. Thousands of Maya Indians fled the Spanish subjugation of Mexico and Guatemala in the 1500s, which reached ferocious heights of cruelty. During Alonso Pacheco's campaign against the Maya of Chetumal, for example, conquistadors routinely garotted Maya men and women, threw them into lakes tied down by weights, chopped of their prisoners' noses, ears or hands, and had others dismembered alive by wild "dogs of war."

Those Maya that survived faced enslavement, the break-up of their families, and relocation. Little wonder that the Franciscan monks who brought the gospel (and demands for Spanish taxes) into the Belizean jungle in the early 1600s provoked open rebellion. The few churches the missionaries managed to build were soon sacked and burned down.

Logwood and piracy: The Maya of Belize got on much better with a few motley Britons who turned up along the Bay of Campeche in search of logwood. The British were out simply to remove a few trees and make

money, and showed not the slightest interest in taxing or converting anyone. Their small camps congregated in Belize's most miserable swampland, where the hard-as-stone logwood was to be found – its black, red and gray dyes were essential for the woollen industry in Britain, fetching logwood £100 a ton, a small fortune in those days.

At first, the Spaniards ignored them. But before long, the barely inhabited coastline of Belize began to attract another kind of British entrepreneur: the buccaneer. It was a perfect

hideout for a Caribbean freebooting operation. The buccaneers sailed fast, shallow draft ships that could chase down a heavily laden Spanish merchantman, capture the cargo and out-pace the pursuing warships. Once inside the Belizean reef, with its low water, treacherous coral heads and mud flats, they were safe. From there, the loot could be transported to the Bahamas, Bermuda or, after the British captured it, Port Royal in Jamaica, where the market for plundered goods was insatiable.

One of these "Gentlemen of the Coast" was Captain Peter Wallace, who in 1634 sailed his ship the *Swallow* into the shallow

Preceding pages: a pirate with his captives. **Left,** a triumphant raid on a Spanish town. **Right,** walking the plank was more artistic license than actual pirate practise.

harbour that would eventually become Belize City. A Scotsman who had served under Sir Walter Raleigh, Wallace remains a shadowy figure. Nobody knows if he was strictly speaking a "buccaneer" (captain who preyed on the enemy) or "pirate" (one who preyed on his own nation's ships); he was reputed to be behind a whole fleet of ships pillaging the Caribbean. Whatever the truth, it is probable that Wallace gave his name, in corrupted form, to Belize. (Others suggest it comes from the Mayan word *beliz*, "muddy-watered," which accurately describes the Belize River for much of the year – but the Wallace connection is usually cited as more romantic.)

The pirates' conversion: Logwood was a valuable enough commodity which many buccaneers logged in their spare time. Some of the most famous names in Caribbean piracy – "Admiral" Benbow, Bartholomew Sharpe, Edward Low, William Dampier, "Blackbeard" Teach, Nicholas van Horn, William Bannister and John Coxon – were all, at one time or other, involved in the trade. Together, they make up a Who's Who of 17th-century villainy.

The legend of Blackbeard: None was as picturesque, or enduringly remembered, as Edward Teach, better known as Blackbeard – who, according to local legend, spent a good deal of leisure time hiding out on Ambergris Caye. According to records of the day, Teach was such a terrifying sight that crews of enemy ships were known to throw down their arms without a fight. His huge black beard, one writer noted, was "like a frightful meteor," hanging down to his waist and twisted with colored ribbons. In battle he wore a leather holster with three pistols over each shoulder. More oddly, he "struck lighted matches under his hat, which, appearing on each side of his face, his eyes naturally looking fierce and wild, made him altogether such a figure that imagination cannot form an idea of a fury from Hell to look more frightful."

This archetypal pirate was born in Bristol, went into training in Jamaica, and embarked on his pirate career by pillaging the coasts of Virginia and the Carolinas. After capturing a large, 40-gun French ship, which he renamed Queen Anne's Revenge, Teach began to roam the Caribbean, often using the Belizean cayes off the Gulf of Honduras as a rendezvous (Ambergris Caye was one of his favorites, and fanciful tales of buried treasure are sometimes still trotted out in the bars of San Pedro).

A surviving fragment of his log shows a typical day under Blackbeard's command: "Such a day, rum all out – our company somewhat sober – a damn'd confusion amongst us! Rogues a plotting – great talk of seperation – so I look'd sharp for a prize – such a day, took one, with a great deal of liquor on board, so kept the company hot, damned hot, then all things well again."

As he captured more ships, several crews agreed to join Blackbeard in his depredations, until he commanded a small fleet. Things were going so well that when one English captain informed him of a royal decree pardoning all pirates who ceased activities, he laughed in derision. The only major problem seemed to be venereal disease, which drove Blackbeard to lay siege to Charleston, Carolina until several hundred pounds' worth of medical supplies were provided.

Finally, desperate merchants and shippers appealed for help to the Governor of Virginia, who hired Lieutenant Robert Maynard of the Royal Navy to hunt down Blackbeard in the heavily armed *Pearl*. They caught him off the North Carolina coast, and the following dialogue was recorded:

Blackbeard: "Damn you for villains, who are you? And whence came you?"

Maynard: "You may see by our colors we are no pirates."

Blackbeard demanded that Maynard come alongside so he could be seen, but Maynard replied: "I cannot spare my boat, but I will come aboard of you as soon as I can with my sloop."

Blackbeard (swilling a jug of rum and toasting his enemy): "Damnation seize my soul if I give you quarter, or take any from you."

Maynard: "I expect none, and will give none."

After this exchange, the two opened up cannons on one another. Maynard hid a number of his men below decks, tricking

Although feared for his ferocity, Teach earned the grudging respect of his enemies. He showed great tactical skill, fought to the death and never harmed his prisoners – a true "Gentleman of the Coast."

From larceny to logging: The death-knell for Caribbean freebooting was tolled in 1670, when a treaty between England and Spain pledged to supress piracy on the high seas. Although it took a long time, the assorted captains and crews eventually realized that the hangman awaited, whoever captured them. Many decided to try logging full-time, and settled around the mouth of the Belize River – a humid, swampy delta chosen not for its setting, which was dismal, but because

Blackbeard into boarding with only 13 men. Realizing his mistake, Teach flew into a drunken rage. As the deck ran thick with blood, several guns were fired point-blank into Blackbeard's body, without obvious effect. He knocked down Maynard in a cutlass duel and received 20 sword slashes before suddenly dropping dead from lack of blood. Maynard, wounded but not mortally, lopped off the pirate's head and hung it from his bowsprit.

Left, Edward Teach, alias Blackbeard the pirate. **Right**, Blackbeard's last stand against Lieutenant Robert Maynard.

this was where logs were floated from the many up-river camps.

The whole was referred to as the Bay Settlement, and its inhabitants, Baymen. By 1700, a rough society of some 300 people was beginning to emerge, commuting to the logging camps, called Banks, up-river. Few English women dared settle here (even the prostitutes preferred the bright lights of Port Royal in Jamaica), although some loggers took Mayan women as common-law wives, starting up the famous Belizean melting pot.

One upper-crust ship's captain who was wrecked here in 1720 was horrified by the lawlessness he found: "The Wood-Cutters are generally a rude drunken Crew, some of which have been Pirates; their chief Delight is in Drinking; and when they broach a Quarter Cask or a Hogshead of Wine, they seldom stir while there is a Drop left... keeping at it sometimes a Week together, drinking till they fall asleep; and as soon as they awake, at it again, without stirring off the place. I had but little Comfort living among these Crew of ungovernable wretches, where there was little else to be heard but Blasphemy, Cursing and Swearing."

The arrival of the slaves: This small society of reformed pirates and drunkards was transformed when the world's best quality mahogany began to be pulled from the river to set up a loosely-structured logging camp. Every slave had a machete or an ax, a few were given muskets and pistols. Each slave had his own tent, wherever he wished to build it, and if the slavemaster had a whip, he probably used it on his mule.

Meanwhile, local slave laws baffled foreign visitors. For example, slaves only worked five days a week. If a slave worked on Saturday, he had to be paid. A slave could buy his freedom, and many did, and any black man who turned up in Belize was declared free unless proven otherwise. Any female slave who was taken as a common-law wife or mistress by a settler was freed, and by the late 1700s a substantial portion of

rainforests. Mahogany was much more valuable than logwood – the rich and powerful demanded it for their furniture in Britain and across the American colonies – and required a larger workforce to extract it. New fortune seekers arrived in Belize, bringing with them boatloads of black slaves from Jamaica.

With names like Congo Will, Guinea Sam or Mundingo Pope reflecting their African homeland, the slaves soon outnumbered white settlers by roughly ten to one. Belizean slavery was a very different institution from that in, say, the southern United States. Instead of rigidly controlled plantations, a white slaver might take a handful of slaves up the

the settlement was recorded in the census as people of "Mixed Colour."

Despite all this informality, slaves had next to no legal rights and slavery could be just as brutal in Belize as anywhere else. Several small-scale rebellions occurred in the bush, including one where six white men were murdered and a dozen slaves escaped to freedom in the Yucatan.

Frontier democrats: The free Baymen ruled themselves by voting for magistrates at a public meeting – much the same way that pirate captains had been freely elected by their crews. All free men could vote, regardless of property or color, to the disgust of visiting aristocrats (although women could only look on from the balconies, waving their handkerchiefs).

Meanwhile, Belize Town was growing, filling up the swampland with wood chips, conch shells and empty bottles of Santa Rita rum. The whites and "free coloreds" lived on St George's Caye a few miles offshore, flanked by a small fortress, while on the mainland a warren of backstreets developed for the black population. As in other Caribbean outposts, African religious practices such as *obeah* were rife, despite attempts to control it. (Slave revolts in other islands had made the white settlers nervous, and the night-long playing of gombay drums was

remote river (after first digging about with your "setting pole" to clear out the snakes and crocodiles). In the dry season, families headed up-river to their Banks, living in tents and eating "bush stew" of gibnut, turtle and peccary, spiced up with fried plaintain and Johnny cakes ("No man should crave more toothsome food," wrote a contemporary).

It was back-breaking work, but lucrative: one Scottish family who moved to Belize bought a moderate holding up-river and earned £5,700 in the first season.

Trouble with the Spaniards: Although vast fortunes were to be made in the Belizean forest, the life of the loggers was desperately insecure. Apart from tropical diseases,

banned as they "deprive the Inhabitants therein from their natural rest.")

A dozen or so of the richer, older white families became known as the "Old Baymen" and made up a minuscule locally-born elite. They made a half-hearted attempt to maintain their British way of life in this malaria-ridden outpost. A Presbyterian church service on Sunday, said under a canvass canopy with the congregation in stifling black coats, might be followed by an afternoon's fishing from a dory, or wooden dugout, and swimming in a

Left, baymen in the swamps. **Above**, dangerous overcrowding on a slaving ship.

poisonous snakes and clouds of mosquitoes, there was the Spanish threat. The Spaniards had never recognized the British presence, and the story of the 18th century is one of constant conflict between the settlers, cut off from Britain or any outside aid, and the surrounding enemy. (And since the majority of settlers were of Scottish origin, they saw an English prejudice in the authorities' indifference.)

Not that the Baymen were blameless. Although a treaty was fleshed out in 1765 to limit their activities, loggers continually crossed into Spanish territory, bribing frontier guards and customs officials, and smuggling anything they could into Mexico. Meanwhile, bandits based in the Yucatán made continuous forays into Belize, often storming the isolated logging Banks. One chronicler records how his young fiancée, fresh off the boat from Scotland, was kidnapped by a bandit named Diego Bustamente while she was paddling a canoe near the camp. Friendly Indians led the Baymen to a remote Mayan ruin, where Diego had holed up and was preparing to force himself upon his captive. The settlers were able to surprise the bandit and his men, cutting them to ribbons with their machetes and rescuing the distraught woman – who, inexplicably, chose to remain in Belize.

Throughout the 1700s, the Spanish kept up raids on the timber camps, but the Baymen could always slip away into the forest. The conflicts with Spain might have remained petty and limited except for the American War of Independence. The Baymen first learned about it when a strange ship, *The George Washington*, pulled into St George's Caye. A few citizens went out in their dories to meet Captain Hezikiah Anthony of the United States Navy, only to be immediately imprisoned as ransom for rum.

Unfortunately for the Baymen, the American struggle prompted Spain to declare war, yet again, on Britain, and use it as an excuse to wipe out Belize. A sizeable Spanish force attacked St George's Cay in 1779, burning it and Belize Town to the ground. Most of the Baymen escaped into the forest, but the unfortunates on the Caye were captured and sent on a forced march 300 miles (480 km) into the Yucatán.

One Bayman, Tom Potts, was captured with his wife Charlotte and daughter. The hard-bitten couple survived the forced march, and had a second child in a dungeon while awaiting trial. After several more years in a prison in Cuba, they were released and headed back, by land and sea, to Belize – and Potts eventually became Belize's Chief Magistrate.

The final conflict: The Bay Settlement was rebuilt, logging recommenced and and new arrivals of British settlers, forced by treaty to leave the Mosquito Shore of Honduras and Nicaragua, boosted the numbers back to over 3,000 souls. Then, in 1796, Britain and Spain started squabbling again in Europe: this time the battle for Belize would be for good.

News of an imminent invasion caused a commotion amongst the Baymen. Public meetings turned into riots over the question of whether to stay and fight. Running away from the Spaniards was an old and honorable tradition in Belize, and many favored it now. After all, the British authorities offered no protection other than a single gunship from Jamaica.

Others were adamant to defend the colony: it had grown too large to abandon, there were too many fine buildings and too much equipment could be lost. Tom Potts, the chief magistrate who had personal experience of Spanish dungeons, wanted out, but Thomas Paslow, a fiery Irishman, thundered that "A man who will not defend his country does not deserve to reap the benefits of it."

In a near vote – 65 to 51 – the majority elected to remain. Many of the deciding votes were cast by a group of free blacks led by Adam Flowers. Despite the acrimony, however, everyone stayed to fight: not a single Bayman left.

The Baymen spent the next couple of years preparing for an attack. Finally, on September 3, 1798, a Spanish force of 32 ships, including 16 heavily armed men o'war and 2,000 troops, bore down on the Baymen. They had managed to dig in on St George's Caye and had armed all the slaves, but their rag-tag naval forces consisted of one Royal Navy battleship, the *HMS Marlin*, five schooners and seven logwood barges fitted out with a single cannon each. But the Baymen had geography on their side: when the Spaniards advanced, four ships were bogged in mud flats and blown out of the water.

Every day, the Spanish advance party was pushed back. Finally, on September 10, the Spaniards made a major effort to land on St George's Caye. This time they were caught in a narrow channel and ravaged by the Baymen's fire. The British naval officers attempted to coordinate an attack on the foundering ships, but the boatloads of slaves and free blacks attacked without orders (and with great success – the sight of the huge slaves, with machetes in their teeth and a pistol in each hand, was terrifying). The Spaniards withdrew, this time forever, and the settlement, for the first time, was secure.

A century later, September 10 was declared a national holiday in Belize, and the battle of St George's Caye is celebrated to this day.

Left, surprise attack on the high seas.

At the smoke cleared after their victory St George's Caye, the Baymen jubilantly looked forward to the 19th century as a new era of peace and prosperity. With the Spanish threat broken, it seemed that they could carry on making fortunes from logging and bathe in a glow of patriotic pride. "Many colonies have been won for England by her brave soldiers and sailors," crowed one Bayman in his memoirs, "but British Honduras is, I believe, the only one in which a mere handful of settlers, without help from home, wrested the lands from a powerful foe and added them to the British Empire."

Things were not, of course, that simple. News of the great victory barely reached the halls of power in London, where the Napoleonic Wars were of far more immediate interest. As far as the British government was concerned, Belize was more of an irritation than a valued aquisition. It was not officially a part of the Empire at all. The Baymen were not even British subjects – they were just a unruly bunch of loggers, working in a godforsaken backwater, entirely on Spanish suffrance.

It was not until 1862 that Westminster officially recognized Belize as the Colony of British Honduras, sending out a proper governor and ordering a colonial parliament. But Central America remained all but unknown to the outside world, and played next to no part in the great strategic struggles of the day. In short, British Honduras may have become a part of the Empire, but to the politicians and traders who orchestrated it, the acquisition seemed almost an irrelevance.

An American in Belize Town: One of the few who took an interest in Belize in this period was the American John L. Stephens, an amateur archaeologist whose memoirs form the basis of modern research on the Mayan empire (they are still in print and widely read to this day). The account provides the classic view of Belizean society in formation.

Arriving in 1839, Stephens found Belize Town firmly established as the settlement's

Preceding pages: South Regent Street, Belize City, at the end of the 19th century. Left, mahogany cutters. Right, a river log jam.

capital (during the battle with the Spanish, the Baymen had burned every building on St George's Caye, so they wouldn't fall into enemy hands). Indeed, when seen from a distance, the town was almost picturesque. Seeing several boats in dock and dozens of canoes plying the river, Stephens was moved to compare it to Venice or Alexandria. Equally impressive were the canoes that came out to his ship, made of single, huge mahogany trees that would have been worth a fortune in New York City.

A fine wooden Government House had been built by the shore, lined with groves of coconut trees, and a bridge over the river. Settlers imported bricks from London – the same used to build mansions on Regent Street, they noted with some pride – to build the Gothic St John's Cathedral. It was Belize's first stone building, its first permanent church, and the perfect place for the British to crown the Indian "Mosquito Kings" of the neighboring Mosquito Coast (present-day Nicaragua), ensuring their allegiance throughout the 19th century.

Landing on shore, however, Stephens's favorable impression evaporated when he found that the "town seemed in the entire possession of blacks." A pre-Civil War American accustomed to a strictly segregated society, Stephens confessed that he "hardly knew whether to be shocked or amused" by the chaotic hubub of African vendors, black soldiers from Jamaica in their red uniforms and women in white frocks with ("I could not help remarking") nothing on underneath.

Slavery had been abolished in Belize in the early 1830s, although the position of the average logging worker was hardly much improved. Even so, Belize's racial melting pot was already well advanced, as Stephens discovered to his horror when invited to lunch one day, only to find British officers

mulatto, was a doctor. The eminent American left the settlement soon after to seek out the Mayan ruins in Honduras (Belize's as yet being hardly discovered), with the soldiers from Jamaica providing a 13-gun salute.

Mexican bandits and Guatemalan warlords: Even as Belize was being drawn into the fold of British colonial rule, the surrounding Spanish Empire in Central America was breaking into independent republics – creating waves of civil war, frontier disputes and domestic chaos that spilled over into Belize. Just as the Baymen had been forced to defend themselves from the Spaniards, so the colonial Belizeans spent the entire 19th century fending off their new neighbors.

dining with mulattoes: "By chance a place was made for me between the two colored gentlemen," writes Stephens bravely. "Some of my countrymen, perhaps, would have hesitated about taking it, but I did not; both were well dressed, well educated, and polite. They talked of their mahogany works, of England, hunting, horses, ladies and wine..." In Belize, Stephens mused, "color was considered mere matter of taste."

Just as baffling to Stephens was the operation of Belize's "Grand Court," where no lawyers argued cases because none of the judges had legal training. Two were merchants, one a mahogany cutter, and one, a

Raids by Mexican bandits made life out on the logging camps a constant peril. Worse came after 1847, when the Maya of the Yucatan rebelled against the ruling Mexican *ladinos* (mestizos) in the great Caste Wars. The conflict would continue until 1900, and spill over the borders into Belize.

At first, the British traders happily sold arms and supplies to the largest Mayan state, Santa Cruz (so named because they worshipped a miraculous speaking cross). But this brought them into conflict with another Maya group, the Icaiche. What's more, British loggers were steadily intruding onto Mayan *milpa* or slash-and-burn lands (the crown in Belize Town distributed permits to the countryside with little interest as to who was actually living there). Traditional good relations between British and Maya soured, and when the Icaiche rebel, General Marcus Canul, attacked Belize, most of the local Maya villages willingly supported him.

In 1866, Canul captured a British mahogany camp on the Rio Bravo and held its members for $3,000 ransom. Next year, he attacked the sugar plantation of Indian Church near Lamanai, forcing local settlers to retreat to Belize Town. Matters were grave enough for the governor to order evacuation ships readied in the harbor, although the expected attack never came. In 1870, the Icaiche

War in 1865, many Southerners decided to escape Yankee rule forever and head for Latin America. Some 7,000 Confederates abandoned the United States for isolated colonies where they hoped to recreate the Old South – complete with plantation houses, belles in hoop skirts, gents drinking iced tea and droves of black workers out in the fields. Most of these voluntary exiles went to Brazil, where slavery was still legal. But around 1,500 decided to try their luck in the wilds of British Honduras.

Southern curiosity in this obscure Central American republic had been piqued long before the Civil war, and when reconstruction began, the interest became intense. Emi-

occupied the town of Corozal, and in 1872 besieged Orange Walk Town. Luckily for the inhabitants, a troop of US Confederate soldiers had settled nearby; fresh from the Civil War, their modern rifles devastated the Indian ranks. Canul himself was shot from his saddle, and later died, taking the wind out of the Icaiche rebellion.

The lost Confederates: How did the soldiers happen to be there in the first place? When Lee surrendered to Grant at the Appomattox Court House, ending the American Civil

Left, banana boat in Punta Gorda. **Above**, prayer group in Belize City.

gration agents sprang up in every Southern city, and a fortnightly steamship service began from New Orleans to Belize in 1866. First reports from settlers were positive, and the British government encouraging: import duties were waved for Confederate families, and London went so far as to promise that the young colony would soon be independent (broadly hinting that the Southerners could take the reins). The British governor even entertained new arrivals at state dinners, when the halls echoed with the song of *Bonnie Blue Flag*, *My Maryland* and *God Save the King*.

From 1867 to 1869, the *Trade Winds* and

General Sherman were bringing 100 settlers a trip. The majority were Confederate soldiers and their families, including many of high rank. The American consul in Belize noted with astonishment that "generals and colonels meet one at every turn."

Most of the new arrivals were appalled by Belize Town with its largely black population, and pressed on into the countryside. Some 300 followed the Reverend B.R. Duval of Virginia south to a spot near present-day San Pedro, setting up a town they named New Richmond (the whole colony was envisaged as "Confederate County"). Another group from Louisiana – including Captain Beauregard, brother of the the famed general, and a certain Colonel Benjamin, brother of the Confederate secretary of war – bought sugar plantations on the New River, south of Orange Walk Town. Other smaller groups of settlers scattered in remote pockets through the Belizean countryside.

The Confederates' stated aim was to withdraw from the rest of the world to recreate an ante-bellum fantasy. But the realities of Belizean frontier life caught up with them quickly. Conditions were much harsher than many had expected: apart from the constant heat, the rain and mosquitoes, settlers faced rampant diseases, problems with food supplies and incessant Indian raids in the north. Even more galling, black employees could simply walk away if pressed too far. Most Confederate exiles packed up and left Belize within a few years, returning to the United States poorer but wiser. But others stayed on, using their skills and wealth to establish themselves in Belizean society, usually in the professions.

Although many Belizeans today can trace their lineage to former Confederate soldiers, the Southern community soon lost any social cohesiveness. Children were sent back to the United States to be educated and find white spouses; many did not return. The families that remained in Belize were drawn into the more relaxed local attitude towards race, soon inter-marrying with the black and Hispanic communities.

Territorial claims: During the last quarter of the 19th century, the British were able to relocate demoralized Maya Indians in towns, mixing their numbers with refugees from Guatemala. Even so, the frontiers were not fully secure after the end of the Caste Wars until the late 1890s. In 1897, Mexico and Great Britain signed a treaty, and Mexico formally renounced its claims on Belize.

Diplomatic problems with the neighboring Guatemalans were not so easily resolved. When it achieved independence in the 1820s, Guatemala picked up Spain's centuries-old claim to Belize, and pressed it enthusiastically. A treaty was signed between Britain and Guatemala in 1859 to settle the dispute, but Britain reneged on a key clause that entailed building a road between Guatemala City and the Atlantic coast (various routes were surveyed, but the price tag of £100,000 seemed a little steep just to secure Belize). Guatemala's threatened invasion and diplomatic pressure over the issue have recurred regularly throughout Belize's history up to the present day.

Haggis in the tropics: As the 19th century drifted into the 20th, the racial amalgamation of Belizean society was proceeding apace. The Old Baymen families of landowners and merchants, with names like Hyde, Haylock, Usher and Fairweather, had largely been "creolized" through intermarriage. Although they lost their monopoly on land and trade, they went into the professions, training as barristers and doctors, as well as setting up the colony's first newspapers.

Meanwhile a steady flow of British expatriates formed a parallel high society, which ran local business. The majority of new arrivals were Scots, forming a clique with its own social clubs and considerable political clout. When a Scottish governor, Sir David Wilson, arrived in 1897, he was met by the local St Andrew's Club, who presented him with a haggis, sang *Land o' Cakes* and performed the highland fling. Every year, a Burns' Night was celebrated, reducing the congregation to tears.

For the bulk of the population, more humble celebrations were the norm. Anglican missionaries had managed to convert almost the entire black population and replace many African rituals. But Christmas was the time when old traditions reasserted themselves in the slums of Belize Town's South Side: work was suspended for over a week, rifles and pistols were shot off into the air and the drinking and dancing went on around the clock. Members of each African nation joined together to revive their homeland's dances and music. The excess of local energy was also channelled into an annual river regatta through Belize Town, in dories (dugouts) or larger pitpans, with crews of a dozen or so. Prizes and betting ran high, and the races had the advantage of improving crews' skills at bringing logs down-river.

Democrats and rioters: Although the remote society of British Honduras seemed to wallow in a heat-induced coma broken only by epidemics of yellow fever and cholera, social upheavals were brewing. The country was rapidly becoming the most backward in Central America. The alliance of white expatriates and old Creole families controlled political power in the form of a five-seat, appointed Legislative Council, often even out-

to a property qualification, only 282 of the 15,118 Belizeans were able to vote.

World War I brought matters to a head. In 1915 and 1916, some 600 loyal British Hondurans signed up to fight in Europe. Unfortunately, instead of being sent to cover themselves in glory on the Western Front, this predominantly black contingent was packed off to dig ditches in the Middle East. Protests were met with the news that "it is against British tradition to employ aboriginal troops against a European enemy." Worse, when they arrived in Cairo and marched in to camp whistling *Rule Britannia*, they were stopped by British officers. One black soldier reports being asked: "Who gave you niggers

voting the governor. There was no income or land tax in Belize, so no railways were built. Roads were no better than mule trails: it would take weeks to get from San Ignacio to Belize Town by land, so most commuters went by canoe. Agriculture, meanwhile, was in disarray or non-existent. Creoles traditionally disdained farming, and even the most basic foodstuffs needed to be imported from abroad.

A half-hearted attempt was made to include the masses in politics by electing a Belize Town Board in 1910. Unfortunately, thanks

Above, the Swing Bridge, Belize City.

authority to sing that? Clear out of this building – only British troops admitted here."

Troops returning to Belize in 1919 brought back the weight of these insults and an awareness of the connections between race, class and Empire. They could not help notice that no black soldiers were invited to tea at the golf club after a sports event held by the governor in their honor. Tensions finally broke out in a riot two weeks later. Soldiers marched down Regent Street in Belize City (as the town was then known), smashing shop windows. Unpopular employers were beaten up. News spread, and the whole population joined in, police included. Some

3,000 people looted the town until dawn the next day, when a gunboat was called in to quell the disturbance.

Between the wars: The riots led directly to the foundation in Belize City of a branch of the United Negro Improvement Association, and a visit in 1921 by its Jamaican-born founder, Marcus Mosiah Garvey. A passionate orator and skilled mass organizer, Garvey traveled around the Caribbean raising black political consciousness. At meetings he was careful to have *God Save the King* sung so as not to terrify the authorities unduly, but his speeches were sharp and damning. Blacks had fought to protect the Empire, he said, and received in return "a kick and a smile."

arrived on the morning of Settlement Day, September 10, 1931, nobody took it seriously. Most of the population, including the governor, was involved in a commemorative parade, which was cut short by a deluge. Retiring to St John's College for patriotic songs, the Imperial Band was soon drowned out by the wind: velocity rose from 40 miles (70 km) an hour at noon to a peak of 132 mph (210 km/hr) at 3pm.

Within minutes the sky had cleared and grateful citizens went to check the wreckage of their homes. Tragically, few realized that this was only the eye of the storm, and many were caught when the hurricane returned with even greater force. Whole houses were

But Belizeans were unable to sustain the emotion for very long, and, when Garvey visited again in 1929, he was easily outshone by a visit from the US aviator Charles Lindbergh, fresh from his solo crossing of the Atlantic.

Meanwhile, Belize was about to be hit by the twin disasters of the Great Depression, which put the fragile economy into a tailspin, and a devastating hurricane. For generations, the citizens of Belize City had thought that any approaching hurricane or tidal wave would be spent on the Barrier Reef. Nothing terribly damaging had been done since 1787, so when a fully-fledged hurricane finally

picked up and smashed by the wind; the Poor House with 41 inmates inside was washed out to sea; the city was flooded and the air was thick with flying sheets of corrugated iron, decapitating passers-by. Some 1,000 people were killed in the disaster, made worse by years of bungled relief work.

A depressed New World: The hurricane only added to Belize's growing economic mire. The chicle trade, which depended on a demand for chewing gum in the United States, was suffering; but, much more seriously, the mahogany trade had collapsed.

During his 1936 visit to Belize, the writer Aldous Huxley observed that a minor fluctuation in British middle-class taste had profoundly affected the lives of woodcutters in the remote forests. "When I was a boy there was hardly a single reputable family which did not eat off mahogany, sit on mahogany, sleep in mahogany," Huxley wrote in the slightly dotty book *Beyond the Mexique Bay.* "Mahogany was a symbol of economic solidity and moral worth. Alas, how quickly such sacred symbols can lose their significance! [Today] my friends eat off glass and metal, sit on metal and leather, sleep on beds that are almost innocent of enclosing bedsteads. Mahogany, in a word, is now hopelessly out of fashion. Result: a falling off of Honduranean exports and a

yellow fever returned as the colony's major causes of death. The situation was so bad that Belize's first labor union was formed, although the leader, Antonio Soberanis, was promptly jailed by the British authorities.

Other political organizations followed, usually starting off as motley public rallies in the sandy Central Park (dubbed "the Battlefield"). For the first time the possibility of independence from Britain was seriously discussed. A "Natives First" movement managed to gain seats on the Belize Town Board in 1939, and in 1941 a firebrand named Joseph Blisset formed a Belizean Labour Party. Amongst its more bizarre proposals was the expulsion of all whites, and Belize

corresponding rise in the death-rate from tuberculosis." There, of course, Huxley's interest ended. He was no more interested in Belize than Stephens had been a century before, and headed straight for the Mayan ruins in Guatemala.

But Belizeans were starting to take a hand in improving their own affairs. The hurricane had left Belize City with a swamp-like appearance, its dirt streets looking like rivers, sewers overflowing and water supply regularly drying up. Dysentery, malaria and

Left, troops march off to the Great War. **Right**, Charles Lindbergh's landing, Belize City.

becoming the next state of the USA. This led to an all-out brawl on the Battlefield between Blisset's men and the largely white loyalist group called the Unconquerables. Blisset ended up in jail, as did several other more moderate nationalists.

The tide of anti-colonialism was growing by the end of World War II and Governor Sir John Hunter, embarrassed by constantly having to throw Creole activists in prison, suggested to London that they try giving Belizeans the vote. The Colonial Office replied that they couldn't "go handing out self-government to all and sundry," and the scene for an extended struggle was set.

On September 21, 1981, the British Union Jack was lowered and the Belizean flag raised in its place. Belize had finally become an independent nation – but many Belizeans who attended the ceremonies or listened to them on the radio that night felt only apprehension at what the future would bring.

Many would have preferred to delay independence – not because they disagreed with the idea but because the 19th-century territorial dispute with Guatemala had not yet been settled. Despite assurances from the British government that they would maintain a garrison in Belize "for an appropriate period," Belizeans were nervous. Some even feared that as soon as the international delegates and media left, Guatemalan troops would swarm over the nation's border.

Long road to home rule: That Belize won its independence at all is largely due to the efforts of the country's first prime minister, George Price, who had championed the cause since 1949. At that time, less than 3 percent of Belizean's met the strict property qualifications required for the vote; many felt that the country was being run like an enormous plantation for the wealthy elite. In 1950, Price formed the People's United Party (PUP) to push for home rule; endless speeches in Belize City's Central Park (dubbed the Battlefield), a national strike and new constitution eventually led to internal self-government in 1964.

But full independence was delayed by hesitancy on the part of the British government and aggressive noises from Guatemala. The latter had renewed its claims to British Honduras in the 1930s; in 1945, it had officially announced that "Belice" (as it is called in Spanish) was a Guatemalan province. Diplomacy was fruitless. Twice in the 1970s, Guatemala moved troops to the border and threatened to invade, only being dissuaded by reinforcements of British troops.

The case for Belizean independence was taken into international forums. The turning point came in 1980 when a United Nations resolution supporting independence finally put the wheels inexorably in motion. But controversy lasted right up to the moment of the transfer of power. The "Heads of Agreement," a document outlining proposed points of negotiation with Guatemala, had caused rioting in Belize City in early 1981; Guatemala closed its border with Belize to show its opposition to independence.

Even so, the ceremony went ahead in September, and Belize became an independent part of the British Commonwealth. Diplo-

matic maneuvers continued with Guatemala until, in 1991, President Jorge Serrana finally announced that Belize's sovereignty would be recognized. Disputes continue, however, about how to arrange Guatemala's access to the Caribbean coast (a key claim); there are strong feelings on the issue in both countries, and old mistrust and resentment has not died. The British government's announcement in 1993 that it would withdraw the last of its troops from Belize sent jitters through the country, although most Belizeans are getting used to the idea of standing alone.

Relative success story: Despite the continuing nervousness about Guatemala and nu-

Preceding pages: the Supreme Court, Belize City. Left, Garifuna settlement day, Dangriga. Right, over 40 percent of Belizeans are under 18.

merous social and economic problems, most Belizeans today feel that life is pretty good in their new nation.

Since independence, the democratic process has proceeded smoothly and voter turnout is generally high. But Belizean politics remains a curious affair to outsiders. Election campaigns operate at a personal level, with candidates handing out T-shirts, caps and calendars and making small talk with their supporters. Politicians provide transportation to the polls and happily grant personal favors. Many Belizeans think nothing of going to a candidate's home to ask for anything from a piece of land to schoolbooks for their children.

ful. Its relaxed immigration policy made it a natural refuge for thousands of Central American refugees. Some were fleeing wars and persecution, but the majority were economic immigrants seeking jobs or land.

The ever-increasing numbers of refugees, combined with a steady outflow of Belizean Creoles, has lead to a substantial shift in the nation's ethnic balance. There are now more Mestizos than Creoles in Belize for the first time since the Caste Wars of Mexico's Yucatán brought a flood of refugees. There has also been a shift in population distribution, since most immigrants have settled in the rural areas. Although a higher percentage of the population now claims Spanish as a

George Price's PUP and the UDP are still the main political parties (the latter winning elections in 1984 and 1993). Party loyalty determines everything from jobs to building contracts; even minor issues become political in some way, and there is tremendous social pressure to choose sides. This partisanship means the public service is turned over after every change of government, while development projects are often scrapped half way through.

Island of peace in Central America: While many neighboring republics were embroiled in civil war during the 1980s and early '90s, Belize's political climate remained peace-

first language, English is still the nation's official tongue.

Some Creoles are deeply concerned about what they call the "hispanization of Belize," and there has been a fair amount of "alien bashing" in the newspapers and on radio call-in programs. But most Belizeans have adopted a wait-and-see attitude, hoping the Central Americans will follow the pattern of previous immigrant groups and embrace the Belizean way of life.

Cultural loyalties: The new demographic realities have shaken up Belize's traditional self-image as a Caribbean nation within Latin America. In truth, Belize's ties to the islands of the Caribbean have been more a matter of tradition and sentiment than actual substance. It shares the Westminster model of government, British heritage and legal system with other Caribbean islands. Cultural connections are also still strong: Belizean youth look to Jamaica in particular as a source of mystical and musical inspiration, often sporting the "Dred" colors of gold, green and red made popular by Rastafarians and musicians like Bob Marley.

Videos of carnival in Trinidad and Tobago also provide examples of costumes and music which Belizeans are beginning to adapt for their own September celebrations. Caribbean television programs and visiting musicians of Caribbean nations. But many complain that Belize benefits little: few of the islands are interested in Belizean products, but Belizeans are still expected to "Buy Caribbean." And most Caribbean nations seem to produce similar products: why import orange juice from Trinidad or matches from Jamaica when there are already steady supplies of these products in Belize?

In recent years, it has been the private sector rather than government that has begun turning to Latin America. Guatemalan manufacturers are eager to trade with Belize, which they see as a stepping stone to the rest of the Caribbean. The need for bilingualism is becoming more apparent in education: prior to

cians also enjoy an enduring popularity.

But these connections are all second-hand. With no direct flights to the islands, visiting them is expensive and complicated. Except for a few politicians, media personnel and students attending the University of the West Indies in Jamaica, it is rare to meet a Belizean who has been to another Caribbean country.

Political and economic ties are also weak. In an effort to promote integration, Belize became a member of CARICOM, an alliance

Left, Salvadorean refugees collecting water. Above, police guard on a bus full of adolescent felons, Belize City.

independence, for instance, most higher degrees were obtained in the US or Britain, but these days Belizean students are also seeking admission to universities in Latin America.

The politics of tourism: One of the most significant developments since Belizean independence has been the dramatic rise in tourism. While Belize hopes not to repeat the mistakes of other small Caribbean countries, which have allowed their landscapes and cultures to be devastated, it still hopes to make increased tourism one of its main economic goals – a balancing act that few countries have been able to manage.

Belizean tourism is still in its infancy compared to other countries. The fledgling Belize Tourism Industry Association is more like a family association of bed-and-breakfast establishments in a remote one-horse town than an alliance of large hotel chains. The Belize Tourist Board, the government's arm in the industry, has failed to maintain consistent policies; in fact, the two groups are more often in conflict than working towards a common goal of promoting Belize. Most Belizean tourism establishments are so small they have only limited budgets; few even have their own brochures.

So far, government duty and tax exemptions have been aimed at attracting foreign investors. As a result, a huge number of new hotels and "lodges" are owned by foreigners, especially North Americans, who have been able to set up ventures for far less than required by their Belizean counterparts. At times it seems as if the remoter parts of the country's coastline has been colonized entirely by foreigners – a situation that has, not surprisingly, caused local resentment.

Belizean nationalists now want to ensure that local operators benefit from tourism. In the early 1990s, an American dive boat was actually met by a flotilla of protestors in Belize City arguing for more local participation. Nationalists cite a law in neighboring Guatemala that makes using a local guide compulsory, and argue that Belizeans need similar protection.

Creating a service culture: The poor quality of service in Belize is another problem plaguing the tourism industry. The indifferent attitude demonstrated by hotel and restaurant employees is so pervasive that the hardest part of traveling in Belize can be trying to get the check after you eat. In response, a few establishments have resorted to bringing in staff from abroad, or conducting classes in hospitality management. Despite these efforts, it may be some time before good service is the rule, rather than the exception, in Belize.

Keeping hotel rooms filled is also problematic. Most Belizean guest houses and lodges average less than 40 rooms, so any unexpected drop in the number of visitors can be disastrous. Several new, large hotels built during a short-lived boom in the late 1980s now compete against the smaller family-owned inns. These smaller establishments have had to be creative in order to attract business, relying on their own home-style Belizean cuisine or "Mom and Pop" atmosphere. "Foreigners usually stay at a big hotel on their first visit," commented one small inn owner, "but when they come back they want to experience the real Belize."

Although some tour operators want a massive increase in tourist numbers, many others argue that Belize should not try to accommodate mass tourism or allow cruise ships to visit, as many other Caribbean countries do. There is concern that unlimited amounts of tourist traffic would put too much strain on the environment and the culture: it is arguable that visitors to Belize are attracted by its small-scale feel, so different from other tropical destinations.

In an attempt to lure visitors from flashier destinations like Cancún in Mexico – which can bring in tourists at a fraction of the cost in Belize – local operators have begun to promote Belize as an "eco-tourism" destination. Whether eco-tourism is just a convenient buzz-word or represents a long-term commitment to the environment is yet to be determined. But for now, the campaign has put Belize on the international map and generated considerable local appreciation for the environment.

Another initiative is the Mundo Maya project, an attempt by tourism operators to join forces with their counterparts in other Central American republics – Mexico, Guatemala and Honduras – on the basis of a shared Mayan heritage. The marketing strategy aims at promoting Belize as the gateway to the region, hoping that tourists will visit archaeological sites in more than one country, but so far it has yielded few results.

A look to the future: Before 1981, this conflict between looking to the Caribbean or Latin America was usually decided along ethnic lines, Creole versus Mestizo. But today, more Belizeans are feeling that it is no longer necessary to make a choice: it may be Belize's unique geography and dual cultural heritage that define her future role in the region.

Most Belizeans now agree that independence was a step forward, although the road ahead is likely to be a difficult one. At least now any improvements, or mistakes, are their own.

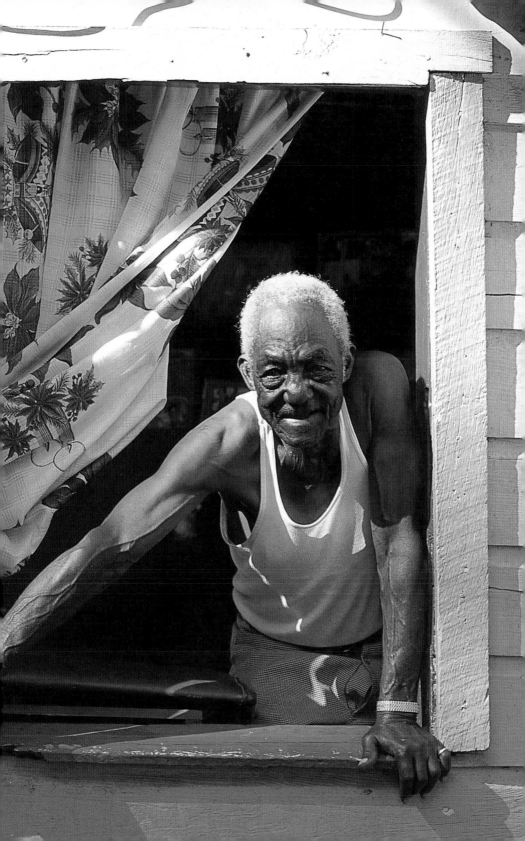

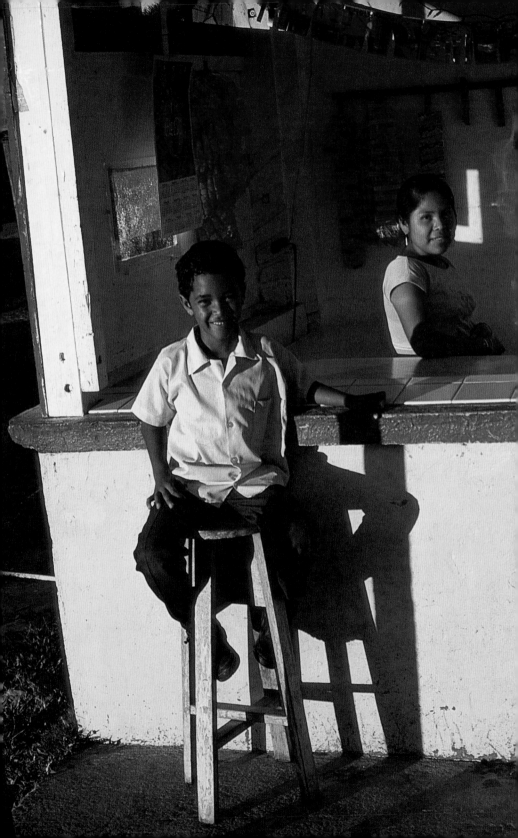

"A tink a si wan new Belize weh di Creole man, di Mestizo, di Garifuna, an di Maya, no separate as a lis dem but instead all da Belizeans."

"I think I see a new Belize where the Creole, the Mestizo, the Garifuna and the Maya, are not separated as I have listed them, but united as Belizeans."

– Belizean politician Phillip Lewis

For most Belizeans, the presence of so many different ethnic groups in their country is as much a national treasure as the Barrier Reef or Mayan ruins. Generations of racial mixing have made it impossible to describe the "typical" Belizean – only a typical room full of Belizeans, whose physical characteristics range from the very darkest to the lightest skin tones, and every imaginable hair and eye color. Even within a single family there is likely to be considerable variation, since the grandparents usually boast ancestors from several continents.

But despite the blurring of racial lines, most Belizeans identify themselves with one particular ethnic group. Belize is not so much a melting pot of cultures as a salad where each element lends a certain flavor or spice to the mix. From an early age, Belizeans are encouraged to feel proud of their own racial traditions and appreciate those of others. "Cultural presentations," displaying the music, dance and dress of the elements of Belizean society, are a regular part of primary school activities, community celebrations and political rallies.

As the Creole saying goes, *All a we mek Belize* – we all make up Belize.

The search for identity: Belizeans have long described themselves as "a Caribbean nation in Central America." Culturally speaking, Belize has long had more in common with the distant islands of the Caribbean than its next-door neighbors. The main difference is that Belize has a British rather than Spanish heritage; English is the official language,

while most of the population are black Creoles, descended from African slaves and British settlers. There have always been Mayas and Mestizos (those of mixed Indian and Spanish descent) like those found in the rest of Central America, but historically the Creole culture has been dominant – making Belize's legal, political and educational systems closer to those of the English-speaking Caribbean, while its music, dance, and folklore share many African elements found dotted around the islands.

Things are changing, however. To the surprise of many, censuses have shown that the Creoles are now only 30 percent of the total population and the ethnic balance has shifted in favor of the Mestizos, who now represent about 44 percent of all Belizeans. Large numbers of Creole Belizeans have been leaving for the United States, while Mestizo refugees and immigrants have been flooding in from war-ravaged Central America.

These refugees have been adding to the numbers of Spanish-speakers who settled in northern Belize in the 1860s, fleeing the bloody Caste Wars in Mexico. Settling around Orange Walk Town and Corozal, these older

Preceding pages: greeting the morning in Gales Point; Mayan family near San Ignacio; food stand, Punta Gorda. Left, young Mayan girl. Right, one of the old-timers.

Mestizo families speak both Spanish and Creole, or a Spanish which is heavily creolized. Firmly established for generations, they feel they have little in common with the Central American refugees, referred to by most Belizeans as "aliens." Some Creoles are concerned that the increase in Mestizos will mean the erosion of Creole culture; others believe the new arrivals will adopt the Creole language and traditions just as many other immigrant groups have in the past.

Ancient inhabitants and recent arrivals: Although they represent only 8 percent of the population, Maya Indians trace their lineage back to the original inhabitants. There are several distinct groups, the largest being the

Odyssey, page 237). Nevertheless, they rose to the challenge: although making up only 7 percent of Belize's population, they have had a great impact on the country, figuring prominently in the professions and the arts.

East Indians also comprise only a small portion of the overall population (3.5 percent), but have become prominent in Belizean business. They first arrived in the 1860s as indentured laborers on sugar plantations established by former Confederate Americans; their cultural identities soon dwindled, but East Indian physical traits are visible in almost every ethnic group in Belize. A second wave of East Indians arrived in the 1970s and set up as shop-owners in Belize City, but still

Mopan and the Kekchi. But like indigenous people elsewhere, the Maya are on the lowest rungs of Belize's socio-economic ladder. Most are subsistence farmers who live in remote villages and maintain their traditional ways. Many exist outside the main economy, with no real access to national health care services or education.

Like the recent refugees, the Garifuna were greeted with prejudice and suspicion when they first arrived in Belize in the early 1800s. A mixture of escaped African slaves and Carib Indians, they ended up in Dangriga on the south coast after an epic 200-year persecution by European powers (*see Garifuna*

make every attempt to preserve their customs – even traveling back to India to arrange suitable marriages.

Adding to the mix are Syrians, Lebanese, Chinese, and Taiwanese, as well as the distinctive Mennonites from the US and Canada (*see The Mennonites, pages 76–77*).

Unity in diversity: Belize is not free from racial prejudice. A visitor might be told by Creoles that the Central American "aliens" are very violent and therefore responsible for Belize's rise in crime; Mestizos often dismiss Creoles as lazy folk who would rather steal than work for a living. But moments later, these same people will proudly tell the visitor that unlike other places in the world, there is no prejudice in Belize and everyone lives together in peace.

The contradiction doesn't seem to bother the average Belizean, who believes that personal feelings do not matter nearly as much as overall racial harmony. Being Creole, Maya, Mestizo is still second to being Belizean, and everyone has the sense that they are helping to "build the nation."

With a population of less than 200,000 in the whole country, this tolerance is not only desirable, it is absolutely necessary. Belize has the intimate, personal feel of a small town. Even in Belize City, strangers usually ask each other how they are related to friends

absorbed in local happenings, and almost everything in Belize is political in some way. Party affiliation is particularly important, since everything from buying land to being hired for a job may depend on which party you supported in the last election. Domestic news is avidly discussed, but there is almost no interest in what is happening in the outside world unless it has some direct bearing on Belize. Foreign films and television programs which mention Belize are always viewed with excitement, as are Belizean travel or wildlife articles on Belize in American or European magazines.

But not everyone sees Belize as the perfect home. An unemployment rate of close to 20

with the same name, or where they attended school. Such familiarity makes it hard to keep things private and gossiping is a favorite pastime. But for most Belizeans, their small society is an advantage: it means lifelong acceptance in the community and the guarantee of a warm welcome wherever they go.

Even so, most Belizeans feel a strong attachment to their homes; many have never left their villages, and residents of Belize City rarely go out to the cayes or neighboring districts. Because of this, they tend to be very

percent, low wages and a high cost of living have prompted many people – mostly Creoles – to head north in search of a better life. Over the past two decades, thousands of young Belizeans have migrated, both legally and otherwise, to major cities in the United States. Many of them have left small children behind to be raised by grandmothers or aunts. The majority are skilled workers and professionals, including teachers and nurses, creating a serious Belizean "brain drain." Scholarships to study abroad now usually insist that recipients return to Belize for several years after graduation.

Almost everyone in Belize has relatives in

Left, faces of Belize. **Right**, Caribbean colors, Caye Cauller.

the United States who send home money, clothing and other goods. The advent of 24-hour American television has made Belizean young people crave not only US fashions and music, but a lifestyle well beyond their means. Many young men seem fascinated by the criminal activity and violence they see in movies, and street gangs modelled on those in urban America have sprung up all over Belize City, complete with drive-by shootings – often carried out on bicycles – drug trafficking and drug abuse. Many wonder whether the search for a better life abroad has cost too much for those left at home.

A relaxed lifestyle: Despite the recent influence of American culture on young people,

together. House parties with lots of food and drinks rage until early the next morning and usually don't end until the liquor runs out.

Sundays are still sacred in Belize. The dominant religion is Catholic, although other denominations have established a following in almost every town and village. While some reserve the day for worship, for others Sunday is a time for family or a trip to the cayes. For Creoles, no Sunday is complete without the traditional stewed chicken, rice and beans, and potato salad washed down with koolaid or a soft drink.

Verbal culture: Belizeans don't read very much and few books by local authors have been published, but this doesn't mean they

most Belizeans are still proud of their culture – and by no means enamored of the US work ethic. Belize's work environment is much more relaxed than in industrialized countries, and people think nothing of dropping by a friend's work-place to chat for a few minutes or stepping out of the office to run errands or go to the bank. Offices and schools close for lunch, when many families sit down together for the big meal of the day.

Belizeans value leisure time and there is no shortage of public and bank holidays. Even though many have to work a half-day on Saturdays, Friday is the preferred night to go out, and any excuse is enough for a get-

don't like words (*see Speaking Creole, pages 80–81*). Because Creole has no written form, people tend to rely on their ears rather than their eyes for information. As a result, Belizeans are often capable of memorizing astonishingly large amounts of information. A waitresses may be serving 10 people at one table, but she won't write a single thing down – and a good waitress can get the order correct even if one of the diners has changed his mind several times.

Belizeans also like to invent names for each other. Some people are so well known by their nicknames that their real name may be a complete surprise when it is announced at a wedding or a funeral. Some reflect the person's appearance ("Big George," "Lagrahead," like the loggerhead turtle, or "Red Boy,") Others, like "January Baboon," seem downright insulting, although they are meant to express affection. Any small idiosyncrasy will also do as the source for a name: in Belize City, a famous old beggar woman with no teeth, said the number 66 as "chicki-chick." Since she also walked with a bamboo cane, she was universally known as "Chicki-chick with the bamboo stick."

Above all, Belizeans are obsessed with giving ordinary conversations sexual connotations, even in the work-place. What North Americans might denounce as sexual har-

A world of superstition: Although Belize has squarely entered the modern world, many traditions linger. Belizeans, whether they admit it or not, are a superstitious lot: there are beliefs and omens pertaining to just about every aspect of life. Those who are having a hard time, or who face numerous disappointments, often fear they have been "*obeahed*," (fallen victim to someone's black magic), and people in love often consult tarot card readers, write their beloved's name on candles, and bathe with special herbs.

The survival of such Africanisms as black magic (*obeah*) and the folklore of both European and Mayan peoples has given Belize a rich variety of magical explanations for every-

assment is viewed as great fun by most Belizeans, and women see it as their obligation to put any man making unwanted advances in his place. A man might suggestively comment on how delicious a woman's meal looks, how she never gives him any of her food, or how he has something which could help relieve her headache, and from there the repartee begins. The goal is to see how long the joke can be sustained and it may even become a running game. Having an audience always makes it more exciting.

__Left__, bread vendors, St George's Caye. __Above__, en route to church, Punta Gorda.

day events. Not only are Belizeans wary of ladders and black cats, but they also look out for Tataduhende, the little bearded bushman who has his feet on backwards (so that you'll think he's coming when he's really going) and Llarona, the weeping woman who lures drunken men to their death.

Stories of these and other mythical creatures have been entertaining Belizeans for generations, and while most people will swear to you that they don't believe a word of it, few will tempt fate and walk alone on a dark night, or along a lonely stretch of beach.

A wealth of pseudo-scientific beliefs relate to medical conditions. A pregnant woman is besieged with warnings of damage to her unborn child if she eats certain foods (conch or pork is said to cause instant death and eating hot pepper will give the baby "spots"). People will go to great lengths to give an expectant mother any food she craves: if she can't have what she wants and touches any part of her body, the child will have a birthmark in the shape of that particular food.

After the baby is born there is constant vigilance lest a malicious person gives the baby the "evil eye," and menstruating women are not allowed near the newborn. Clothing must be washed carefully and diapers can never be left out on the line after dark in case a drunken man passes by. Tickling a baby

Good fortune is continually being sought and dreams are considered a reliable source for lucky boledo (lottery) numbers. Dreams, both good and bad, can signify all sorts of future events from the birth of a child (fish) to death (a wedding). If you see a dead person's face in a dream, it is believed that you will follow shortly, but if they do not look at you, it's good luck.

Even people who do not believe in dreams or ghosts cannot escape the numerous small rituals Belizeans are constantly engaged in throughout their day. Most women, for instance, will go to great pains to keep their purses off the ground (you'll always be broke if you leave it there) and walk only to the

can cause it to stammer when it grows up, and you must never look at a child from above or it will become cross-eyed.

Even the most common household activities have magical overtones. Most housewives, for instance, will never sweep all the dirt out of the house (thereby loosing all their luck) and a dropped spoon or fork means that visitors are coming. A guest who overstays his welcome can be made to leave by turning a broom upside door behind a door. Ghosts can be stopped from entering by scattering wangla (sesame seeds) on the front step (the ghost will stop and count each one and by the time he finishes, it's morning).

right of a statue (to avoid bad luck).

Traditions of machismo: Other relics of the Belizean past are less picturesque. In many ways, Belize is still a man's country and swaggering macho attitudes and customs go back to the days of logging and piracy.

The need for constant excitement makes many men incapable of accepting responsibility or forming lasting attachments. Married men work to support more than one family or numerous "sweethearts." Others hardly work at all, preferring to "catch and kill," or make money only when they really need it. The old tradition of "spreeing," or going on a drinking binge at the end of the logging season, is a regular habit for men, who may spend their entire paycheck in one night on liquor for friends. There is tremendous pressure to go along with the crowd and those who don't measure up are ridiculed.

Belizean women often feel that they don't have any choice but to accept men's infidelity and carousing. Many accept common-law marriages or spend years being a married man's sweetheart. Fifty percent of all children in Belize are born outside of wedlock and it is not uncommon to find a single mother who has several children by different fathers. A woman with few or no children is pitied: children are seen as an insurance against a lonely old age and a compensation

secretarial work, increasing numbers are obtaining degrees and becoming managers, or entering the legal and medical professions. Others, who don't have these advantages, work from their homes, taking in washing or baking pastries. Many immigrant women become domestics or shop assistants and some are even taking jobs collecting garbage or cleaning the streets. Women's wages tend to be very low and few receive any form of child support.

A young nation: Not only is Belize one of the newest nations in the world, it also has one of the youngest populations: more than 40 percent of Belizeans are under the age of 18. With many absentee parents, very few adults

for a hard life. One grandmother summed up the philosophy: "Men come and go, but your children are always with you." With fathers largely absent from the domestic scene, grandmothers and aunts usually help with child care, and cousins are often raised as closely as siblings.

Women make up a large percentage of the workforce. Although they tend to occupy traditional jobs like teaching, nursing and

Left, sugarcane workers, descendants of Mexican immigrants, Corozal District. **Above**, afternoon training. **Right**, Belizeans don't stand on excessive formality.

are actually responsible for the care, education and training of the country's future nation builders. Crime, child abuse and unemployment are certainly cause for great concern. Yet in some ways, just as the grandmothers have always believed, so many children may be a blessing: it is easier to be optimistic about the future when so many of the nation's citizens are young, energetic and have little or no memory of a more restrictive colonial past.

While visitors may be most impressed by Belize's natural beauty, Belizeans themselves consider their population's diversity and youth to be their country's greatest assets.

They stand out in any Belizean crowd: blond, blue-eyed men in denim overalls and cowboy hats, their skin glowing an almost albino pink; severe women whose outfits – ankle-length, long-sleeved frocks and wide-brimmed hats tied down with black scarves – seem in outright defiance of the tropical heat. Polite and reserved, they hang back from the general hubbub, talking quietly amongst themselves. If you should overhear, the language isn't Spanish, English or Creole, but gutteral German.

The Mennonite settlers of Belize are part of a resilient religious sect that traces its roots back to 16th-century Netherlands. Starting off as an obscure Anabaptist group during the Reformation, they took their name from a Dutch priest Menno Simons. Like the Amish of Pennsylvania, to whom they are distantly connected, Mennonites seek to exist in isolated farming communities without modern technology (calling themselves, at times, *die Stillen im Lande*, the Unobtrusive Ones). They reject state interference in their affairs and are committed pacifists.

From Russia to the tropics: Belize is only the latest stop in the Mennonites' three-century search for a homeland. Their more radical beliefs – particularly a refusal to bear arms or pay certain taxes – led to persecution, driving them from the Netherlands to Prussia in the 1600s, then on to southern Russia. When the Russian government revoked the Mennonites' exemption from military conscription in the 1870s, they packed up again and headed for Canada, setting up their closed, autonomous colonies again in the wildernesses of Alberta and Saskatchewan.

Even here the modern world intruded: after World War I, the Canadian government demanded that only English be taught in Mennonite schools and, spurred on by anti-German feeling, reconsidered the conscription exemption. Again many Mennonites moved on, this time to the barren highlands of Mexico – only to find in the mid-1950s that the Mexican government wanted to include them in their social security program.

The Mennonites were running out of obscure frontiers to settle when they decided to try out Belize (then British Honduras). A delegation soon established that this was virgin territory, and that the British authorities were more than enthusiastic to have them: the Mennonites were renowned for their farming skills, and the colony had virtually no agriculture. Local Creoles had always held farming in complete contempt, and even eggs were imported from abroad.

In 1958, the first of some 3,500 Mennonites began arriving in Belize. Although the Mennonites had largely been able to maintain their religion through their endless odyssey, there were still many divisions within the ranks – particularly on the matters of language and the use of technology. The most conservative groups spoke German and used only those farming implements available in the early 1900s (when an edict had been passed against the engine and science). More progressive Mennonites, meanwhile, had learned English in Canada, and were happy to use tractors and fertilizer.

Agricultural success story: The progressives – a group called the Kleine Gemeinde, who bought land around Spanish Walk near San Ignacio – soon became successful in Belize, clearing their land and starting production. A more conservative group, called the Altkolonier, purchased 115,000 acres (46,000 hectares) of wilderness at Blue Creek on the corner of Mexico and Guatemala, with a break-away contingent settling near Orange Walk Town at Shipyard and Richmond Hill (where, coincidentally, US Confederate soldiers had tried to settle a century before). They suffered from language barriers and the difficulty of hand-clearing their land: almost half left within a few years, although new arrivals maintained the numbers.

Today the Mennonites have ironed out their initial problems and are the most successful farmers in Belize. They supply most of the country's produce (Mennonites can be spotted in the central market in Belize City every morning) and carve splendid mahogany furniture for sale and export.

Even so, there are still serious divisions within the Mennonite Church and splinter groups regularly form and are absorbed. The progressives have relaxed their traditional dress, use power tools and drive pick-up trucks, while their villages look little different from places in the US Midwest. But hardliners can still be seen on the highways driving their horse-drawn buggies, the men with close-cropped hair and flowing Santa Claus beards, the women modestly dressed in black to ward off prying eyes.

Typical of these conservative Mennonites is William Freisen, an elder at Barton Creek – a break-away group from Spanish Lookout which became disgusted with progressive ways. Freisen lives with his wife, 10 sons and

memory should be left of a person after they die). Although they are unlikely to do anything more than glare at you if you take a shot, their wishes should be respected.

Communal society: The community works on a straightforward basis, rather like a 19th-century version of communist society. "We believe that too much property, like too much beer, is not good for one," says Freisen. Strict Mennonites are accepted from any quarter (one member was brought up in Bolivia), and disputes are settled by popular vote.

three daughters (contraception is definitely beyond the pale for strict Mennonites) in a remote community of a dozen families, linked to the highway only by a rough dirt road. Despite the isolation, Freisen and others are happy to meet and talk with interested visitors ("We want to show what Christian people do," he explains).

There is one caveat: like the Amish in Pennsylvania, strict Mennonites object strenuously to having their photographs taken (some will explain that they believe no

The family's wooden house, a combination of a European dwelling and a Mayan hut, is without electricity or telephone. Angered by the lapses of progressive Mennonites, Freisen says steadfastly: "We *know* that the world moved before machines and electricity." The law is strictly observed: even when one of his family falls sick, Freisen drives them the 7 miles (11 km) by buggy to the highway – although there a car will be hailed to take the patient to a hospital.

And is this the last stop in the Mennonites' seemingly endless peregrinations? Freisen shrugs philosophically. "Belize has been good to us, but if this changes, we leave."

Preceding pages: Mennonite family, Spanish Lookout. Above, dawn duties.

Fowl caca white an tink e lay egg.
– Belizean proverb: A chicken shits white and thinks she has laid an egg. (Used to describe a person who is self-important.)

The official language of Belize may be English, but as any visitor soon realizes, the language of the street is rather different. *Weh mek unu no lef' me 'lone an' mine unu own business?* one might hear a Belizean tell a group of listeners. Many of the words are not far removed from English. *Weh mek* is

literally "what makes," and means "why?" *Lef' me 'lone* means "leave me alone." The queerest word is *unu*: of African origin, it means "you" or "your." So the whole sentence translates as: "Why don't you leave me alone and mind your own business?"

A more perplexing example: *Da weh da lee bwai mi di nyam?* ("What was that little boy eating?") Here, *Weh da lee bwai* can be traced back to the English "what that little boy." The rest is all but unintelligible to English speakers. *Da* means "is." *Nyam* is an African word for "eat," from the vegetable yam, while *mi* and *di* are grammatical words indicating the past imperfect tense.

Belize Creole, it should be obvious, is very different from English.

There was a time when the Creole languages of the world (and there are dozens in the Caribbean region alone, as well as the version in Louisiana) were regarded as "uncivilized" or "broken" speech – imperfect, childish copies of the colonial languages from which they were derived, whether English, French, Portuguese or Spanish.

Today, with more scholarly and objective scrutiny, Creole languages are being recognized for what they are: new linguistic creations with fully-fledged, highly nuanced grammatical systems. The process of standardization in many Creole-speaking countries is well under way, with grammars and dictionaries being commissioned and panels of scholarly experts working on problems.

Linguistic hybrid: In Belize, the Creole people are the products of centuries of interbreeding between the British colonizers and their West African slaves. The language, Belize Creole, is the linguistic result of this meeting of north and south: English (including many English and Scottish regional dialects) blended with the diverse language groups of West Africa.

Belize Creole's nearest relative is Jamaican Creole, also based on English, although the two are quite different. Adding to the Belizean mixture are words from Spanish (*goma* for a hangover, for example) and others from the Miskito Indians of Nicaragua (*konka* for a house fly, amongst others).

Although Belize Creole was the creation of the Creole people, today it is far from their exclusive property. It is the country's lingua franca, spoken by Mestizos, East Indians, Mayans and Garifunas. To speak it is part of being Belizean – so much so that the US Peace Corps has decided to teach Creole to its volunteers. Although everyone in Belize understands English, speaking a dash of Creole doesn't hurt, and many travelers have taken quick courses to pick up some of the language.

Perhaps the most fascinating – and frustrating – aspect of Creole is that, amongst the rhythmic and pulsating sounds, are hundreds of recognizable English words. You might make out *table*, *chair*, *man*, *woman*, *sun*, *moon*, *sea* or *boat* in a conversation, but because the grammar of Belize Creole is so different, the meaning is quite lost.

A good place to start solving the mystery is a small book called *Creole Proverbs of Belize*. Proverbs have always been a storehouse of folk wit and wisdom in any language (witness the Icelandic proverb, "Every man likes the smell of his own fart," or, from Nigeria, "The bad dancer blames the dance floor.") Belizean Creole proverbs are an

what part of the barbed wire to rub its balls." "When cockroaches make a dance, they never invite the fowls."

Cross-cultural fertilization: Some Belizean Creole words have infiltrated the standard English language. The word *jook*, for example, is used by all Belizeans to mean "stick," although its secondary meaning is "copulate." The term migrated to many southern black communities of the United States, where a brothel was often called a "jookhouse" – so that when music-playing boxes

amusing way of getting to understand local cadences, as well as customs. Some can be read in the original, like *Ax me no question, I tell you no lies, If you ax me again, I spit in your eyes*. Others require only minor translation. For example, *Dis-ya time no tan like befo time*, means literally "This here time doesn't stand like former times," or, "In the old days, things were different." Others are worth reading for the translation. "The man who has lifted his horse's tail knows that the bottom is red," goes one. "The bull knows on

began to appear in nightclubs and whorehouses, they were naturally referred to as "jook-boxes" or, as it is usually spelled, "juke-boxes." Another Belize Creole word still current in the southern US is *pinda* (spelled "pinder" in American English), an old African word for peanuts.

One final warning to the would-be student of Belize Creole. This is a vernacular, folk speech. Reading or writing it is never taught in schools, and there is still no systematic way of spelling its words. This, however, is one reason why many educated Belizeans have trouble writing in English. It is, after all, a foreign language.

Preceding pages: chewing the fat. **Left**, Creole cool. **Above**, laying it on the line.

You'll never find Belizeans sitting politely through a concert or throwing a party without dancing. In Belize, music of any kind is an irresistible invitation to move, and any social event without a live band, or at least a disc jockey and his "box," is hardly worth attending.

While some radio stations and nightclubs do play American pop and country music, more often you'll hear Caribbean reggae, soca, and dance hall. There is also a healthy appetite for Latin American ballads and salsa beats. But as much as Belizeans enjoy these foreign imports, the music Belizeans love most is home-grown. Whether they come from Dangriga, Belize City or Orange Walk Town, Belizean musicians can always find a loyal following and creative – if not financial – success.

These days, the Belizean music attracting the most attention, both at home and abroad, is Punta Rock. Based on traditional Garifuna music and lyrics with some contemporary electronic alterations, Punta has won the hearts of every ethnic group in Belize. When the Garifuna drums start to beat in the shops, streets or discos, everyone moves to the steady, energetic rhythm. Punta lyrics cover topics from social commentary and humorous jibes at community members to the loss of a loved one. No one seems to mind that they are in a language that only a small part of the population understands – everyone tries to sing along anyway, and many feel this even adds to the music's appeal.

Besides Punta Rock, there are local groups that specialize in reggae and soca; several bands from Mexican-influenced northern Belize promote tunes with a salsa or merengue beat. Traditional music is still popular: Creoles can claim *brukdown* and a large number of original folksongs, while the Mayas and Mestizos occasionally explore their musical roots in the few villages that still boast a marimba band.

Patriotic party time: With so many holidays on the Belizean calendar, it's not hard for

visitors to find some type of music or celebration during their stay – especially if you're passing through in September. This is when Belizeans are at their most patriotic and spirited, celebrating both St George's Caye Day on the 10th – marking the victory of the British Baymen and their slaves over Spanish invaders in 1798 – and, on 21 September, Independence Day. Weeks on either side of these dates are filled with activities, most taking place in Belize City. Banners with patriotic slogans, red, blue and white

streamers and twinkling lights festoon the streets, which are crowded with the Queen of the Bay beauty pageant, bicycle races, concerts, military displays – even a fire engine parade. Many "Bel-Ams" (Belizeans residing in the US) choose this time to come home for a visit, adding to the festive atmosphere.

Music, both old and new, plays a vital role in the celebrations. Every year an assortment of favorite old "Tenth songs" – some patriotic march tunes, others sentimental ballads – hits the airwaves, while Belize's contemporary musicians try to release at least one new song, or perhaps an entire album, in honor of the season. And the party simply

Preceding pages: carnival parade, Belize City. **Left,** glittering marcher, Carnival. **Right,** Garifuna drummers, Dangriga.

couldn't go on without at least one calypso or soca band from the Caribbean to give the Belizean crowds something to help them *wine dey waist* (wind their waists).

Throughout the country, the eve of both holidays is celebrated by going to discos and parties; next morning, nursing their *goma* (hangover), people crawl out of bed to watch the more traditional parades weave through town. In the past there were separate, competing parades for each political party; today the PUP and UDP march in the same parade – separately, of course. They are joined by friendly societies, including (in Belize City) the "Loyal and Patriot Order of the Baymen." Trucks bearing huge speakers are followed

friends. Everyone would celebrate the temporary reprieve with two solid weeks of drinking, dancing, singing and parading through the streets.

Drinking is still a central part of a Belizean Christmas, especially for men – some of whom pride themselves on staying intoxicated for the entire two weeks. As in the old days, most people still turn their houses inside out for a Christmas cleaning, hang new curtains, make *rum popo*, (an egg nog with the emphasis on the rum, not the eggs!) The traditional holiday meal, served on both Christmas and New Year's Day, is ham and turkey, rice and beans, and cranberry sauce. The season is filled with visiting and ex-

by crowds *bramming* to the cacophonous music.

The flag-raising at the courthouse on Independence Eve and the official ceremonies the next morning are very solemn events, but the party atmosphere prevails later in the day as people swarm the parks or main streets for the "jump up" or street fair, with lots of food and music.

Ole time Christmas: With so much party spirit in Belize, Christmas is no simple affair. Many of the traditions go back to logging days, when slaves and apprentice woodcutters would get a break from life in the "bush" to come to town for a visit with family and

changing Christmas cards and rum-preserved fruitcakes, usually personally delivered.

Until very recently, no Christmas was complete without the *bram*. A group of revelers would travel from house to house, push the furniture against the walls and use any household object that could function as a musical instrument to make *brukdown* music. Anything from a broom handle, wash basin or a metal grater to drums, banjos, guitars, accordions, cow bells and even the jaw bone of an ass could be used. The Creole lyrics, invented on the spot, would be about famous people or local village happenings. These days, even though *brukdown* has lost its appeal for many young people, there are still several "Boom and Chime" bands and singers who are much sought after for private parties throughout the year.

In Dangriga, the Christmas season is greeted by Joncunu (John Canoe) dancers. Outfitted in a pink wire mask, white tunic with flowing ribbons, an elaborate crown with tall feathers and hundreds of tiny shells attached to their knees, the dancers go from door to door dancing the *wanaragua*, with their arms outstretched and legs together. Some say the dance is meant to be an imitation of white slave holders and their behavior, which may be why it was popular at Christmas when normal master and slave relations

The best place to witness this convergence is in Dangriga, the town which boasts the greatest number of Garifuna in Belize. Don't plan on getting any sleep, however, because the previous night is filled with music and dancing in the streets and at the Roundhouse. As well as performing the *wanaragua*, or Joncunu, Settlement Day is a chance for the Garifuna to show off their most most popular dance, the Punta. In what is supposed to resemble the courtship ritual, a couple circles each other shaking only their hips and plowing the earth with their toes as they alternately propel themselves towards and away from each other.

The *hunguhungu* is also performed for

were traditionally more relaxed.

New Year's in Belize is really a continuation of Christmas and although people "ring in" the coming year with parties and champagne, New Year's Day is usually spent quietly with family or friends.

Garifuna pride: Garifuna Settlement Day, on the other hand, is anything but quiet. Celebrated on November 19, the day commemorates the 1832 arrival of the largest group of Garifuna to Belize's southern shores, and is a non-stop cultural fête.

<u>Left</u>, Garifuna dancers with attitude, Seine Bite.
<u>Above</u>, afternoon singalong.

Settlement Day (although it usually has a more ceremonial function as part of the *dugu* ritual – see "South to Dangriga", pages 227–236). The *hunguhungu* may use up to three drums and requires the whole clan, or even entire community, to participate in the dancing and call- and response-chanting.

At dawn the next morning there is a re-enactment of the arrival of the early settlers in their dories. As they enter town from the mouth of the river, the travelers are greeted by women singing, drums beating, and the waving of cassava sticks and Garifuna flags of yellow, black and white. Everyone then proceeds to the church for a lengthy Thanksgiving Mass: the European choral-style hymns are given Garifuna lyrics and ritual is Roman Catholic.

Amongst the Mestizos: A blend of religious traditions can also be clearly seen in Mestizo communities of northern Belize, particularly at Easter. Costume parades begin the weekend before Lent. In Orange Walk, *los mascaradas* wear scary disguises and drag chains through the streets, while others perform humorous skits or *comparsas* door to door. A dummy made of old clothes with a calabash head is dubbed "Juan Carnival" and burned in a ritual at sundown. In San Pedro, skits tell the story of the Mestizos' arrival in the village last century or relate other significant

events. In both towns, children roam the streets carrying raw eggs, flour and paint to ambush each other – and hapless adults – "painting" them from head to toe, a tradition said to be inspired by the mischievous Mayan god, Momo.

Good Friday is often observed with a religious procession through the streets. In Orange Walk, the devoted dress in mourning and carry images of Jesus at various stages of his life as they head to the church for a symbolic burial. In San Pedro the mourners carry a coffin to the church, stopping at each station of the cross to recite prayers.

In many communities no liquor is served on Good Friday and in some towns no one is supposed to play loud music or ball games. Many Belizeans are superstitious about swimming or using boats on this day, while others joke that swimmers will turn into fish or mermaids.

By contrast, the next day is filled with action as the country's most prestigious bicycle race, "The Holy Saturday Cross Country," captures national attention. On Easter Sunday people attend sunrise services and go on family outings; the American-style Easter Bunny has also begun to make his presence felt in recent years.

Most Mestizo and Mayan villages also have an annual fiesta in honor of the town's patron saint. The most prestigious of these is the Benque Fiesta held in July in Benque Viejo del Carmen near the Guatemalan border. Although it is heavily commercialized with imported carnival rides and game booths, there is still a mass at the Catholic church with marimba music.

In memory of Baron Bliss: One of Belize's most popular holidays, held every March 9, celebrates the life of a man who not only wasn't Belizean, he never even set foot on Belizean soil.

The English aristocrat Baron Bliss spent two months fishing in Belizean waters from his yacht the *Sea King* in 1926; already partly paralyzed by polio, he fell ill and died on board. Even so, he enjoyed his stay so much, and was so impressed by Belizeans' hospitality during his illness, that he left the bulk of his estate in trust for the country.

This gift made possible many of the public facilities Belizeans enjoy today, and helps finance the annual Baron Bliss Day regatta in Belize City. Held in the waters off Fort George near the Baron's grave, this spectacle continues to draw Belizean sailors – some third- or fourth-generation seamen – piloting every form of craft. The waters are packed with fancy sailboats, working "sandlighters" (boats which bring sand to shore) and brightly-trimmed dugout dories, which need a man to *kindola* over the side (hang by the mast) for balance. At the same time, the skies over Belize City are filled with hundreds of kites, strung up to take advantage of the March winds.

<u>Left</u>, Punta bump-and-grind. <u>Right</u>, Joncunu dancer.

For Belizeans, eating is a communal act. There is no such thing as a diet in Belize: denying oneself food means rejecting the good intentions of others and the years of tradition behind every dish. Food is to be shared – if an old woman has only one creole bun she will gladly give you half, and plates of dinner appear from all directions whenever someone is ill or falls on hard times. Waste is considered a sin and so is refusing a stranger a glass of water if he or she asks at your door.

Despite this enthusiasm, Belizean cuisine can be mystifying to visitors. The country has an abundance of fresh fruit, meat and fish, yet there is a peculiar fondness for tinned foods imported from Europe. This may be the legacy of Belize's years as a British colonial outpost, or a taste acquired during the days of famine following this century's two major hurricanes. Whatever the case, many Belizean families would be at a loss without their salad cream, tinned luncheon meat and condensed milk.

Equally baffling is how a country that possesses so many different ethnic dishes embraces one of the world's most monotonous daily diets. With an almost religious devotion, the entire country sits down every day at noon for the main meal – which, nine times out of ten, is either "rice and beans" or its variation, "stew beans and rice." The former is a pinkish mash of red kidney beans cooked together with rice; the latter is where the beans and rice are cooked separately, often with a piece of pigtail thrown in for extra zest. The best versions of both dishes use coconut milk in the rice.

Some Belizeans' love of rice and beans borders on addiction. Many eat it every single day of the week, insisting they just don't feel satisfied by anything else. No matter what the house specialty, new restaurants quickly discover they must include rice and beans on the menu if they want to attract customers – especially at lunchtime. Late night partygoers in Belize City simply cannot go home unless they stop for "Meegan's," the rice and bean dinners sold by an elderly vendor and his sons from a bicycle cart in front of a bank. Even Belizeans living abroad continue to cook this filling staple, at least for the traditional Sunday dinner of rice and beans, stewed chicken, potato salad and fried plantain – the meal many consider Belize's national dish.

Down to the bone: Chicken is certainly Belizeans' favorite meat, and each bird is stretched to the limit. Except for the head,

every bit of the chicken – including the feet – is stewed and served up. The bony rather than meaty pieces are considered the choicest, especially by those who like to suck out the marrow. Even the former Prime Minister, George Price, is said to always ask for the chicken neck, making him a welcome guest in even the poorest homes.

Many Belizeans complain that they would starve if it weren't for Chinese take-out windows selling "dolla chicken" – a small bag containing one piece of chicken and some french fries for a dollar. After a hard night at a bar or club, many Belize City residents grab an order of chicken and head for "the

Preceding pages: Garifuna meal, Pelican Beach Resort, Dangriga. <u>Left</u>, Brenda's Caribbean cuisine, Placencia. <u>Right</u>, fresh fish on the barbie.

Fort" – the sea wall near the Baron Bliss Lighthouse – to continue drinking or prolong a romantic evening. Fund-raising groups set up Saturday barbecues on street corners.

Belizean steaks are rarely worth the money, or the jaw-power they take to chew, but pork is plentiful, as is mutton and venison. Adventurous diners should try at least one of the unusual game meats in Belize – usually served stewed and seasoned with red ricado, a spice ball whose main ingredient is anatto seed. One classic is "bamboo chicken," which is actually a type of iguana known for its tender white flesh. In an effort to conserve the species, the dish is banned during the months of February and March. Another is

of choices, but standards include red snapper, mackerel, grouper, shark and barracuda (also called "barro") and fresh- and salt-water snook – a light textured fish considered "the steak of the sea."

Besides being baked, barbecued or stewed, fish often appears in soups, the richest of which is "serre." This traditional Garifuna dish requires numerous "ground foods" such as yams, cassava and okra, as well as plantains and lots of coconut milk; it is often served with thin, crispy cassava bread. The thinnest version of the fish soups is called "fish tea," typically made by fisherman camped at the cayes. It uses only onions, black pepper, and live fish – they have to be

armadillo, known locally as "hamadilly." Restaurant owners say this armor-plated mammal is a particular favorite with members of the British Forces stationed in Belize.

But of all the game meats, the one Belizeans recommend most is gibnut. This large rodent is considered so delectable that it was presented to Queen Elizabeth on one of her visits. The British press had a field day, with headlines blaring QUEEN EATS RAT IN BELIZE. Ever since this auspicious occasion, the animal has been known by the distinguished title of "Royal Gibnut."

Bountiful waters: For less exotic tastes, seafood is a lifesaver in Belize. There are dozens

still jumping when they hit the boiling water.

Shellfish, whose supply seemed limitless only a generation ago, now have strictly regulated harvesting seasons. Lobster, unavailable from mid-March to mid-July, has become a lucrative export and fetches handsome prices locally. Shrimp, whose season is closed from mid-April to mid-August, is a little cheaper, especially the fresh water variety sold in Chinese restaurants, but is still a luxury for most. Conch (pronounced *conk*) is the most affordable and widely consumed shellfish, although unavailable from the beginning of July until the end of September. It is often chopped up and cooked in lime juice to make "ceviche," a dish common to many Latin American countries; it is also fried in batter as the "conch fritters" sold on the streets or in snack shops.

Although conservationists warn that their numbers are rapidly decreasing, turtle is a beloved Belizean delicacy as a steak or stew. Salt-water varieties, called simply "sea turtle," have a closed season from April to October, but the two most popular fresh water species, the "Bucatora" and "Hicatee," are available most of the year.

Many seafood dishes are reputed to have special sexual powers. If a woman wants to conceive a child, she and her husband are encouraged to eat *behave bruda* ("behave

Mayan Soul Food: Perhaps the greatest contribution the Mayas and Mestizos have made to Belizean culture emerged from their fire hearths and kitchens. Traditional Spanish dishes have become such important components of the Belizean diet that many consider foods like *escabeche* and *panades* to be of Creole origin. One Creole restaurateur even coined the phrase "Mayan Soul Food" to describe a variety of Spanish foods served in his establishment.

Tamales can be obtained anywhere, anytime in Belize. Whether cooked at home, in restaurants, or sold in buckets on the streets, they are made from ground corn meal or *masa* mixed with shredded chicken or pork,

brother") a soup made from snapper and ground foods with an entire grouper head thrown in (the eyes are said to be the most potent ingredient). If a man wants to increase his sexual prowess or "strengthen his back," he should drink seaweed shakes or eat thick white conch soup. (Cowfoot Soup, which really is made of cow's feet, is another back-strengthening creation, particularly sought after following a hard night of drinking – although the uninitiated may be put off by its gummy, gluey texture.)

Left, Mexican plate, Corozal. **Above**, haute cuisine at Maruba Resort.

wrapped and steamed in a plantain leaf. *Tamales de chaya* are a spinach variation which may include cheese. A smaller version (*tamalitos* or *dukunu*) are steamed in a corn husk and may have no meat filling at all.

Completely unconcerned about their cholesterol levels, many Belizeans enjoy several other corn-based, deep-fried Spanish minifoods. The undisputed nationwide favorites are fish or bean *panades* made from corn *masa*, folded over and fried until crispy and served with an onion and vinegar sauce spiced up with habanero pepper. These can be quite small, so you may have to fill up on *garnaches* – flat, crispy corn tortillas topped with refried beans, grated cheese and tomato sauce. *Salbates* are a thicker alternative, topped with shredded chicken and cabbage. Especially popular for breakfasts on the run are soft corn tortilla *tacos*, sold on the street from bicycle carts under colorful umbrellas.

Spanish soups are more substantial. *Escabeche* is a clear onion soup with large pieces of chicken and a tangy flavor, *chimirole*, also using chicken, has special seasoning which makes it black. *Relleno* is made from an entire chicken stuffed with pork and may also contain hardboiled eggs. Fish lovers will enjoy *chichac*, a clear broth which may be spooned over a whole fried fish or contain fish patties.

Fruit lover's fantasy: Some say it is because the colonial masters discouraged farming, but whatever the reason, today the closest many Creole families get to serving vegetables is from a can. If you are determined to taste a typical Belizean vegetable, however, try a wrinkled green squash called *cho-cho* (which it's said resembles a granny with her teeth out).

On the other hand, fresh fruit is everywhere in Belize. Street vendors sell everything from the familiar bananas, watermelon, papaya and pineapples to exotica like *craboo* – small yellow balls that are often made into wine or ice cream – and hard little green

plums topped with hot pepper and salt. Little bags of pumpkin seeds called *pepitos* or macobi seeds are supposed to help keep your mind off a failed romance or absent lover, and yellow cashew fruit is stewed with brown sugar (delicious!) or made into cashew wine. During April and May, there are several varieties of mangoes, which can be eaten green (sliced and served with salt and pepper), served as chutney or eaten fresh when ripe and sweet.

Plaintains, rich in potassium, are often served with rice and beans or mashed to make Garifuna dishes like *fufu* or *matilda foot*. Coconut is also a key cooking ingredient, with every part used: the milk, the meat, the oil for frying and the husks for fuel. Orchards in southern Belize produce endless fresh citrus fruits – although watch out for too much lime juice, said by Belizeans to "cut your nature" (decrease your sex drive).

Breads and sweets: Breads, buns and other pastries are baked in Belizean kitchens almost daily, to be consumed in the morning with a cup of coffee or ovaltine, or eaten with cheese, beans or "fry fish" for evening "tea." Favorites include the small, flaky biscuits known as "johnny cakes" (the original name for which may have been "journey cakes," because they travel well), and "Creole bread," made in round dense loaves using coconut milk for extra flavor. A favorite with hot tea are "Suny and Tan buns" sold at a Belize City bakery of the same name. These sweet brown loaves filled with raisins are so popular they are sent to relatives living in the United States and much sought after by Belize-Americans visiting home.

For Belizean women, being told they are losing weight is no compliment. Belizean men admire full, rounded figures and pity those who are too slim (*magre*). As a result, desserts are rich, gooey and filled with calories. The sweetest of all is lemon pie, also known as "merengay pie," which has a rich filling of condensed milk and lime (not lemon) topped by light, fluffy meringue. There are coconut pies, tarts and trifles, as well as coconut "crusts," made of grated coconut and brown sugar sealed in a flour shell and cooked over an open fire. Coconut candies include *cutubrut*, chopped coconut meat crystalized in brown sugar, and its cousin, *tableta*, made with shredded coconut.

"Stretch me guts" is a taffy-like confection

created from a mixture of coconut water, lime and sugar – when set, it is pulled out from a nail on the wall. The British heritage emerges in desserts such bread pudding, rice pudding and "potato pung," a heavy cake made of grated sweet potatoes and sprinkled with brown sugar and ginger. Finally, Christmas is always greeted with rum-preserved fruit cakes and *rumpopo*, a sort of rum egg nog.

Liquid refreshments: Despite being in Central America, Belizeans aren't great coffee drinkers. As you might expect in a former British colony, tea is the preferred hot brew, especially in the evenings. It is drunk with condensed milk and, although no one seems

lizean social scene, with men doing all the buying. A woman who refuses to accept a drink from a Belizean male, especially an older one, may cause a severe blow to his pride – the offer is often made out of courtesy and contains no ulterior motive. (The only bigger insult is for a woman to offer to buy a man a drink; this implies that he hasn't enough money!)

Although many villagers pride themselves on their home-made wines – concocted from everything from berries to rice and sorrel – the liquor most widely consumed in Belize is rum. This can be mixed with anything from Coke to pineapple juice. There are several local brands, of which *Caribbean* and *Durleys*

to know why, people traditionally knock the spoon against the side of the cup while stirring, to make a tinkling sound.

Belizeans are noticeably addicted to soft drinks. Along with the standard international brands which have been invading the market, a local company, Bradley's Bottling Works, quietly continues to sell its product (with a noticeable boost in sales at Christmas time). Its drinks are known as "lemonade" regardless of flavor, and the Belizean clientele is fanatically loyal.

Drinking is an important part of the Be-

(which is also called "Parrot rum" because of its company logo) are the top sellers.

The most successful local beer, *Belikin*, with a Mayan temple on the label, has withstood several challengers over the years and somehow manages to reign supreme. Although it holds special appeal for tourists and sentimental Belizean-Americans, status-seeking local males shun it in public: many will drink Belikin at home or with friends, but only order imported brands when at a bar or trying to impress their date. Whiskey drinking follows a similar etiquette, with the imported and costly Black Label burning a hole in many a drinker's pockets.

Left, take-out *tamales*. <u>Above</u>, medicinal teas.

The seaward rim of Belize's Barrier Reef, referred to as the outer fore-reef, is a favorite locale for scuba divers. It's not hard to understand why.

Imagine floating along an underwater mountain ridge. To the east stretches an abyss of nothing but deep blue. Below lies an 80-degree slope, covered by a quilt of magnificently-colored coral plates and swaying fronds. A formation of eagle rays cruises past, their 3-ft (1-meter) wings lazily flapping; groupers lurk in the shadow of coral heads, their skins darkening to blend into the surroundings; 3 inch (7 cm) long damsel fish defend their territories against all intruders (including divers); and parrotfish, the grazers of the sea, browse on algae while fluorescent blue chromis float above coral gardens.

Out of nowhere, panic hits. Clouds of fish explode and dart for cover as the silver streak of a barracuda flashes by and collides with a careless hogfish. Scales and bits of fin erupt from the impact. The tail half of the hogfish slowly sinks, undulating through the water like a pendulum; the barracuda crushes its prey in its powerful jaws, while yellowtail snappers and bluehead wrasses converge on the entrails in a frenzy, tugging and tearing at pieces of floating tissue.

Within a minute everything below the waves is as serene as before, except there is one less hogfish on the reef and one more satiated barracuda.

Understanding the Barrier Reef: Coral reefs, it has been said, are visual poems, filling a diver's sense of sight with form, color and patterns. If so, Belize is a master poet, and the Belize Barrier Reef is an epic of colossal proportions. At 185 miles (298 km) in length, dotted with around 200 cayes, the Belize Barrier Reef is the second largest in the world after Australia's Great Barrier Reef, while the variety of reef types and marine life within its borders is unequaled in the northern hemisphere.

Belizean waters are perfect for coral growth. Corals are surprisingly finicky, requiring warm, clear water, steady sunlight and a shallow, firm foundation to grow on. The vast mass of marine life now following the Belizean coast actually grows on a prehistoric reef. This thrived over a million years ago, when water was imprisoned in gigantic northern glaciers and sea levels were 300 ft (90 meters) lower than they are today. The underlying Pleistocene reef structure contains many of the same coral species divers still see, as scientists found from cores

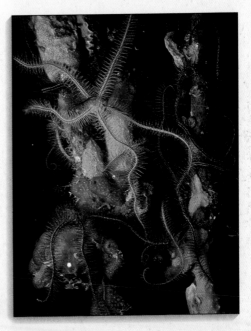

drilled 175 ft (53 meters) below the surface of present-day reefs.

Closer to the surface, at Reef Point on the northern shore of Ambergris Caye, lies further evidence of these ancient reefs. Here, portions of the Pleistocene coral reef intercept the shoreline in an area no larger than a football field. Sharp, skeletal remains of staghorn, elkhorn and brain corals lie exposed, cemented together in a matrix of coral sands. During the winter, heavy surf pounds this coast, fracturing the ancient reef and tossing limestone fragments upon a 15-ft (4.5-meter) rubble wall, but in calmer weather charter boats slip through a narrow channel

Preceding pages: breakers on the reef; flowing sabellidae. Left, a diver at Southwater Caye floats across Yellow Pencil coral. Right, life amongst the mangrove roots.

from San Pedro. The eroding limestone and fossil corals conjure up images of prehistoric landscapes, but you don't have to go far to see the images come to life.

"Hard" and "soft" coral: South of Reef Point, the "hard" coral begins to form a true barrier reef, snaking south into the Bay of Honduras. Its structural framework is limestone; upon this, billions and billions of individual coral polyps form colonies, connected by living tissue.

Each coral polyp essentially consists of a set of tentacles, a mouth, and a gut perched atop a limestone skeleton. The polyps have special cells on the outside of their bodies which secrete calcium carbonate. As the

allow disease or infection to develop. And since the entire colony is connected by living tissue, a small, seemingly inconsequential injury may eventually kill a whole colony that might have taken thousands of years to grow to its present size.

Other coral groups have forsaken a hard skeleton on the outside of their bodies for a more flexible, internal skeleton. These "soft" corals also secrete calcium carbonate, but they imbed small pieces of limestone in a horny protein substance inside their bodies. Soft corals, with trunks and branches waving gracefully in the water currents, come in a range of hues – yellows to reds to purples – and create colorful underwater forests.

colony grows, the polyps build their skeletons from underneath, pushing themselves up or out into a myriad of sizes and shapes. Growth rates vary with different species and different conditions, but coral reefs in warm, tropical waters grow only around 5 inches (13 cm) every century.

A coral reef, then, is actually a thin layer of life on top of ever-growing pieces of limestone. When an inattentive swimmer or errant boat hits or brushes against a piece of coral, the damage may not be immediately apparent. But much like a small wound on a human which can become infected if not properly cared for, the damaged piece of coral may

Diving on the reef: The Belize Barrier Reef is not one continuous wall of coral, but is splintered into segments separated by relatively deep channels. The oxygen and plankton (free floating microscopic plants and animals) carried by the Caribbean Sea flush the Belize coastal zone twice daily through these channels, feeding billions of hungry coral polyps and other reef creatures. Attracting large numbers of fish as a result, they are often excellent for diving and snorkeling (the most popular and accessible is Hol Chan Marine Reserve on Ambergris Caye).

There are over 460 species of fish that a snorkeler or diver is likely to see while swimming over coral reefs. Though some look formidable, most fish are unconcerned by your presence. Barracudas for example, have an unnerving habit of approaching swimmers and following them about. This is pure curiosity – there has never been a report of an unprovoked attack by a barracuda, and they normally move away when approached. Eels have a nasty reputation, although they are generally non-aggressive. Alarmingly, they open and close their mouths as if preparing to bite, but they are merely pumping water through their gills. But be careful: eels can inflict a nasty bite if annoyed, especially the green moray eel.

Sharks are not commonly encountered in shallow water. Characterized by a smooth surface and a uniform mustard color, it grows in two distinct forms, plate-like or encrusting. Though it looks like one, fire coral is not a true coral. This hydrozoan has tiny silica needles which break off on contact and can cause intense stinging. Some sponges cause irritation, as does the bristle worm.

The best way to avoid any potential problems when exploring the coral reef is never to touch anything – for your own safety and the health of the reef.

Research on the reef: The basic structure of the Barrier Reef is similar all along its 185-mile (298-km) length. At Carrie Bow Caye, a marine lab perched atop the edge of the

Belize, with the exception of the docile nurse shark. Chances are that sharks will sense you long before you see them, and move away. However, all sharks should be treated with caution. Even the normally docile nurse shark can become aggressive if molested.

Probably the most serious underwater hazard is the long-spined urchin, returning after the population was severely reduced by an epidemic in the 1980s. Needle-like spines will pierce gloves or wet suits, and the tips easily break-off. Fire coral is a danger in

Left, sponges and anemone. **Above**, squirrelfish and coral.

Barrier Reef, scientists from the Smithsonian Institution's National Museum of Natural History have divided the reef up into the basic zones, or habitats. A zone is an area where local environmental conditions – temperature, sunlight, water movement – allow certain groups of animals and plants to exist together. Usually one or two species in the group are more abundant than the rest and are used to characterize a habitat.

Starting from the shoreward, or western side of the Barrier Reef, four major and 12 minor zones have been established along an east–west line north of Carrie Bow Caye. These zones include grass beds, where conch and striped grunts feed; reef flats, where crabs, small corals and anemones lie concealed among the rubble and sand; and spur and groove formations, where the coral grows in long linear mounds separated by coral sand gullies.

Moored as close as 10 miles (16 km) off the Belize Barrier Reef lie three of the finest coral atolls in the Caribbean: Turneffe Island, Glover's Reef and Lighthouse Reef. The origin of these atolls – shaped like underwater table-top mountains, with gardens of coral on the summit – is still a matter of speculation. Most geologists agree that the atolls grow over protrusions created by the movement of the tectonic plates of the re-

gion. The combination of uplifting and subsequent sinking land masses has created magnificent underwater drop-offs, some plunging to depths of 10,000 ft (3,000 meters) to the east of Lighthouse Reef. The reef systems surrounding these atolls rival the Belize Barrier Reef in length, with almost 140 miles (225 km) of lush coral growth. Within the coral barrier surrounding the atolls lie thousands of patch reefs; in the case of Turneffe, the largest of the atolls with an area of over 200 sq. miles (520 sq. km), there are hundreds of small mangrove-covered islands. Together, these three atolls provide some of the finest wall diving in the world.

(For more details on diving possibilities in the outer reef, see *Northern Cayes* chapter, pages 163–169).

The mangrove coastline: Coral reefs do not exist in isolation. Mangroves line much of the Belizean coastline, the cayes and lower reaches of the rivers. Seagrass beds, their blades swaying in the current like prairie meadows, blanket the sea bottom between reef and shore.

These mangrove and seagrass beds may not look as spectacular as coral reefs but, as giant marine nurseries, they form the foundation of the continuing long-term health of the Belize coastal zone. The quiet, protected water of the mangrove roots and grass blades provides plentiful food and shelter for countless juvenile marine organisms. In fact, most of the shellfish and the fish caught for food or sport off the Belize coast rely on mangroves for at least part of their lives.

Four different species of mangrove thrive in Belize – red, white and black mangrove and buttonwood. As well as stabilizing the coast-line against erosion and presenting a natural buffer against destructive hurricane winds, mangroves link the rich nutrients on land with the billions of hungry mouths at sea. Every year Belizean rivers transport tons of sediment and debris to the sea from deep within the interior. The nutrients in these loads, deposited along the coast, are often in forms unavailable to marine life. But mangroves thrive on the frequent deposits, producing branches, leaves and seeds.

When a mangrove leaf drops into the waters below, the process of decomposition begins. The leaf slowly releases thousands of minute particles, each coated with millions of voracious micro-organisms. Small invertebrates like worms, shrimp and crabs begin to feed on the microbes; these small invertebrates are in turn eaten by larger creatures, until the nutrients in river silt are passed on through the food chain.

Many of these smaller fish also become prey for flocks of wading birds combing the surf line for food. Belize's coast has an abundance of water-birds and nesting colonies, with over 50 mangrove-covered cayes reported to have nesting sites on them. Roseate spoonbills, ibis, herons, and cormorants nest on many of the small mangrove islands in Chetumal Bay to the north. The magnificent frigate bird and brown boobies have established large nesting colonies on many cays to the south. Man-O-War Caye, 10 miles (16 km) east of Dangriga, has one of the largest colonies of frigate birds in the Caribbean. Meanwhile, ospreys locate the highest trees on the cayes, usually black mangroves, and construct a loose pile of sticks on top to raise their young.

A living treasure: The entire coastal zone of Belize is a treasure of sea life, pristine and as yet mostly unexploited. Jewels of evolution are continually being found. For example, scientists from the Smithsonian Institution's marine lab on Carrie Bow Caye recently stumbled upon a tiny bay that may be unique in the Caribbean – if not the world. A quirk known as sea squirts) cling to the prop roots, competing for the limited amount of space.

Smithsonian researchers have identified 43 different tunicates in this one location, more than was previously known throughout the entire Caribbean. The fish are so abundant that they form layers, with the smaller fry near the surface, the larger ones a level down, and the fat-bodied herrings blanketing the carpet of lettuce coral.

The location of this bay will stay a closely guarded secret until scientists, the government and conservation groups within Belize can agree on the proper management of the area. The risk to any pristine environment can not be overestimated. After all, these

of nature allows mangrove to grow on the edge of a series of deep sink holes. Healthy colonies of lettuce coral carpet the steep slopes of the depressions. As the slopes rise into shallow water, the scene explodes into activity, with bright oranges and reds, deep purples and blues streaming past; crinoid arms perform silent ballets between 3-ft (1-meter) high loggerhead sponges; star and brain corals flourish among seagrasses and mangrove trunks. Sponges, anemones and tunicates (tiny barrel-shaped creatures better

Left, cushion sea star. <u>Above</u>, a sailfin blenny, **Carrie Bow Caye.**

marine organisms evolved over millions of years within a stable or gradually changing environment. Any sudden stress – whether from pollution, siltation, overfishing or injuries from a careless diver – can be devastating. For a visitor, kicking a piece of coral is hardly noticed; for the coral it is a matter of life and death; for Belizeans it is slow destruction of a priceless resource.

At present, the bay – and countless others like it – are a gauge of the environmental health of Belize's marine systems. Areas such as these expose Belize as a country of raw, uncut wilderness, below the waves no less than in the rainforest.

FISHING

Before the scuba divers and eco-tourists came to Belize, there were the fishermen. For decades, anglers have been coming to Belize seeking the excitement of jumping a tarpon or stalking the elusive permit, choosing their locale from the country's mud flats, the rivers, or the deeper waters near the reef.

Fishing in Belize has changed. Thirty years ago, there was only one fishing lodge on the Belize River, patronized mainly by retirement-age men. These days, there are at least eight fishing resorts located on the cayes, rivers and coral atolls; the sport is no longer limited to men, as more and more women become passionate and skilled anglers.

And whatever type of fish they seek, environmental awareness has rubbed off on fishermen: there is general agreement that Belize's lush, pristine foliage and abundant wildlife add immeasurably to the total fishing experience. It is not uncommon during a river trip to see monkeys, iguanas and crocodiles as well as orchids and bromiliads, and even the cayes are completely different environments from what North Americans and Europeans are used to at home.

The fly fishing craze: Belize has also seen changes in fishing technique. Bait fishing, once the most popular, has given way to fly fishing – a result of the fever that has taken hold of sport-fishers throughout the world.

Fly fishers describe their technique as an art rather than a skill, and consider themselves to be conservationists as well as sportsmen. They are the first to argue in favor of preserving both the fish and their natural habitats in order to ensure healthy populations in the future; for this reason, most fishing in Belize is now catch-and-release with very few fish actually being killed. This new breed of anglers is more concerned with skillfully landing the fish than in making it a trophy or filling an ice chest to take home; success is not measured by the number of fish brought to the boat, but by achieving a flawless cast, or choosing just the right lure.

Most fly fishers do not consider themselves to be on vacation in Belize – it's more

like they are on a mission. Often they are in the boat before dawn and back at the lodge only at sundown. For these passionate fishermen, Belize offers exotic surroundings and several of the most sought-after salt-water game fish, the most popular of which is undoubtedly the tarpon.

Known for its spectacular jumps, tarpon in Belize range in size from 5 to 150 lbs (2 to 68 kg), but most commonly weigh between 20 and 60 lbs (9 and 27 kg). Even the smaller tarpons will twist and turn somersaults, but

the real thrill comes when a big one takes the bait, fly or plug. A large tarpon will leap into the air shaking its head violently, and for a brief instant will appear to hang in mid-air. This amazing action has led Belizean fishermen to dub him the "silver Michael Jordan" after the American basketball player.

A tarpon is capable of keeping up the fight for two hours, so it is no wonder so many fishermen consider it a real challenge. Guides say most anglers visiting Belize have a good chance of landing a tarpon, although success is measured by how many jumps a fisherman achieves that day or week.

Hunt for hidden prey: Bonefish are Belize's

Preceding pages: the morning's catch. <u>Left</u>, the battle is joined. <u>Right</u>, showing off the spoils.

second most popular game fish. These fish may be small (1 to 10 lbs/0.45 to 4.5 kg) but they have great power for their size. A bonefish can provide a fantastic run once it is hooked, but getting one to take your fly is by no means easy. The bonefish's mirror-like scales also give him almost perfect camouflage as he travels over green sea grass or the gray bottom of the mud and coral flats.

Although a bonefish can be practically invisible in the water, it is the permit that is known as the "ghost of the flats." These members of the jack family average between 10 and 12 lbs (4.5 to 5.4 kg) and have been described by one fisherman as 10 times more elusive than bonefish. They may also be 10

times more powerful: once hooked, a permit takes off with explosive force. The experience has been described as being similar to a grenade going off underwater and amazes most anglers the first time they feel it. Fishermen stalk the easily spooked permit by wading through the water, or standing silently in a skiff as their guide poles it.

Another popular salt-water fish in Belize is the snook. Unlike tarpon, bonefish and permit, which are not considered very tasty, snook are delicious. Dubbed the "steak of the sea," snook used to be standard fare at some fishing lodges, but these days more and more are being released as environmental aware-

ness grows: there has been a marked decrease in the average size of snook from the record of 47 lbs (21 kg) over a decade ago to between 6 and 8 lbs (2.7 and 3.6).

Out on the reef: Barracuda, snapper and jacks are also plentiful off the Belizean coast, and many tourists charter individual boats from Ambergris Caye to try their luck. There is some commercial sport fishing for billfish, and the Belize Fishing Association holds yearly ocean tournaments and rodeos for those who want to catch marlin and sailfish. Despite increasing pressure to release these large fish taken in competitions – which can weigh in at up to 450 lbs (200 kg) – most are cut up for their meat.

The recommended way to fish in Belize is through an established lodge or fishing resort, which uses qualified guides, rather than simply chartering a boat. There are lodges at Ambergris Caye, the Turneffe atoll, South Water Caye and Glover's Reef, all of which specialize in salt-water fishing, and two fishing resorts in Belize City which provide both river and coastal fishing. Individual guide services are also available on Ambergris Caye, Caye Caulker and at Placencia.

Belize looks set to remain one of the western hemisphere's great fishing venues. The year-round warm weather continues to draw fishermen season after season: while those in colder climes are scraping winter snow off their cars, visitors to Belize's fishing lodges are coating themselves with sunscreen before beginning their day in a skiff. And with many years of experience under their belts, Belizean guides are good at what they do. Not only do they know the waters and where the fish are most likely to be, but some can tell great stories about the fish and other exotic local wildlife.

Most fishermen enjoy being a part of nature, and return to their lodge each night full of stories about the orchids and iguanas they have seen during the day. But that doesn't mean tradition is thrown entirely by the wayside: for many, fishing still means competition and exaggerated stories about four-hour battles with a tarpon or the sighting of 30 or more permit. As one angler joked, "A good day for me is when I see more fish than my guide."

Left, fisherman on the cayes. **Right**, bringing in the big one.

For centuries, Belize's small population, limited agriculture and lack of industry doomed it to being a backwater of civilization. Today, Belize boasts the most accessible tropical wilderness in the Western hemisphere, and wildlife that lures travelers from around the world. Though not as biologically rich as the Amazon or Costa Rica, Belize, for its size, is unique in the number of different habitats and species within its borders.

The reason can be traced back to its climate and geological history. Set in the heart of Central America, Belize is part of a land mass bridging two great continents. This has not always been so. Around 100 million years ago, Belize formed part of an ancient archipelago, isolated from North and South America by primordial oceans. During this time of isolation, many animals evolved that were endemic, or native to the region.

Then, roughly 2 million years ago, giant continental plates began to rotate, grinding against each other and thrusting up mountains. As water became imprisoned in the colossal ice sheets of the poles, the seas receded, exposing new land. Central America became a land bridge between North and South America, allowing a free flow of migration. The resultant mixture of endemic and immigrant creatures spawned one of the most varied faunas on earth.

Thanks to its complex geological history, Belize's landscape mixes mountains, savannas, and coastal lagoons, while the tropical climate provides wet and dry seasons, hurricanes and heat. The resulting environmental mix creates an astonishing variety of animal and vegetable habitats: although only the size of New Hampshire in the United States, Belize has over 4,000 species of flowering plants, including 250 orchids and over 700 species of trees. In contrast, the whole of the US and Canada supports only 730 species, giving Belize on average 1,000 times the diversity of trees per square mile.

Scientists have catalogued over 70 kinds of forest in Belize, grouping them into three

basic types: 13 percent are open forests of pine and savanna; 19 percent are mangroves and coastal habitats; and by far the largest type, 68 percent, is covered by broadleaf forests and cohune palms, the rainforests of Belize. This vegetation determines to a large extent what animals will thrive and where.

Into the rainforests: The broadleaf forests (rainforests) support by far the greater diversity of wildlife. They are the result of the most favorable possible conditions for life on land – abundant sunlight, warmth, and

moisture. Most of the plants are trees, which grow to form a dense canopy. Lower down are multiple layers of smaller trees and shrubs, tied together by twisting vines. Finally, leaves, fallen branches and fungi litter the forest floor, quickly broken down into minerals by soil decomposers and recycled through the forest. Each layer is an animal habitat in itself, allowing space for a multitude of creatures to evolve. The secret of the rainforest is that most of the nutrients are stored not in the soil, but in the biomass – the roots, trunks, leaves, flowers and fruits, as well as the animals – of the forest.

Despite this, many visitors to the tropics

Preceding pages: dawn in the rainforest; puma surprised. **Left,** a kinkajoo, nocturnal mammal. **Right,** red-eyed tree frog.

are disappointed with the apparent lack of wildlife. Don't be. The animals are there. Most creatures of the rainforests see, hear, smell or feel human intruders long before they themselves are noticed, and the seemingly solid wall of green and tangle of vines provide innumerable hiding places. But to the patient, perceptive and informed visitor, the biological wealth of the forest eventually reveals itself.

Midday is a poor time to visit the rainforest. The heat of the overhead sun and the stillness of the air force most creatures into the shade, and humans should probably follow suit: the chainsaw buzz of flies and cicadas, along with the heat and humidity,

reptiles, the most easily spotted are snakes: of Belize's 54 species, 45 are harmless to man, and even the most poisonous are as eager to avoid you as you are them. Staying on trails is probably the surest way to stay clear of snakes; unless you are sure of identification, do not attempt to handle them.

Rainforest nights: After the sun sets, the rainforests come alive with the creeping, the crawling and the jumping, making it the perfect time to scrutinize vegetation on well marked trails. Red eyed tree frogs, gaudily colored lizards, and delicate salamanders awake and roam the blackness.

Insects abound in an astonishing array of shapes and sizes. Spiders are one of the most

make walking hard work. For birdwatchers, the best time is sunrise, when the air is cool and filled with the sounds of birds feeding and declaring territories. (*See "A Birdwatcher's Paradise," pages 131–133.*)

On the ground, it's easiest to spot leafcutter ants, also known as "wee wee" ants, carrying a load of leaves along the wide, clean highways they've cleared on the forest floor. The pieces of leaf are carried into huge underground chambers, where they are chewed and processed to grow fungus. The fungus in turn feeds the ants. This incredible relationship is so finely evolved that the fungus can no longer reproduce without the ants. Of the

conspicuous creatures encountered at night, the glinting reflections from their multiple eyes visible up to 50 ft (15 meters) away. Delicate crickets, iridescent beetles and mantis prowl the night in search of a meal. Many insects sport antennae two to three times their body lengths, using touch in the inky blackness to catch or avoid becoming prey.

Night is also the best time to view mammals. Bats dart above trails, gathering insects and startling hikers. Opossums, armadillos and ant-eaters are nocturnal, foraging along the many stream banks and fallen logs of the forest. Most nocturnal animals have large eyes to sense the jungle by moon or starlight, so pointing a flashlight at rustling in the leaves often produces eyeshine.

The paca, known as gibnut in Belize, is a nocturnal rodent the size of a large rabbit, often heard chewing on cohune nuts and thrashing around the litter of the forest floor at night. It has a large head sprouting from a chestnut colored body with four distinctive lines of white spots running along its back. This small animal, with enlarged cheeks, often gives out a hoarse bark or deep grumbling. Gibnut is a favorite item in restaurants – though similar in texture to beef, gibnut meat has a taste all its own – and a favorite prey of the five species of Belizean wildcats.

Famous felines: As Central America's largest spotted cat, the jaguar is probably the most celebrated creature of the rainforest, and Belize has created the world's first wildlife sanctuary specifically for the jaguar's protection (*see "The Jaguar," page 127, and the Cockscomb Basin Wildlife Sanctuary chapter, page 241*). But roaming beneath the rainforest canopy and along the banks of mountain streams, four other wildcats share the same territory as the jaguar – the jaguarundi, the margay, ocelot, and puma. Though all are endangered throughout their ranges, Belize supports healthy populations of each. That five species of cat, so similar in their ecological needs, can coexist and thrive within the same rainforest is a tribute to the health of the Belizean habitat.

Smallest of the wildcats (and most abundant), the jaguarundi moves like a fleeting shadow. The long, lanky body, slender tail and short legs make the jaguarundi unmistakable. No bigger than a house cat, this wildcat feeds mainly during the day on small rodents, birds and insects.

The margay is the most nocturnal of the cats: its large eyes and extremely bright eyeshine attest to its highly developed night vision. Superlative balance and great leaping ability – one researcher recorded a vertical leap of 8 ft 2 inches (2.44 meters)! – make the margay ideally adapted for life in the forest canopy. Smallest of the spotted cats, the margay prefers primary or old growth forests and is rarely seen in the wild.

The ocelot's name comes from the Aztecan word *tlalocelotl* meaning "field tiger,"

although it seems to prefer second-growth or recently cut forests. Known locally as the "tiger cat" (a name also used for the margay), it is about the size of a medium dog. It keeps to the forest floor, feeding occasionally on larger prey such as anteaters and brocket deer. Due to the exceedingly soft and beautiful spotted pelt, the ocelot was hunted nearly to extinction around Central America to produce fur coats.

While the jaguar inhabits lowland forests near streams and swamps, the puma, known as cougar or mountain lion in the US, prefers the highlands and drier ridge areas of the forest. The puma is extremely shy and secretive and probably the least likely to be seen.

The puma and jaguar are not the largest mammals of the rainforest. That distinction belongs to Belize's national animal, the Baird's tapir, known locally as "mountain cow." Although weighing up to 650 lbs (300 kg), tapirs can dissolve silently into the forest at first sign of danger; they are cautious creatures not prone to aggressiveness unless protecting young. Their most distinctive feature, despite their size, is a long prehensile lip which grabs plants and strips them clean.

Tapirs can survive in just about any type of terrain, though they prefer rainforest rivers and swamps. Despite this adaptiveness, the tapir is endangered throughout its range

Left, an iguana amongst the leaves. **Right**, the edible gibnut, once served to Queen Elizabeth II.

(Mexico to Ecuador) by hunting and deforestation. Belize is one of the last remaining strongholds of this magnificent creature.

The call of the wild: Another celebrated inhabitant of the Belizean rainforest is the black howler monkey, whose gutteral cry is often mistaken for the roar of a jaguar. "Baboons," as they are known in Belize, live in troops of four to eight, carving out a territory of between 12 and 15 acres (5 to 6 hectares). They defend their territories from intruding troops by using their remarkable voices to let other troops know their location. Howlers often begin and end their days by roaring, and the noise can carry for several miles.

The black howler monkey's range is lim-

ited to southern Mexico, northern Guatemala and Belize, but the populations are rapidly declining due to increasing deforestation throughout Central America. Belize supports one of the last strongholds of the baboon in the region: at the Community Baboon Sanctuary, a grassroots project where landowners agree to manage their properties to benefit the baboons, there are an estimated 1,200 monkeys. The roaring is deafening at sunrise and sunset around the sanctuary. A project is now underway to transfer howler monkeys from the sanctuary to some of their former homes, including the Cockscomb Basin Wildlife Sanctuary.

In the pine and savanna forests: In contrast to the mountainous tumble of rainforests blanketing the interior of Belize are its many areas of flat, relatively dry savanna. With the exception of the pinelands covering the Mountain Pine Ridge in the Cayo District, much of the savannas, locally referred to as "broken ridge", occur along the level lowlands of the north and the coastal strip east of the Maya Mountains. The new coastal road between Belize City and Dangriga meanders through some of the most beautiful savannas in Belize. Islands of limestone, surrounded by oceans of wind-blown grasses and knurled trees, attest to the harshness of the habitat.

Savanna flora in Belize evolved to take advantage of the extremes of climate and soil. The plants must deal with alternate water-logging during the rainy season and severe drought during the dry season. The savanna soils are generally acidic and nutrient-poor, allowing only hardy plants like craboo, oaks and palmettos to flourish. (The craboo is a small tree with tiny, yellow flowers which turn red with age. The fruit – cherry sized and also yellow – is a favorite of Belizeans, used in jams, ice-cream and wine. The slightly pungent odor of ripe, fermented craboo permeate towns and villages during the summer months.)

As the name suggests, Caribbean pine is a prominent feature of pine and savanna woodlands. Driving along stretches of the Northern Highway, the new coastal road and much of the Southern Highway, formations of pine align themselves like silent sentries awaiting review. Many of these pines have scorched trunks, blackened by fire – usually lit by lightning strikes in the spring and early summer. The fires start atop dead pines or in the tinder-like grass and may burn and smolder for days. The thick bark of the pines allow many of the trees to survive, while the underground root system of the grasses and shrubs allow them to resprout. In fact, savanna plants are often referred to as pyrophytes, meaning they are adapted to frequent burning. However, not all fires start by natural causes. Though the practice is discouraged, hunters will often start fires to flush deer and other game.

Despite the often scorched, inhospitable appearance of the savannas, many species of mammal forage there. Most commonly seen is the gray fox, one of the most abundant mammals in Belize, and one that often darts in front of cars or sprints along the side of the road before dodging into roadside vegetation. About the size of a house cat, with a large bushy tail, this member of the dog family feeds on small rodents and birds; it is an excellent climber, spending much of the hot mid-day in the shade and breeze of the upper branches of the forest. Often seen after a fire is the white-tailed deer, emerging during early morning and browsing for tender new shoots. Though some luck is required to spot mammals in the pine and savanna woodlands, the wide open spaces are ideal for bird watching – over 100 species are common. The striking vermilion flycatcher, a sparrow

stork in the Americas. Standing nearly 5 ft (1.5 meters) tall, the jabiru is entirely white except for a black head and a red band around the neck; it constructs a distinctive 8-ft (2.4-meter) diameter nest atop a lone pine, often visible from a mile away. In pre-protection days, this exposed nest made the endangered stork easy prey for hunters, and jabiru meat was often peddled in Belize City markets. Now fully protected, the jabiru's figure graces the backside of Belizean $20 bills.

Mangrove and coastal habitats: Near the coast, savannas and pine woodlands often blend into brackish water swamps and lagoons shared by mangroves. Though not requiring salt water to survive, mangroves

sized, bright red bird, is often seen "hawking" or making repeated sorties to nab flying insects on the wing. The fork-tailed flycatcher, another unmistakable inhabitant of the savannas, has 10-inch (25-cm) long tail feathers called "streamers" which provide increased maneuverability for catching insects flushed up by fires. Often, coveys of quail explode from the tall grasses lining roads in the broken ridge.

By far the most spectacular bird of the savanna and pine habitat is the jabiru, largest

Left, baby howler monkey on the lookout. **Above**, Baird's tapir, the national animal.

grow better in salt and brackish water than other terrestrial plants. Much of the Belizean coastline and lower reaches of the rivers are lined by three different species of mangrove.

The most common and distinctive is the red mangrove, found in frequently or permanently saturated areas. Numerous stilt-like prop roots arch from the main trunk into the soft mud, while aerial roots drip down from the branches, providing additional support in the loose sediments. The red mangrove seed sprouts while still on the tree, forming a 10-inch (25-cm) spear that, when released, embeds itself into the soft mud or sand below.

The black mangrove is commonly found

in slightly drier areas. The soft sediment around the tree trunks are punctured with armies of spiky projections (pneumato-phores) which rise above the soil or water to assist the plant with gas exchange.

Found on still drier ground are white mangroves, whose distinctive oval leaves sport a pair of salt glands for exuding excess salts at their stems. Bunches of wrinkled, grape-sized seeds crowd outer branches. After dropping, the seeds are dispersed by currents.

The easiest way to see mangroves is by taking a short boat ride up the Belize River from Belize City, where they form a majes-tic, cathedral-like tunnel over Haulover Creek. But mangroves reach their greatest

mammals which feed primarily on plants. Like most herbivores, they are normally slow and lumbering, but can exhibit tremendous burst of speed when startled, leaving behind swirls of mud. Manatees are found all along the Belizean coastline, but the largest con-centrations occur near the village of Gales Point near Dangriga.

A long history of harvesting manatee has led to a general population decline. Manatee was once an ingredient in the diet and cer-emonial activities of the Maya. In the 1800s, logwood cutters relished the manatee meat; the tails were reportedly pickled and eaten cold, while the tough skin was made into durable boot soles. As recently as the 1930s

size along the lower reaches of the remote Temash River in the Toledo District. Here, red mangrove trunks send up 10 to 15-ft (3 to 5-meter) high stilt roots, forming open for-ests of arches.

Manatees and crocodiles: Compared to other ecosystems in Belize, mangrove wildlife is not diverse or abundant. In fact, few terres-trial animals are restricted only to mangroves. Yet two endangered animals, the American Crocodile and the West Indian Manatee, rely on the mangrove environment.

Manatees are vast, docile, amiable crea-tures that can easily grow to 15 ft (4.5 meters) and 3,500 lbs (1,585 kg), the only marine

manatee meat was sold in local markets.

Today, manatee enjoy special protection, and the population is no longer declining: in fact, a recent survey showed that Belize has the largest population in the Americas (they were once common on the eastern coast of the US, but hunting drastically reduced their numbers). But, while hunting has been con-trolled, water and noise pollution are taking their toll: increased boating and fishing ac-tivities have damaged the coastal habitat and are affecting manatee numbers.

Hunted reptiles: The other endangered ani-mal in the Belizean mangroves is the Ameri-can crocodile. Feeding on fish, crabs, birds and small mammals, this species can grow to lengths of 22 ft (6.5 meters). During the dry season, females build nesting mounds, depositing up to 60 eggs inside. The eggs hatch near the start of the wet season and the parents often feed and protect the newly hatched young for some weeks after.

The American crocodile is much less aggressive than its much maligned cousin, the American alligator, which has overrun southern Florida. The crocodile typically shuns human activity. But despite its shyness and a thick hide which protects it from most natural predators, the American crocodile is threatened across its range by hunting and habitat destruction. The mangrove and coastal habi-

churn up the nutrient-rich soil. Though relatively poor in diversity, a mangrove forest remains a crucible of birth and decay.

Vital precautions: Belize may be a naturalist's heaven, but it can become purgatory for those ill-informed about the dangers of tropical wildernesses. The first rule is: don't go alone. All forests begin to look alike very quickly, off the trail. If you wander off into the rainforest after a bird sighting or the croak of a red-eyed tree frog, it is easy to lose your orientation. The dense vegetation tends to swallow up sound; calls for help won't travel far. It is best to travel with someone who knows the area – or hire a guide.

The second rule is: watch where you place

tats of Belize are one of the last remaining strongholds of this magnificent reptile.

Other above-water life in the mangroves is not quite as spectacular. The mangrove warbler, a tiny yellow bird with a rust-colored head, hops from roots to branches, picking up ants and flies. Nephila spiders (3 inches/ 7.5 cm long) spin golden webs to capture the abundant flying insects, while clouds of dragonflies dart through the open spaces as though locked in aerial combat. Fiddler crabs and 1-ft (30-cm) long great land crabs continually

Left, spotted skunk and American crocodile. Above, speckled racer.

you hands and feet. Some palms have needle-like thorns sticking out horizontally from their trunks, and will cause a nasty wound if a carelessly placed hand grabs hold. Checking where you sit down may save you the discomfort of pants full of ants.

"What about snakes?" is probably the most-asked question by visitors to the forest. Of the 54 species of snakes found in Belize, 45 are harmless to man. That, of course, leaves nine that are poisonous. Snakes such as the deadly fer-de-lance and coral snake live among the litter of the forest floor, but they are more eager to avoid you than you are them: they will sense the vibrations of your feet long before you see them and probably scurry away. Staying on trails is the surest way to avoid snakes – and unless you are sure of their identification, never handle them.

Much more annoying is the multitude of Belizean insects, though they are not the holiday-destroying nuisance they can be in other parts of the tropics. During the rainy season, mosquitoes can chase you inside as the sun sets. Also, during the heat of the day, tiny simulid flies (related to black flies and known locally known as bottlas – pronounced *bottle-ass*) bite and leave little red blood spots which itch for a short time. If you plan to walk through fields of tall grass where cattle sometimes graze (such as in the Com-

remove the larva without killing it (if you kill it inside your skin, there is the chance of infection). Wait a few weeks until the larva is about ⅛-inch (¼-cm) long, then squeeze it out slowly with continuous pressure to either side of the wound. Other than the psychological stress and chance of infection, this insect is harmless.

Most insect problems are solved by applying insect repellent during the day and draping mosquito netting around you while sleeping. Lightweight long trousers and shirts will protect you from insects and the occasional scrape and cut – bacteria and infections thrive in the hot, humid tropics.

Finally, always check your shoes or boots

munity Baboon Sanctuary) beware of ticks. Minute hatchlings can sometimes grab hold of your trouser legs by the thousands.

One insect deserves special mention. If you're exceptionally unlucky, a small bite might begin to enlarge on your skin rather than shrink and heal. After a few weeks, the wound will periodically sting or burn like hot needles for a few seconds at a time. This is caused by a larval botfly (*Dermatobia hominis*). An egg, placed on the skin by a blood-sucking fly, hatches and burrows its way down for food and shelter. If left alone for 40 or 50 days, the larvae will emerge and pupate – not a pretty sight. The trick is to

and shake out your clothes before putting them on in the morning: scorpions, though generally rare, can be locally common, especially in thatched roofed jungle resorts around San Ignacio. Some of these are a horrifying sight, about 6 inches (15 cm) long and shiny, metallic black – but, unlike the scorpions of Arizona, are not deadly. This may not be much comfort if one strolls into your bedroom at night, and even the sternest ecotourist has been known to pick up a heavy book and crush an intruding scorpion.

Above, sphinx moth larvae. **Right**, a jaguar prepares to pounce.

THE JAGUAR

The jaguar, largest cat in the Americas and largest spotted cat in the world, is a superbly designed predator whose legendary stealth in the rainforest has allowed it to stay at the top of the food chain while remaining an enigma to most of the world.

Each piece of the jaguar's physical equipment plays a role in the hunt. The body – with oversized head, short back and legs, and large, steady feet – is built for power rather than speed. The dish-like eyes, which see color, provide unusually sharp binocular vision to accurately track and seize prey. Within the shadowy habitat of the rainforest floor, the jaguar's sight is six times more acute than a human's.

Long, pointed canine teeth, specialized for crushing bone, complement a set of blade-like premolars to shear meat. The lithe body, sharp retractile claws, and strong shoulders allow the jaguar to single-handedly grasp and immobilize a 600-lb (240-kg) tapir. Even the name, derived from the Maya Indian word *yaguar*, meaning "he who kills with one leap", attests to this animal's great hunting skill.

Because of these fearsome qualities, jaguars are often depicted as vicious and cruel by people who equate anger and murder – as manifested in man – with aggression and killing of prey in cats. On the contrary, there is nothing vindictive in a jaguar killing its prey, any more than in a deer decapitating a plant stem. Each requires food to survive. And, contrary to legend, there is little evidence of jaguars attacking man.

But decades of bad press, bounty hunting and fragmentation of the forest habitat have left the jaguar an endangered species. Once ranging as far north as Arizona and as far south as Argentina, only isolated populations now survive in Central America and the Amazon. Belize supports the largest concentration of jaguars north of the Amazon Basin.

Some of the first behavioral data on the large cat in Belize was collected by New York Zoological Society researcher Alan Rabinowitz, who headed into the Cockscomb Basin (now the jaguar reserve). Rabinowitz found that most male jaguars lead rather solitary lives, ranging within an area of about 13 sq. miles (33 sq. km). While many other male cats in the wild, such as the tiger and puma, maintain exclusive territories, the jaguars in Rabinowitz' study shared up to 80 percent of their territories with neighboring cats. Yet there was little evidence of aggression between males. Only one captured jaguar showed signs of facial scars which would indicate aggressiveness.

Avoiding potentially deadly encounters requires some form of communication between cats with overlapping territories. Rabinowitz found that jaguars use visual and olfactory cues in the form of feces, urine and scrapings. Such sign were found most often where the adult male's ranges overlapped (they are also about the only evidence of a jaguar's presence that most visitors to Belize will see, outside the zoo). Besides providing clues to the jaguar's social behavior, the collected scat provided clues to the great cat's diet. The jaguar is a nocturnal hunter. It is not surprising, then,

that armadillo, paca (a rabbit-sized rodent) and red brocket deer, all nocturnal creatures, make up over 70 percent of the jaguar's intake. More important, the jaguar is an opportunist, eating whatever prey is available, provided it can be caught easily.

The almost mystical hunting skills of the jaguar weren't lost on the ancient Maya. "Our ancestors considered jaguars as living symbols of the gods and their power," says Cockscomb Basin Wildlife Sanctuary director Ernesto Saqui. "The skin was prized as much for what it stood for as for its beauty. Today, we consider the jaguar an intricate part of our lives. By protecting it, we maintain a window to the health of the forest." ∎

Birdwatchers don't have to tromp around the deepest bush to run across their quarry in Belize. A casual stroll along a caye, at an archaeological site, or even near your hotel will reveal a surprising number of resident and migratory species. But don't call them by their English names. Few Belizeans can tell you about jacanas, finches, jays or orioles; instead look for the resonantly Creole "dickie bird," "georgie bull," "pyam-pyam," or "banana bird."

In Belize City alone, you can find at least 100 species of birds living around the parks, residences and undeveloped land. Members of the Belize Audubon Society say the best places to start looking are near the Baron Bliss Lighthouse and Radisson hotel; the marshy lands behind St John's College; open spaces around the MCC grounds and the Ramada Hotel; the trees near the Port Authority and Customs; the area around the Government House; and Bird's Isle at the end of Regent Street.

With relative ease, you may see everything from ordinary blackbirds (or grackles) to the vibrant banana birds (known elsewhere as orioles). These beautiful little birds are hard to find in the trees; you're more likely to spot one as it swoops down like a falling yellow leaf to catch an insect.

You'll probably hear the pyam-pyam (brown jay) before you see him because this bird is a real busybody, chattering or "talking" whenever someone passes by. In Belize, anyone who talks a lot, or makes comments about others is said to be "going on like a pyam-pyam." The tropical mocking-bird is also very noisy and has been known to be very protective of its young. During the nesting season, they have been known to dive-bomb small children and people with light colored hair, so watch out.

Like the mocking-bird, the georgie bull (jacana) can be very aggressive, but only with males of his own species. These birds have spurs on their wings, rather than on their legs, so that when two males fight they look like they are boxing. But these macho creatures also have a softer side, for it is the male, not the female, that hatches the eggs.

Also common within the city limits are several species of humming-birds, giant fly-catchers (kiskadee), royal and sandwich terns, brown boobies, little blue herons, gaulins (egrets), scissor-tails (magnificent frigates), laughing gulls (sea gulls), and kites.

Into the countryside: If you want to join a tour, or take a drive out of town, you can find hundreds of birds along the Northern High-

way en route to the Mayan ruins at Altun Ha and the Community Baboon Sanctuary in Bermudan Landing. This is the area in which the Belize Audubon Society conducts its annual Christmas bird count. In recent years they have documented almost 600 species of birds, one third of which are migrants.

From the road and down by the Belize River, you're sure to see gaulins (egrets), with their long white necks, and several species of hawks and kites circling above, looking for live prey. The John Crow (king vultures) are also common in this area. Because they live on garbage heaps and hover near rotting animal carcasses, these ugly

Preceding pages: tri-colored herons on red mangrove, Shipstern Caye. **Left**, great egret. **Right**, brown booby.

birds are so scorned by Belizeans they are even the subject of several piquant Creole proverbs (for example: *Ebrey John Crow tink'e picney white* – Every black bird thinks his children are white or, No one sees the flaws in his own child). Any chicken or game bird that tastes tough is also ridiculed as being "John Crow."

The Crooked Tree Wildlife Sanctuary (also off the Northern Highway) is another great place to find birds since the nearby lagoon attracts hundreds of migratory and resident species. Belize's largest bird, the jabiru stork, likes the marshy waters here: it stands about 4 ft (1.2 meters) tall and, with its wide wingspan, looks like a small airplane when it is

taking off. Belizeans have always respected jabirus, so when a newly arrived hunter from another Central American country shot one recently, the incident caused a violent public reaction. The offender got off with a warning, but the incident prompted the Audubon Society to increase its protection efforts.

Jabiru adults are efficient providers, and have been seen carrying snakes, rats and lizards up to their young nesting in the ceiba trees. They also transport water (siphoning it into their beaks) which they spray on their chicks, or give them to drink. Unlike the adults, which are mostly white, jabiru young have matted gray feathers which resemble those of a sick or dying bird, perhaps intended to discourage predators.

Guanacaste National Park near Belmopan is another favorite stop for naturalists and birdwatchers. Just off the Western Highway and easily accessible by car or bus, Guanacaste has many varieties of hardwood trees and hundreds of birds including flycatchers, tanagers, yellow bill cacique and bamboo clappers (motmots).

Motmots can also be found at just about any archaeological sight because they like to hide in the limestone. A nesting motmot burrows a tunnel in the side of a temple, then turns 90 degrees and makes a cavity in which to lay her eggs. (If you're lucky, you may see one of these little birds poking its head around the corner.)

Glories of the toucan: Keel-billed toucans and their smaller cousins, the toucanets, are also common near archaeological sites and wooded areas. Belizeans love this colorful creature so much they have made it the national bird.

The toucan's image is everywhere, from billboards to T-shirts. There's even a brand of matches bearing the name. The most famous toucan of all is Rambo, a charming fellow who roams freely at the Belize Zoo, captivating the nation's children with his multicolored beak and sociable nature.

Although images of majestic red and blue macaws are also plentiful in the commercial art of Belize, seeing the real thing is a little more difficult. These long-tailed birds reside mainly in the Mountain Pine Ridge and over in the forests of Guatemala. You may have to rely on a local guide to help you find them since there are reportedly less than one hundred pairs remaining in Belize.

The many species of parrot, including the tiny aztec parakeets, are much more common, both in the bush and in many Belizean homes. "Pollies" are as carefully raised and cherished as any other member of the family; senior citizens are particularly fond of these talkative birds, which can live for 30 years or more. The yellowhead is considered to be the most intelligent: they are capable of learning just about any song, phrase or words, and are especially adept at mimicking family members or other pets.

In the wild, parrots are active from dawn until dusk so Belizeans describe a job requiring long hours as "working from polly to polly." These smart birds take advantage of nests or holes created by other animals such as termites; often they simply enlarge an existing nest to suit their own purposes.

While it is not illegal to take parrots from trees to keep in your home, it is against the law to take a polly out of the country. But because they are so popular in the United States, there have been horror stories of smugglers drugging the birds and trying to pass them through American customs in everything from suitcases to plastic piping. Although there are very stiff jail sentences in the US for wildlife smugglers, the practise has proven difficult to stamp out.

In contrast to the clever parrot, the "who

Birds of the sea: Along the coast or out at the cayes, you can't miss the brown pelican perched on piers or flying in formation, often riding the wind low and close to the waves. His placid nature has inspired the Creole proverb: *Sea breeze always blow pelikin wey 'e wan go* (The pelican goes wherever the breeze takes him).

Laughing gulls (sea gulls) are also everywhere, and there are numerous species of frigate birds. The king-bird (osprey) is particularly exciting to watch as he drops into the water to catch fish with his feet.

female curassow mate for life and are so devoted that when one is shot, the other expires soon after.

you?" (whip-o-will) is supposed to be rather stupid: these birds like to sit in the middle of the road and are often hit by cars.

Hunters also poke fun at the top knot chick (also called the "rotten ass") because its meat spoils quickly after it is killed. Other species to look for in the bush are the owl (barn and spectacled), hawk eagles (which are very rare), and the trogan (which is related to the quetzal of Guatemala). Game birds include the oscelated turkey, the crested guan, and the curassow. Hunters say that the male and

The best places to search for sea-birds is on Caye Caulker, San Pedro (many migrants stay north of the village) and at Half Moon Caye Natural Monument. Because of the distance and expense involved, the reserve at Half Moon is mostly frequented by divers, but excursions are occasionally available for birdwatchers who want to see the island's huge colony of red-footed boobies.

There are also several small mangrove cayes which have been declared bird sanctuaries because they support nesting populations of wood storks, three species of egrets and two kinds of herons, white ibis, magnificent frigate birds and anhingas.

Left, jabiru nest. **Above**, scarlet macaw. **Right**, endangered agami heron.

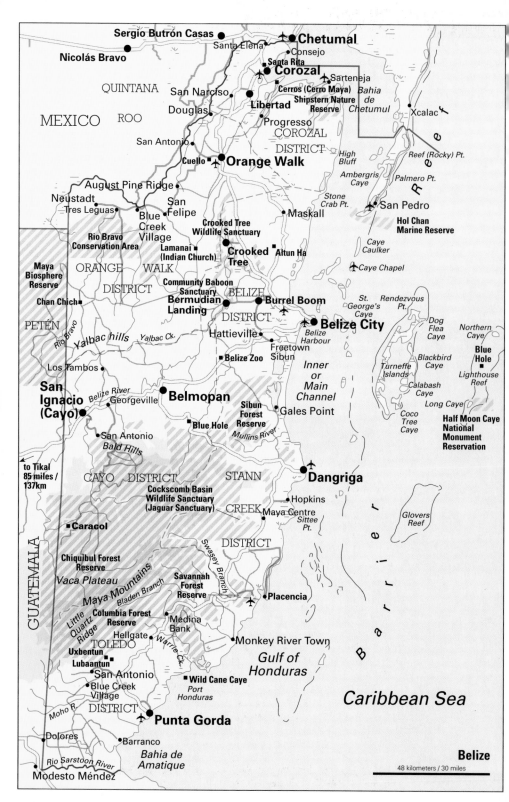

Belize

48 kilometers / 30 miles

PLACES

Old travel hands like to say that Belize has the look and feel of the Caribbean in the 1950s, before it was "ruined" by commercialism. Everything is small-scale in Belize: the biggest hotels rarely have more than a couple of dozen rooms, and, although this is a tiny country, transport can be tortuous. Roads are either unpaved or pot-holed; traveling up and down the coast is best done by small, 10-seater propeller plane; getting out to the off-shore cayes is often in small, high-speed motor boats bumping across the waves.

No matter which part of the country you visit, most journeys begin at the least appealing point: Belize City, a ramshackle outpost that one writer cruelly remarked looks like "an African ground nut port after 20 years of ground nut blight." Grubby, noisy and troubled by petty street crime it may be, but Belize City still retains a fascinating atmosphere of *Casablanca* intrigue.

Most visitors head quickly to Belize's other attractions (often hopping a light plane directly at Belize City airport). Best known are the 200 or so small islands or cayes (pronounced *keys*) dotted along the Barrier Reef. Some are tiny and uninhabited, with only a few palm trees, looking as if they were plucked straight out of *Gilligan's Island*; Ambergris Caye (San Pedro) is the American-style getaway venue, for those who like their home-style luxuries. Caye Caulker is the choice if you want Belizean-run hotels, tiny local restaurants and a pace so slow it's almost in reverse.

Back on the mainland, Belize's menu of eco-tourism attractions are often combined with visits to remote Mayan ruins. North of Belize City lie both the Community Baboon Sanctuary and ancient ruins of Altun Ha; a visit to the ancient city of Lamanai includes a river trip through pristine savannah. Further north, the little visited Orange Walk and Corozal Districts have a distinct Mexican flavor.

Ground zero for the eco-tourism movement remains San Ignacio, in the rainforests of the Maya Mountains close to the Guatemalan border; comfortable, thatch-roofed jungle lodges have spread across this remote countryside, which are riddled with nature walks to waterfalls, underground caves and jungle-covered streams. En route to San Ignacio is the nation's capital, Belmopan; further into the wilderness lies Caracol, Belize's most significant Mayan site.

The attractions south of Belize City can be most easily reached in a series of 20-minute plane hops: first comes Dangriga, center of Garifuna culture and jumping-off point for the Cockscomb Basin Nature Reserve; next is Placencia, a tiny fishing village shaping up as a laid-back coastal resort (see it while you can); third, for the committed eco-tourist in search of the truly remote, is Punta Gorda, the base for exploring the far south.

Last but not least, almost all visitors to Belize now take advantage of daily tours to Tikal in neighboring Guatemala, considered the most spectacular of all ancient Mayan cities.

Preceding pages: Caribbean calm, Belize City; enjoying the cayes; backroad in the Cockscomb Wildlife Sanctuary.

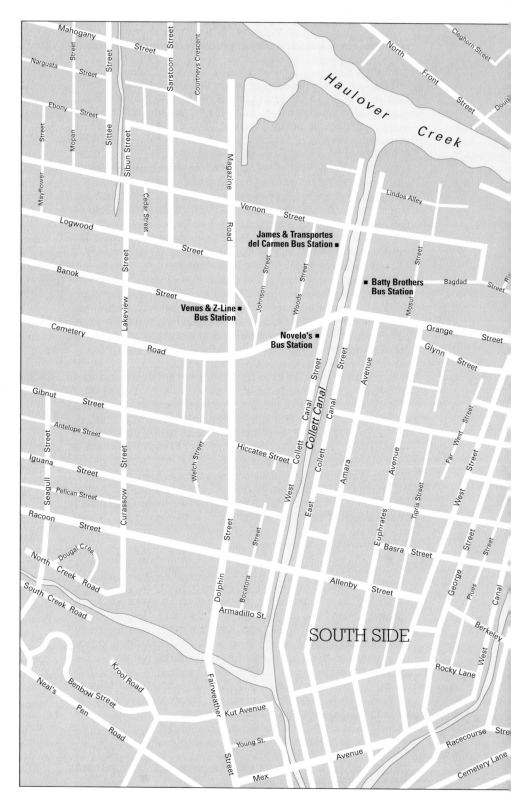

SOUTH SIDE

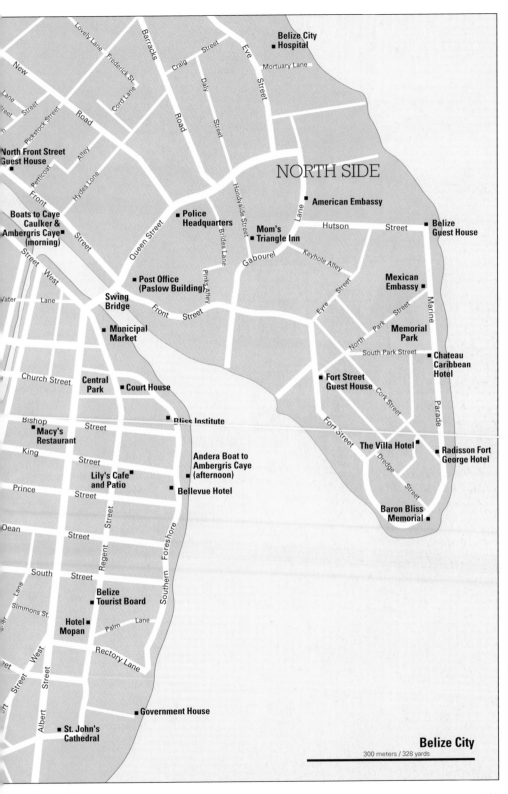

Belize City Hospital

Mortuary Lane

NORTH SIDE

American Embassy

Police Headquarters

Mom's Triangle Inn

Hutson Street

Belize Guest House

North Front Street Guest House

Boats to Caye Caulker & Ambergris Caye (morning)

Gabourel

Keyhole Alley

Mexican Embassy

Post Office (Paslow Building)

Swing Bridge

Memorial Park

Municipal Market

South Park Street

Chateau Caribbean Hotel

Central Park

Court House

Fort Street Guest House

Bliss Institute

Macy's Restaurant

Andera Boat to Ambergris Caye (afternoon)

The Villa Hotel

Radisson Fort George Hotel

Lily's Cafe and Patio

Bellevue Hotel

Baron Bliss Memorial

Belize Tourist Board

Hotel Mopan

Government House

St. John's Cathedral

Belize City

300 meters / 328 yards

143

BELIZE CITY

"Amandalaaa! Amandalaaa!" shout the newspaper boys as they push through the crowds with the latest edition. Street vendors' carts, loaded down with fruit and cheap Guatemalan goods, squeeze pedestrians onto miniscule sidewalks or force them to step out directly into the traffic. Drivers curse as bicycle riders cut recklessly in front of them; taxis stop without warning in the middle of the street. As the sweat pours down their faces, all many can think about is the cool air-conditioning in the bank just a few blocks away.

It's always the same in Belize City – congested and miserable – yet in this small place, where everyone seems to know everyone else, friendliness prevails and business still takes a back seat to pleasure. From shop clerks to bank executives, no one is too busy to inquire about the family or exchange a bit of gossip on the street corner. Friday after-noons are downright festive as every-one discusses weekend plans, keeping one eye on the clock and the other on the cash box.

People move slowly in Belize City, and so does everything else. The heat sets the pace, regulating everything from business hours to just how long it will take the clerk at the income tax depart-ment to answer the phone. Visitors are invariably frustrated by the intermin-able wait at the brand new traffic lights and ready to walk out of restaurants where the simplest order – and often the check – seems to take an eternity. But everyone else is on Belize Time (mean-ing you're lucky if they show up on the same day, let alone at the right hour) and rarely annoyed by delays.

Nor does anyone seem particularly distressed by the city's *brukup*, or di-lapidated state. In fact, Belize City's denizens pay no attention at all to the peeling paint and potholes. This is not to say the citizens don't "rail up," or com-plain, about the nauseating smells ema-nating from open sewerage canals or

Preceding pages: the Belize River. Below, the Supreme Court building.

poor water pressure (so low at times they can't bathe or flush the commode). It's just that most have learned it's useless to expect those in authority to do anything – at least not until election time rolls around again.

Life on the swamp: After all, this hot, humid sea-level town was never supposed to be located here in the first place, and it seems to be only sheer obstinacy that keeps it afloat now. Belize's original 18th-century settlers preferred the cool, mosquito-free life on St George's Caye, just a few miles offshore but the expanding logwood trade required a camp closer to the river. Belize Town was established at the mouth of Haulover Creek (so named because cattle had to be "hauled over" to the other side before they built a ferry) only as a temporary solution. But as the years passed, permanent wooden structures became more common, while the swampland north and south of the river was reclaimed and connected by a bridge.

It may be hard to imagine today, but journal accounts from the early 1800s describe the settlement as positively charming, the streets lined with gracious colonial homes and lush gardens. Naturally, only the privileged few were part of such a genteel picture; the African slaves who made possible the white and upper-class Creoles' pampered lifestyle lived in places like Eboe Town, where Yarborough or "Yabra" is now. This was composed largely of "negro houses," long rows of separate rooms sharing a single roof. Indentured servants from India and Garinagu (Garifuna) settlers also occupied less than idyllic quarters in an area known as Queen Charlotte Town, or Frenchmen Town, which was located east of today's Caesar Ridge Road.

Today the situation is not much better. While the more affluent areas of Belize City boast large, gleaming cement structures sitting well back from the street and their neighbors, the rest of the town is a hazardous fire trap. Small wooden buildings, many built on stilts to avoid flood waters and catch more

Giving a little lip.

breeze, are crowded closely together on narrow streets. Demand for housing far exceeds supply, every bank is inundated with requests for building loans, and desperate families have squatted in outlying areas far from water and electrical lines. Not surprisingly, housing is a recurrent election issue in Belize City, with every candidate vowing to build more low cost homes, fix the streets, dig more drains and fill more land – but few keep their promises.

End of the "good old days": Until recently, Belize City was one of the world's safest cities, but now everyone is worried about crime. Street gangs now terrorize many neighborhoods; crack addicts "sprang out," stealing whatever they get their hands on, to raise quick cash. Although Belizeans love to buy and give gold jewelry, these days people are on the lookout when they walk the streets for louts ready to "tief you chain." Gone too is the freedom to leave doors and windows open, and many have resorted to living behind burglar bars or chain link. Private security companies regularly patrol the homes of the wealthy and foreign embassy staff members, but most citizens are left to defend themselves. Most people have learned they cannot even rely on the police for assistance because they usually take too long – if they make it at all – when called for help.

Although they may have seen better days, most of the city's 45,000 inhabitants say they wouldn't live anywhere else in Belize. Such loyalty flies in the face of bitter experience: residents have had to completely rebuild their city twice in the past six decades alone, when hurricanes literally turned it into a pile of wooden sticks. The 1931 hurricane leveled almost 80 percent of Belize City and claimed thousands of lives (including those of virtually all the East Indians in Queen Charlotte Town). Exactly 30 years later, Hurricane Hattie demolished the town for the second time.

The present face of Belize City is the result of a massive rebuilding effort. In 1971, the government decided to avoid further destruction by relocating the

Left, the new city market. **Right**, taking produce to the streets.

capital to Belmopan, a newly-built city 52 miles (84 km) inland. To date, few people have been willing to move. While Belmopan, with its population of under 4,000, may be Belize's political capital, Belize City remains the nation's commercial, social and historical center.

The view from downtown: For many, Belize City's main attraction is economic. Every morning, lunchtime and evening, the streets fill with professional women in their color-coordinated uniforms and men in freshly starched shirts, all making their way to and from their respective offices downtown. There is no shortage of opportunities for domestics and shop assistants, and the city's construction boom also attracts manual laborers from all over Belize, as well as from neighboring republics.

On **Albert Street**, members of the East Indian, Lebanese and Chinese communities have literally taken over, establishing shops which stock everything from shampoo to stoves and mattresses. The major commercial banks are also located here. **Regent Street** is home to many legal and medical practices, accounting firms and specialty shops.

While Belize City has no organized building preservation effort, most historically significant structures are maintained simply because they are still in use. Within walking distance of downtown at the very end of Albert Street is the oldest Anglican church in Central America, **St John's Cathedral**. Built by slaves using bricks brought to Belize as ship's ballast, the building was completed in 1820 and became the coronation site of four Mosquito Kings, whose people (Native Americans who once inhabited the Mosquito Coast, in what is now Nicaragua) maintained good relations with the British government in Belize, even though they eventually came under Spanish rule. The interior of the church contains wall plaques commissioned by the families of some of the earliest parishioners, and a more recent wooden sculpture depicting the dove of peace by one of Belize's most revered artists, George Gabb.

Just across from the cathedral is

St John's, the oldest Anglican church in Central America.

Yarborough Cemetery, named for the land's owner, the magistrate James Yarborough. It was used from 1781 to 1882, first as a burial ground for the colony's more prominent persons and later opened to the masses. There are no mourners these days, but you may find groups of school children scampering over the graves deciphering the intriguing tombstones or playing ball. Not too far from the graveyard is a statue of the first self-made Belizean millionaire, Emmanuel Isaiah Morter, a devotee of Marcus Garvey, who owned a great deal of property along Barracks road and donated much of his fortune to the UNIA (United Negro Improvement Association). The monument also marks the entrance to what was Eboe Town in the 19th century. Albert Street ends with a lane leading to **Bird's Isle**, site of weekend concerts and sporting events (and rapidly becoming part of the mainland through a build-up of silt from the river).

Around the corner towards Regent Street lies the spacious **Government House**, completed in 1812. This colonial mansion was home to British governors appointed to Belize, but today its only inhabitant is the Governor General, whose duties are largely symbolic. Even so, colonial etiquette still prevails. A view of the mansion's interior requires a special invitation – an honor generally issued only for a black-tie reception on Independence Eve and restricted to the society's upper echelons.

Further down Regent Street – once known as Front Street because it faces the sea – are many of the city's best preserved examples of 19th- and early 20th-century architecture. (Although No. 45 appears to be a particularly well maintained example, it is in fact a strikingly accurate replica of its colonial predecessor.) Several structures survived the hurricanes because they were made of bricks. Although local legend holds that they were stolen from St John's Cathedral, official records show the work was in fact legally contracted. The bricks date these buildings to the early 19th century; iron slave shackles can still be found embedded in some of

Boats come back from the cayes.

their interior walls (including the building at the corner of Prince Street), a startling reminder of the darker side of Belizean history.

Legal eagles and political scandal: Also on Regent Street is the white **Court House**, where lawyers and judges still wear British-style robes. It replaced the one destroyed by fire in 1918; the clock tower was erected in memory of the colonial governor, Hart Bennett, who was fatally wounded by a falling flagpole during the disaster. The **Public Building**, on the same compound, used to be the seat of the Legislative Assembly until it moved to Belmopan in 1971; it is now used by several government offices, including the Treasury and Central Bank.

Facing the Court House, **Battlefield Park** seems quiet now; it got its name in the 1930s and 1940s for the heated political arguments that took place there. A labor organizer, Antonio Soberanis – whose likeness was recently erected in the park – and political activists like George Price and Philip

Goldson attracted crowds with their emotional speeches on social justice and self-government.

The new **City Commercial Center** was one attempt at urban renewal, but the marble-floored high-rise – high for Belize City, at least – has always been the center of controversy. Few Belizeans wanted to lose the old market, a steel arched structure built in 1845 which was reputed to be one of the few of its kind left in the Caribbean; meanwhile, the circumstances surrounding the building contract with an Italian construction company were dubious. Public outcry led to the old market being carefully dismantled and stored away, to be rebuilt sometime in the future as part of a proposed tourist center. But, as with many Belizean development schemes, the resurrection remains uncertain.

The venerable old **Swing Bridge**, one of three connecting the city's south and north sides, may soon face a similar fate. Constructed in 1922 for what was then primarily pedestrian traffic, the bridge is notorious for its narrowness

On the Swing Bridge.

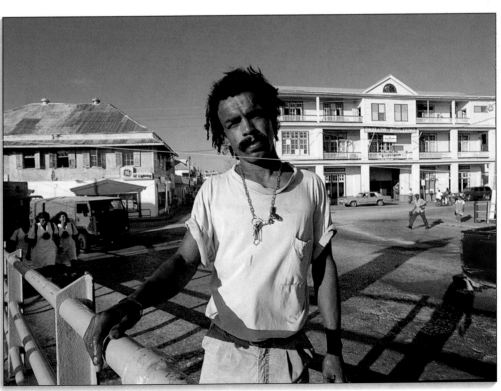

and steep incline (one of the town's first cars, a model-T Ford owned by a doctor, always rolled back down again unless it was given a push by helpful bystanders) and can hardly accommodate today's heavy traffic. The biggest drawback, however, is that the bridge must be manually swung open every morning and evening to allow sailboats and other large craft to exit or enter the river, stopping traffic on both sides for some time. Plans are underway for an automated replacement, but many city residents will undoubtedly be sorry to loose this old veteran which weathered both the 1931 and 1961 hurricanes (although it did have to be retrieved from some distance up the street in 1931).

Belize City's Nob Hill: Across the Swing Bridge is the district residents call, logically enough, "the northside," where many of the city's hotels and nicest mansions can be found.

Almost directly opposite Swing Bridge is the **Paslow Building**, named for Thomas Paslow, a landed gentleman who is reputed to have been less than kind to his many slaves; it now contains the **post office** and lower courts. Along North Front Street is the **Biddle Building**, a lovely old structure with lots of Victorian gingerbread trim, which used to be a popular shoe store but which has also been appropriated by the post office. The old **fire station** across the street on the riverfront houses many antique examples of firefighting equipment – all still in use.

At the end of North Front Street is **The Fort**. This area was formerly Fort George Island; it did have a fort until 1803 and was separated from the rest of the city by a creek. In 1924 an American construction company reclaimed the land and built some lovely homes on **Cork Street** and facing **Memorial Park**, which commemorates the battle of St George's Caye in 1798. The **Fuller home**, at the entrance to the park, survived the 1931 hurricane almost completely intact by floating off its foundations and ending up across the street; it contains about 90 percent of its original interior woodwork. The **Fort Street**

The Paslow Building.

Guest House directly behind the Fuller house used to be a small hospital run by a Spanish doctor called Perez de Scofield; the seaside **Chateau Caribbean Hotel** is also a former hospital.

With several guest houses and two of the city's largest hotels, the **Fort George** and **Villa** (whose bar and restaurant on the top floor has the very best panoramic view of the city), the Fort may have more tourist accommodations than anywhere else in town. Locals also enjoy the view from the Fort, particularly on Sunday afternoons when families and lovers take a walk out to the **lighthouse**, past the **Baron Bliss memorial**. The Baron, a wealthy British invalid who fished Belizean waters for several weeks and then died aboard his yacht, the *Sea King*, left the bulk of his estate to the Belizean people in gratitude for their hospitality during his final days. The lighthouse and children's park across the street were built for public enjoyment with funds from the Baron's Trust, as was the **Bliss Institute** on the Southern Foreshore, which contains a library, an art gallery and auditorium.

Another part of town worth exploring is **Gabourel Lane**, base for the United States Agency for Development (USAID), the Peace Corps, and the **US Embassy** – housed in a beautiful old colonial building dating back to the turn of the century. Although there was an abundance of the finest wood in the world in Belize at that time, the Americans chose to build their consulate in New England and ship the whole thing to Belize City.

Also on Gabourel Lane, just over the fence from the embassy, is the **Sisters of Mercy Convent** and one of Belize's most prestigious high schools, **St Catherine's Academy** for girls, both of which were rebuilt by American soldiers after the 1931 hurricane almost completely destroyed them. A building in dire need of assistance these days, is **Her Majesty's Prison** at the very end of the street. Built in 1857 to accommodate less than 100 prisoners, the facility is now so overcrowded and understaffed that prisoners escape almost every week,

or elude police while on their way to court at the Paslow Building.

Conditions are not much better around the corner at the **Belize City Hospital**. Despite recent renovations in this rambling colonial relic, reports still emerge of hospital personnel administering the wrong medications or failing to respond to patients in a critical condition. Any Belizean who can afford it goes to Mexico or the US for treatment, but most people have to take their chances.

Modern urban sprawl: The newer areas of Belize City are more spread out, and should be visited by car. A taxi ride can be quite an adventure in Belize City as cabs speed through traffic, brushing past pedestrians with only a fraction of an inch to spare, and sail over the bridges seemingly unconcerned with the law of gravity. (On the plus side, many taxi drivers are very talkative and can be counted on to recommend good restaurants or sightseeing.)

Newtown Barracks, which eventually becomes Princess Margaret Drive, takes you past the **Ramada Hotel** and the **MCC grounds**, a sporting arena built by the famous Marylebone Cricket Club of Great Britain. Although cricket is rarely played here anymore (although it is still extremely popular in some villages outside the city), football games draw crowds every Sunday afternoon and the MCC grounds are sometimes used for concerts or cultural events. Just up the road is the **Belize Pickwick Club**, a more exclusive, members-only sporting facility featuring tennis courts and one of the city's few swimming pools. However, everyone is able to enjoy the nearby **Ramada Park**.

Opposite the park, those looking for a little nightlife head for a popular open air bar, **Lindbergh's Landing** (pronounced "Linsberg" by locals). Named in honor of Charles Lindbergh, whose *Spirit of St Louis* was the first airplane to land in Belize, back in 1927, the bar boasts photographs of the aviator meeting his Belizean fans. There are also paintings by proprietor, Jerry Nisbit, who likes to serenade his customers.

Around Princess Margaret Drive is

Caribbean languor.

the area of Belize City the more prosperous call home – named, appropriately enough, **King's Park**. Here and in the adjacent **West Landivar** are also many of the city's schools, the oldest of which is St John's College, established by Jesuits in 1887. Nearby are the **University College of Belize** and the **Belize Teachers' College**. Needless to say, drivers have to proceed cautiously in the mornings and at noon when the uniformed students spill into the streets on their bicycles for the long, hot trek home. Near the river is the new **fire station** built with assistance from Italian contractors, and Belize's first-ever **supermarket** with automated doors and conveyor belts – a sure sign to Belize City residents that they have entered the age of high technology at last.

Over the **Belcan Bridge**, built with Canadian assistance in 1969 (just as the city's third and newest bridge, the **Belchina**, was made possible by Taiwanese funds) is the **City Center**, a large sporting and public performance auditorium (the ventilation is so poor that large crowds nearly suffocate).

Belize City's longest thoroughfare, **Central American Boulevard**, runs through depressed communities like **Lake Independence** and **Port Loyola**. Caesar Ridge Road, at the end of the Boulevard, passes through **Mesopotamia** (land originally given to soldiers who returned from fighting there in World War I) and **Yarborough**, also neglected areas, before ending back at St John's Cathedral.

The **Western Highway**, which runs to Belmopan, San Ignacio and the Guatemalan border, also begins at its junction with Central American Boulevard. As one last bizarre touch in this bizarre city, the highway runs straight through **Lord's Ridge Cemetery**; above-ground tombs, crucifixes and plaster statues extend on both sides of the road, as well as on a median strip. Belize City's small town closeness is never so evident as during a funeral here, when the traffic stops and people line the streets to sympathize with mourners making the long, hot walk to the burying ground.

Shades of Conrad: view of the Bliss Memorial.

BELIZE ZOO

What many people fail to realize when they come to Belize is that their chances of seeing the larger land animals are limited. The tangle of vines and thick foliage makes it difficult to see even a few feet off a forest path or road. Also, many tropical creatures are nocturnal, finding safety under the cloak of night. Except for a flash of fur dissolving into the roadside bush, or the snap of branches and rustle of leaves, most visitors will end up experiencing the habitat where wildlife live instead of viewing the creatures themselves.

But there is one place where you are assured of seeing a jaguar or a tapir in a natural setting. The Belize Zoo is an oasis of ponds, forests, and flowers among the sprawling savannas 29 miles (47 km) west of Belize City. It has no cages or bars, unlike zoos in most of the world.

Over 60 indigenous Belizean animals are comfortably harbored in large, naturally vegetated enclosures. In fact, during the heat of the day, many of the animals are difficult to see because of the thick cover. This is because the welfare of the animals takes precedence over the viewing ability of visitors. You will often feel that you are in the forest, peering through a tangle of vines and shrubs to catch a glimpse of a jaguarundi or ocelot. Just as when searching for wildlife in the rainforest, patience and persistence are necessary to view the beauty of the creatures at the Belize Zoo.

The animals and grounds are meticulously cared for by the Belizean staff. Shiny pelts, bright eyes and, in most cases, pleasant dispositions attest to the health of the animals. Raised gravel paths lead from exhibit to exhibit through natural savanna and pine ridge vegetation, as well as transplanted rainforest. Hand-painted signs call attention to the natural habits of each animal and its endangered status, reminding Belizeans and visitors that "Belize is my home too!" The Belize Zoo is as much a botanical garden as it is a zoological park. The message: we need to save the habitat to save the animals.

Sharon Matola, the North American founder and driving force behind the zoo, **Eco-tourists please note.**

arrived in Belize after a colorful career that included a stint with a Romanian lion-tamer and a circus tour in Mexico. Today, she often recounts an incident that helped convince her that she was on the right track during the zoo's difficult founding years of the early 1980s. A very old man showed up at the gate after closing. At the time, Matola was keeper, janitor, tour guide and accountant rolled into one, so she let the man in and gave him a personal tour.

At first the old man commented freely at each cage about well-entrenched Belizean myths – how ant-eaters kill dogs with their tongues, or that boa constrictors are poisonous during the day. Soon he grew silent. Finally, as they stood in front of a sun-lit jaguar, Matola noticed tears in the old man's eyes. "I'm very sorry, Miss," she recalls him saying. "I have lived in Belize all my life and this is the first time I have seen the animals of my country. They are so beautiful."

That was in 1983, when the zoo consisted of chicken wire cages sheltering animals left over from a natural history film. Matola was hired by the film maker to care for the animals, and when the film was completed, she was left to decide how to dispose of them. Many were tame and unaccustomed to life in the wild, so the idea of an unusual zoo cropped up. With characteristic energy, Matola hung signs beside the cages soliciting funds to buy feed; she began to visit schools around the country to raise awareness about the wealth of Belizean wildlife and its deteriorating habitat; and she went outside Belize to raise money from environmental groups.

Today, the Belize Zoo covers 30 acres (12 hectares), employs 17 Belizeans and is part of a larger complex that includes a Tropical Education and Research Center. It is the focal point for environmental awareness in Belize. An innovative visitors' center features the artwork of local school children, freshwater aquariums, and explains the Zoo's sophisticated solar system; there is also a children's playground with natural motifs.

The Belize Zoo can be visited on a half-day trip from Belize City and may be the only chance you have of feeling what an old man felt when viewing the magnificence of the jaguar. ∎

Look into my eyes...

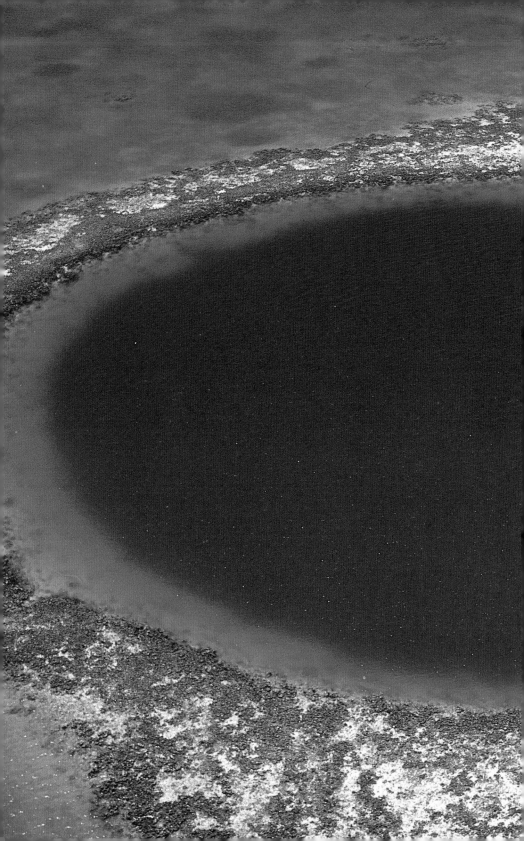

THE NORTHERN CAYES

While most visitors to Belize simply hop on a plane and go straight to a hotel on San Pedro, Ambergris is by no means the only caye in Belize worth exploring. Each of the northern islets offers something unique, although getting to them can be an adventure in itself. Air travel is possible only to a few select spots, but water taxis (speed boats which leave Belize City at regular intervals and charge only a small fee) and boat charters from a hotel or tour operator can take you just about anywhere.

Not all cayes in Belize are the beautiful coral islands featured in travel brochures. Most are little more than a tangle of mangrove trees filled in with mud. Yet even the most homely cluster of roots plays a vital role in the coastal eco-system; for fishermen, they are small paradises, and sportsmen from around the world now come for the fly and light tackle fishing for snook, tarpon, bonefish and snapper.

Many of the cayes' names date back to the days of pirates and buccaneers. Near Belize City, for example, in what are known collectively as the **Drowned Cayes**, are such titles as **Frenchman's Caye** and **Spanish Lookout**; **Bannister Bogue** is a channel named after a pirate who later became a logwood cutter in the late 1600s; while **Gallow's Point** was where criminals and freebooters were hanged. The pirate John Colson anchored his ship at **Colson's Cayes**, further south, but today lobster fishermen use these mangroves to collect booty of a different sort. **Robinson's Point** was once the center of Belize's boat building industry with a shipyard run by the Hunter and Young families; all that remains is an old lighthouse.

Fishing village cum tourist mecca: One of the most popular northern cayes is **Caye Caulker**, just a few minutes south of San Pedro. This working fishing village was originally settled by Mestizos fleeing the Caste War in Mexico's Yucatán in the 1800s; today it has about 500 year-round residents, mostly of Mestizo descent. The population swells considerably on weekends and holidays, when hundreds of Belize City residents descend on the island's small guest houses and hotels. Easter is Caye Caulker's busiest season and those who arrive without advanced reservations are likely to find themselves walking from one end of the caye to the other, looking for a friend to give them some floor space in their room.

Many Belizeans prefer Caye Caulker to San Pedro on Ambergris Caye, and not just because hotel rates are lower (although you may have to share a bathroom). Most importantly, they feel more at home here than in the Americanized San Pedro. Caulker has a typically Belizean atmosphere, with many of the restaurants and sidewalk stands offering local cuisine and the bars providing raucous nightlife. Drinking is a favorite pastime (except on Good Friday or election days when no liquor can be served), and there's usually a live band. It's not uncommon to see tourists and Belize City visitors struggling to find their way

Preceding pages: Half Moon Caye; the Blue Hole. **Left,** relaxing at "the Split". **Right,** peak hour on Caye Caulker.

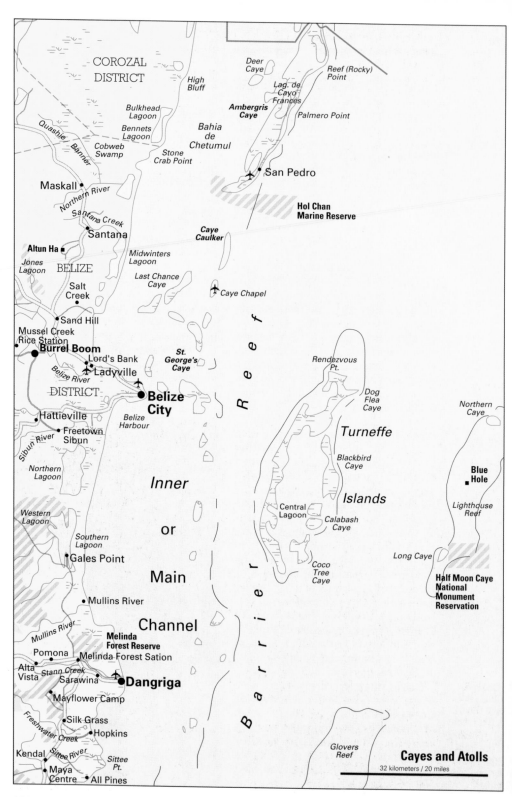

Cayes and Atolls

32 kilometers / 20 miles

home through the sand, or taking a snooze in an beached dory.

Although there are really no good beaches on Caye Caulker, this doesn't mean there is nowhere to swim. **The Split**, a channel cut through the island by Hurricane Hattie in 1961, may be the most popular gathering place on the island, with a nice swimming area (be careful of the strong current and speed boats, however) and an open-air bar. European tourists who like topless sunbathing are often the cause of some excitement at the Split, but unless a policeman strolls by, no one is likely to tell them that it's illegal in Belize. For those who want to do more than sun themselves, day trips to the reef for diving and snorkeling are also available and water taxis make runs to San Pedro throughout the day.

Because of its relaxed, Bohemian lifestyle, some visitors like Caye Caulker so much they never go home. As a result, the caye now has a number of expatriate artists, and several restaurants and gift shops are run by gringos determined to find their own piece of paradise.

Pleasant as Caye Caulker is, the island has its share of problems – including a rising crime rate and reputation as a haven for drug traffickers. Determined not to let their island be overrun by criminals, residents frustrated by police inactivity have organized an extremely successful citizens' patrol program, similar to one pioneered at San Pedro. At the other end of the social scale, residents want to ensure that tourism growth is controlled and the island does not become over-commercialized.

Site of the first settlement: Just 9 miles (14 km) from Belize City, crescent-shaped **St George's Caye** is the most historic of all the off-shore islands. It was here that the British buccaneers established the territory's first real settlement around 1650; a century and a half later, they defeated Spanish invaders in the famous Battle of St George's Caye in 1798.

One account, written by a traveling Spanish cleric, reveals that in the mid-

T-shirts for sale.

17th century, the British pirate Bartholomew Sharpe used St George's Caye as a command center for an impressive fleet of 23 vessels manned by several hundred buccaneers. The Spanish priest reports that he was captured by Sharpe's men and taken to the caye, but since he didn't speak any English and Sharpe didn't speak any Spanish, the two communicated in Latin. (Sharpe is reported to have acquired the language in Britain while he himself was training to enter religious orders.) Fortunately for the Spaniard, the gentleman pirate decided not to kill him but put him to good use conducting mass and hearing confessions, until he was released a few months later.

Today the only reminders of these colorful times at St George's Caye are a mounted cannon on the beach and a small **graveyard** near **St George's Lodge**. A white picket fence encloses what little is left of the cemetery; the elaborate tombstones and many graves of the caye's early settlers were carried away during the 1961 hurricane. The rest of the island is occupied by the vacation homes of Belize's more affluent families, two small hotels and several fishermen's homes.

The caye is very quiet during the week, but on the weekends many Belize City residents come out for fishing and water-skiing, or sunbathing on the kraals (an old colonial system of enclosing an area of sea water, supposedly to protect swimmers from sharks). A mile (1.6 km) offshore is an area of shallow water called **The Spit** (or Miami Beach), a great place to anchor a boat and hop over the side for a swim. The water is only about 1 to 3 ft (0.3 to 1 meter) deep and the sand is completely free of sea grass and other vegetation.

Spaniards' haunted graveyard: Those looking for even more seclusion may want to try **Caye Chapel**. Although no one has ever found any evidence to verify the claim, legend has it the defeated Spaniards buried their dead on this small coral island after the Battle of St George's Caye in 1798. Rumors of wandering Spanish ghosts don't seem

St George's Caye, site of Belize's first capital.

to keep visitors away from the caye's one hotel, **Pyramid Island Resort**, which was once a particular favorite with British army officers. This caye also has an airstrip and thanks to a good deal of cleaning up, one of the best beaches in Belize.

If you want a caye all to yourself, the best thing to do is charter a boat and head south. Tiny **Sergeant's Caye**, named for an 18th-century merchant, is almost always deserted except for five guardian coconut trees. Although there is very little shade, this island is an unforgettable place to swim and have a picnic. **Goff's Caye**, visible just to the south is not much bigger but has an even better swimming area, so tends to get very crowded on the weekends. The waters surrounding Goff's Caye are incredible, ranging from deep blue to pale green. Depending on the tide and size of your boat, you may have to wade ashore – the pier stops short of the caye due to constantly shifting sands.

English Caye, further down the line, sits alongside the main shipping channel. Its steel frame lighthouse, built in 1935, marks the entrance to the channel for deep draft vessels coming into the port of Belize City. There are also several homes here.

Beyond the Barrier Reef: Diving and fishing enthusiasts may venture further into the Caribbean to Belize's three coral atolls. Although most water-sport activities take place from charter boats, a surge of interest has fueled the development of a few island-based resorts.

The **Turneffe Islands** are the surface elements of the largest atoll running some 30 miles (48 km) from north to south; it has several shallow lagoons and two lighthouses. The northernmost beacon, built in 1885, is on **Caye Mauger** ("Skinny" in Creole) while a second lighthouse can be found on **Caye Bokel** ("Elbow" in Dutch). **Turneffe Island Lodge** is located here, nestled among palms by a coral sand beach. It offers guests world-class fishing trips and dive trips to such spots as **Elbow Reef** and **Black Beauty**, an area known for its black coral. **Blackbird Caye**

Sea kayakers ready to roll, St George's.

Resort, located on the central eastern shore of Turneffe, is a new enterprise catering to nature-based tourism.

Lighthouse Reef is another atoll with a treacherous boundary of coral. Like Turneffe, there are also two lighthouses here, one on **Sandbore Caye**; the other, first built in 1828 and replaced in 1848, is on **Half Moon Caye**, a crescent shaped island that is easily one of the most beautiful places in Belize. The abundance of nesting sea-birds and marine life made Half Moon Caye and its surrounding waters a natural choice to become the nation's first Natural Monument in 1982. Around 4,000 red-footed booby birds nest on the island; the population is unusual for being white instead of the usual dull brown (the only other similar booby colony is near the island of Tobago in the eastern Caribbean). An observation platform allows unrestricted viewing of the boobies, along with some of the 98 other species of birds that have been recorded on the island. Lighthouse keeper John Lambey is happy to chat with visitors about the endangered sea

turtles that have chosen this beach as a nesting site.

Forests of black coral sprout like weeds from **The Wall** near Half Moon Caye. This vertical drop-off is sliced by canyons and narrow passages, many of which have overhangs that often coalesce into short caves wide enough for divers to swim through. Closer to shore lies a wide sand bank covered with thousands of garden eels swaying in the current. These creatures are extremely shy, quickly pulling back, tail first, into their holes in the sand at the approach of a diver.

Cousteau's stomping ground: Just 7 miles (11 km) north of Half Moon Caye is one of the world's most famous dive sites, **The Blue Hole**. Looking from the air like a dark blue cavity in a field of turquoise, this dive site gained fame in 1972 when Jacques Cousteau maneuvered his ship *Calypso* through narrow coral channels to moor and film inside. The Blue Hole is actually a sinkhole created by a collapsed underground cavern; over 300 ft (90 meters) in diameter and 450 ft (135 meters) deep, with huge stalactites hanging from the ceiling of caves at depths of 100 to 150 ft (30 to 45 meters). Sharks and turtles abound here, though their presence is rarely predictable. This dive is usually reserved for the more adventurous and experienced, under the strict supervision of a dive master. It is definitely not a plunge to be attempted by the novice.

Finally, **Glover's Reef** has six cayes, all crowded on the southeast end of the atoll. Due to the great diversity of reef types and their almost pristine condition, 25 percent of Glover's Reef is a conservation area. The government of Belize has plans to establish a marine lab on **Long Caye** in conjunction with the atoll's reserve status. Few dive boats make regular visits to Glover's Reef as it is further away from Belize City than the other two atolls, and regular dive sites are not well established. But a full service dive facility on **Southwest Caye**, **Manta Reef Resort**, provides access to fantastic wall diving. Also, a small family-run operation on **Northeast Caye** caters to the budget-oriented adventurer.

Left, conch shell mountain. **Right**, palm tree mosaic.

AMBERGRIS CAYE

On a typical Saturday night in the village of **San Pedro**, a crowd gathers outside the local church. The event seems to be a typical wedding, with a girl dressed in white and her groom in a black tuxedo as the centers of attention. But, after the service, the happy couple hops into a golf cart decorated with palm leaves; the rest of the church party follows in a train of bouncing buggies, the main form of transport on this almost car-free island. The reception is nearby, in a canopy-covered basketball court; in the center stands a huge white cake, decorated with 30 plastic dolls.

The event, it turns out, is actually the girl's Quince Años, or 15th birthday – an old Mexican tradition that is celebrated with 15 other couples about the same age. The festivities bring half the population of San Pedro together and carry on late into the night – part of the strange innocence that still permeates Belize's most popular tourist resort, **Ambergris Caye**.

Hispanic touch: It's not surprising that Mexican is the predominant influence on Ambergris Caye and San Pedro (the only settlement here, effectively synonymous with the caye). In fact, Ambergris is technically not an island at all, but a 25-mile (40-km) peninsula extending from the Yucatán and separated from Mexico only by a small trench originally dug by the ancient Maya.

In the early 1980s, fishing was still the major industry on San Pedro – which is why the town and church were named after St Peter. Now many of the fishermen use their locally-made mahogany boats to take tourists to the Barrier Reef that parallels the island. But although this is the most touristy part of Belize, the population is still only 4,000. If you like your tourism slick and well-orchestrated, with raging nightclubs and elegant dining, this may not be the place for you. San Pedro and the Caye have lots of charm, but sometimes the eyes and the heart need to make the distinction between rundown and quaint.

The population of San Pedro is determined not to become one more high-rise Caribbean resort: laws have been passed prohibiting any building more than three stories tall. The idea is to maintain the small scale of Ambergris and give owners of small hotels a chance to stay in business. According to local activist Patty Arceo, there is concern that too much tourism would overwhelm the values of the "host population." Locals should never start seeing tourists as dollar signs, nor should Belize become "a country of waiters."

There is plenty to enjoy in Ambergris, where the living is so casual that going barefoot is appropriate just about anywhere. Even His Honor the Mayor of San Pedro, Baldemar Graniel, goes to the town hall without shoes (the rest of his work clothes consist of a black baseball cap and button-down shirt, mostly unbuttoned). At town board meetings, he even stomps out his cigarette butts with his feet. Like any good politician, the mayor is in step with his people. The streets of San Pedro are of soft, foot-

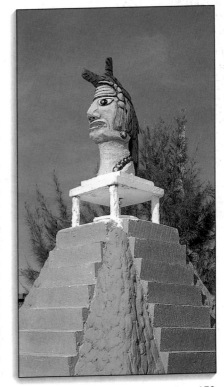

Preceding pages: San Pedro's laid-back high street, Barrier Reef Drive. Left, Ambergris dreaming. Right, monument to the Mayan past.

friendly dirt. Many bars, restaurants, and stores have soft sand floors, with a constantly changing pattern of barefoot imprints.

A large percentage of the owners of diving shops, bars and restaurants owners in San Pedro are Americans, creating a thriving expatriate scene. Even the publishers of the weekly newspaper, *The San Pedro Sun*, are Californian. Like the folks in City Hall, Bruce and Victoria Collins tend to work barefoot; their explanation of their "island fever" could apply to most US escapees. "We wanted to get away from the rat race and from making money," Bruce Collins says with a smile. "And we have achieved both."

Belize's largest caye: Ambergris, 35 miles (56 km) from Belize City, can be reached by water taxi in two hours or small propeller plane in about 20 minutes. San Pedro's airport has a rugged appeal to it, far removed from the crowded world of international terminals. The "waiting room" is a white wooden bench outdoors, dogs snooze beneath the parked planes and, between arrivals and departures, kids ride their bikes across the lone runway.

Located near the southern edge of San Pedro, the airport is a good orientation point. Facing the road that parallels the landing strip, the town proper is to the immediate left; to the right, the road leads through the quiet resorts of the south. Straight ahead, beyond a few buildings, is the Caribbean; behind is the lagoon.

Three streets run north–south through San Pedro: **Barrier Reef Drive**, which parallels the shoreline; **Pescador Drive**, in the middle; and **Angel Coral Street**, closer to the lagoon. The heart of town is midway along Barrier Reef Drive. On one block, there is the **Town Hall** and **police station** (the police have little to do except remind tourists to turn on their golf cart headlights when travelling at night). On the next block is **San Pedro Church**, an airy, tropical building. The large windows have jalousies so that the congregation can be cooled by the Caribbean breeze.

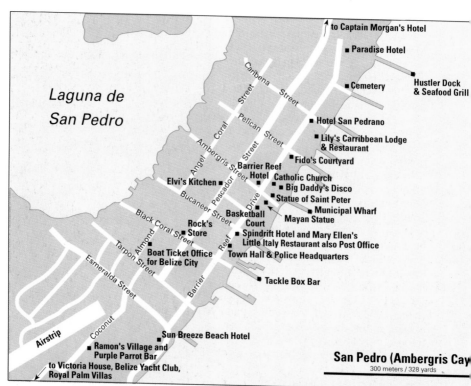

San Pedro (Ambergris Cay

300 meters / 328 yards

174

Opposite the church is an open-air concrete **park**, with a painted bust of a Mayan chief, not too far from the churchyard's painted statue of St Peter, himself a chief in his own way. Neither statue could qualify as great art, but both have a naive charm. The park also has a basketball court, played on every night. People gather to watch the games, if for no other reason than to take advantage of the sea breeze: games are subject to being interrupted during the rainy season by sudden storms.

Evening vibrations: Directly down on the beach from here is the center of the caye's nightlife, namely **Big Daddy's Disco** and **Fido's**, home of the island's second **Purple Parrot Bar** (the original is at Ramon's Village Resort). The **Pier Lounge** is known for its promotional gimmicks, especially the Chicken Drop Contest on Wednesday night, where people bet a dollar per square on which numbered square a chicken will defecate on. The Pier is also the home of the annual Beach Queen contest held in July. One year, the winner was a 300-pound (135 kg) retired cook from Brazil who had more leg to show than some guests wanted to see.

Not far from The Pier is **Mary Ellen's Little Italy Restaurant**, which may be the island's swankiest eatery – but not so swanky that beach dress isn't acceptable. **Elvi's Kitchen** on Pescador Drive features native dishes including chicken or pork served with the ever-present rice and beans. **Celi's Restaurant**, located in the **Holiday Hotel** offers specials like cheese-stuffed fish and Louisiana-style Cajun dishes. There's nothing at all fancy about **Lenny's Place** across the street from the airport, but the food has a native, home-cooked quality.

While strolling along Barrier Reef and Pescador Drives, step back and look at the buildings themselves; many are classic versions of Caribbean architecture. The **Barrier Reef Hotel** is perhaps one of the most splendid examples, but even some of the apparently decrepit wooden houses are architecturally interesting. Some visitors to San Pedro have been looking down instead of up:

Shooting a wave.

In a lot on Pescador Drive, across the street from Elvi's Restaurant, a team of archaeologists has been spending summers digging, gradually finding relics from the island's remote past as a Mayan settlement.

Heading north: Many of the local inhabitants live towards the north end of town, some in the vicinity of an unsightly landfill. Beyond this, the island is divided by a stream: a hand-pulled barge ferries people across to the northern part where the development is almost non-existent and the mood, if possible, even more laid back.

This is the place for those who find even the subdued village life of San Pedro too much and who really, really want to get away from it all. A rugged sand path runs along the shore, which can be traveled by foot or bike. But the preferred way to head north of San Pedro is by boat. There are no towns here, so activity centers around the resort **Journey's End**. This has *casitas* (one-room huts with thatched roofs), villas and the only full-time tennis court on the island.

Journey's End once hosted the presidents of Central American countries for a summit on the drug problem, and some of the *casitas* facing the Caribbean are named for the heads of state who stayed in them.

At a distance of several hundred coconut trees to the south, along a sand path, lies the **Belizean**, an elegant resort that ran into financial problems, was closed, but has been scheduled to reopen. Its swimming pool faces the sea.

Only a bit farther south is **Captain Morgan's**, named after a Caribbean pirate. It consists of a collection of *casitas*, a swimming pool and an observation tower that provides a gull's-eye view of the sea and the back lagoons. In the restaurant, the *tostadas* are excellent and the cold lemonade is a good medicine for countering the tropical sun. Nearby is **El Pescador** (The Fisherman), which is more like a traditional inn. As the name suggests, the place specializes in vacation fishing trips.

As peaceful as this end of the island is, it has created a lot of noise politically.

US investors have proposed a large-scale residential and tourism development project here. The familiar arguments for and against such projects are echoed many times over in northern Ambergris: jobs and growth versus local control and maintaining native integrity. No development is expected in the near future, but the controversy remains alive.

The road south of San Pedro: Ambergris Caye owes much of its physical existence to the mangrove, which can be most easily seen to the south, following the sand road from the airport. Untouched except for the occasional plastic wrapping or old shoe washed in by the gentle waves, the mangrove swamp is like a trip into the womb that gave birth to the island.

Before the mangroves is a clearing developed as a park by the local Lions' Club. The area was used as a set for some of the scenes in the Harrison Ford movie, *The Mosquito Coast*. There's no shortage of the devilish insects here, and having repellent on hand is a good idea, especially at night. Mosquitoes are seldom a problem on the beaches, however, from which they are pushed back by the steady trade winds.

Victoria House Resort is the gem not only of the southern part but, perhaps, the entire island. The 29-room facility has a glamorous mix of hotel rooms, *casitas* and villas in a laid-back, very tropical setting. One of the villas, the Windsor suite, has an original linear mural of native animals and birds. Guests who are staying at some of the nearby places often dine at the Victoria House. Admiral Nelson's Bar has the expected assortment of tropical drinks plus occasional surprises. Some evenings, a band of Garifuna boys makes music with turtle shells, tambourines and drums.

Don Pearly, who, along with his wife Eli, manages the Victoria House, is a tourism activist. There is now no serious drug problem on the caye, but when there was, Pearly was part of an effort to equip the police more effectively. One of the new items was a network of two-way radios. The efforts paid off quickly:

Left and right, snorkelers take the plunge at Hol Chan Marine Reserve.

a burglar fleeing from a rare break-in was spotted by a security guard. On this island, where everyone knows everyone else, the villain's name was relayed to the police, and by the time the suspect reached his home, there was a force waiting to arrest him.

As a member of the local Chamber of Commerce, Pearly worked to create an annual Sea and Air Festival, which was designed to draw well-to-do visitors during Ambergris Caye's usually slow summer months.

Back in the direction of town is the **Belize Yacht Club**, which is not a yacht club at all but a condominium development. (Local officials aren't enthusiastic about vacation condo complexes, which create few jobs; rents usually go to out-of-town owners rather than circulating in the economy.) For an island with few gas-driven vehicles, there is an extremely attractive Shell gas station located at the front of the Yacht Club. It is built in Spanish colonial style and features a mahogany door with Mayan relief figures.

Still nearer to town is one of the island's more famous resorts, **Ramon's Village**. The resort, which has casitas as well as suites, is the home of the original **Purple Parrot**, a poolside bar with a mostly young and hip following. Mississippi-born owner Jerry Gilbreath hopes one day to have a flock of Purple Parrots from Mexico to New Orleans. More than just drinks, the bars do a lively business in T-shirts with the Purple Parrot logo.

Into the Caribbean: Like any self-respecting tropical island, Ambergris Caye looks to the sea. The island is set in the Barrier Reef, and it is off-shore that one heads for swimming, fishing diving and snorkeling. There are no real beaches or even waves along Ambergris' shoreline. Most of the water between the coast and the reef is shallow and grassy – a shoreline for lounging, not surfing.

It was the Maya who discovered a natural cut in the reef, which attracted a wide range of marine life. They called it "Hol Chan," Little Channel. In 1987, the area around the cut was declared the **Hol Chan Marine Reserve** – only 10 minutes away by boat, it is Ambergris' principal local for snorkeling and scuba diving. Snorkelers look for the coral formations and for fish, many of which like to congregate beneath the anchored boats, while scuba divers are attracted to a sinkhole and an underlying cave (see chapter *Beneath the Waves*, pages 103–107, for Belize's marine life).

Fishing is not permitted in the preserve, but there's plenty of sea left for that. Most fishing consists of either trawling in the open sea or dropping anchor in one of the lagoons, where the water is calm. Snappers and groupers are plentiful, and an occasional barracuda puts up a good fight. There is also a lobster industry provided by the sea. Over the years, however, the lobsters have been over-fished, and between March and July the crustaceans are off limits.

Ambergris Caye exists in a fragile ecology, both socially and biologically. Its future faces the same challenge as most of the world's tourist areas – to be able to grow while, in the ways that are important, remaining the same.

Left, a burst of energy on the courts. **Right**, sails at the ready.

ary. This string of four separate lagoons, connected by swamps and rivers, is one of Belize's richest bird habitats – nesting here are migratory flocks of egrets, tiger-herons, roseate spoonbills and hundreds of other species. Perhaps the most impressive, although elusive, is the jabiru stork, the largest bird in the Western hemisphere, with a wingspan of up to 8 ft (2.4 meters).

Covering 3,000 acres (1,200 hectares), Crooked Tree was set up by the Belize Audubon Society in 1984 and is now managed by volunteers. Before entering, sign in at the tidy **visitors' center**, just outside the village of **Crooked Tree**, one of the first "Banks" founded by British logwood cutters in the 17th century. The manager here will provide information on nature trails and birdlife (although the best information can be obtained from the Audobon Society office in Belize City). It is possible to stay with local families here, and the Audubon Society runs the **Crooked Tree Resort**, seven pleasant cabanas set by the lake. The ideal way to visit is by taking a hired boat trip into the swamps and lagoons (call the visitors' center well in advance of your visit to arrange this, as the village is not over-endowed with boats). Peak birdwatching season is between April and May, when hatching begins; (most migratory birds arrive in November, and many leave before the rainy season starts in July). As usual, start at dusk.

Apart from birdlife, the waterways of Crooked Tree have thriving communities of turtle and Morelet's crocodiles; it is also one of the last places in Belize where logwood can still be found.

Alternative route: Running closer to the coast than the new Northern Highway is the rather rougher **Old Northern Highway** (the turnoff, on the right, is 6 miles/10 km past the turnoff to the Baboon Sanctuary). The tiny villages of **Cowhead Creek**, **Lucky Strike** and **Santana** pass by in a colorful blur – the houses all seem to be painted baby blue or fru-fru pink, framed by the lush green of surrounding palm trees. **Maskall**, although no more impressive, passes as

Dusk at Bermudian Landing.

the region's local administrative center.

An unlikely addition to this remote Belizean setting, marked at Mile 40.5, the **Maruba Health Resort**, one of the country's more luxurious and eccentric hotels. White stucco buildings are spread out across statue-studded grounds, with each guest room designed along a theme, decorated with plucked frangipani flowers and the manager Franziska Nicholson's own art works (which use everything from twisted copper to animal skulls, Arizona-style). One room is designed like a chapel, complete with stained glass over the double bed, while the *pièce de résistance* is the huge Tree House Suite, set amongst the palm fronds on the third floor of the tallest building. The room is completely open-air, with wooden slats instead of walls, and only a layer of mosquito netting to hinder the cool breeze wafting across the trees. In the morning, dozens of birds – including toucans – flit around the sills. When one wearies of nature there's a CD player with 3-ft (1-meter) high speakers.

Many Belizeans and North Ameri-cans make regular visits to the hotel for the health cures – massages, seaweed wraps and the like – or for the excellent restaurant, but Maruba also makes a good base for visiting the nature reserves and ruins of the area.

Only a short drive away are the impressive Mayan ruins of **Altun Ha**, a Classic Period ceremonial center with two large plazas (large enough, in fact, that kids from the nearby village of **Rockstone Pond** are often found playing football in them) and 13 ancient structures, which were probably occupied from 1100 BC to AD 900. Some 3,000 Mayans are believed to have lived here, mostly supporting themselves by farming and trading. Excavation of the site began only in the mid-1960s. The dominant pyramid of Plaza A, known as the **Temple of the Green Tomb**, is actually several temples built on top of one another. Around 300 artefacts have been found inside it, from skins to jewelry, stingray spines and parts of an ancient Maya book.

The tallest structure at Altun Ha, the **Temple of the Masonry Altars** (also known as the Temple of the Sun God) looms over Plaza B with a height of 60 ft (18 meters). Five of the seven tombs found in the pyramid had already been ransacked, but in 1968 archaeologist David Pendergast discovered the untouched remains of an elderly priest. Interred with him was the famous jade head of the Mayan Sun God, Kinich Ahau, at 5.8 inches (14.9 cm) in height and weighing 9.75 lb (4.42 kg) Belize's most precious Mayan artefact. Although obviously of great religious significance for the Maya, archaeologist still have no clues as to what its purpose was.

Other digging at this temple showed that local priests indulged in an unusual form of sacrifice, whereby beautifully carved jade objects were smashed and flung into fires. And one of its seven tombs showed signs of desecration during the end of the Mayan period, which has led archaeologists to speculate that Altun Ha was abandoned after a violent encounter, possibly a peasant revolt – one more clue in understanding the abandonment of the great Mayan cities.

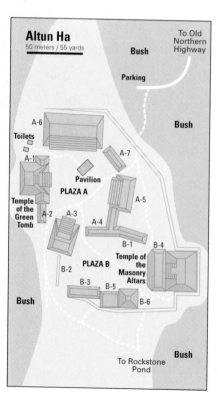

Altun Ha
50 meters / 55 yards

To Old Northern Highway

Bush

Parking

A-6

Toilets

A-1

Bush

A-7

Pavilion

PLAZA A

A-5

Temple of the Green Tomb

A-2 A-3

A-4

B-1 B-4

PLAZA B

Temple of the Masonry Altars

B-2

B-3 B-5

B-6

Bush

To Rockstone Pond

Bush

LAMANAI

Appreciating an ancient ruin is largely an act of the imagination. Even the most impressive Mayan city, when reached in a tourist bus on a paved highway, can seem just a pile of dead rocks (which, of course, is exactly what it is). But arrive via a rugged dirt road and a boat trip through the sinuous waterways of a remote jungle swamp and, magically, the scene is infinitely more exciting.

That's why a visit to **Lamanai**, although physically nowhere near as prepossessing as some of Mesoamerica's more famous ruins, is often more memorable. Located on the banks of the **New River Lagoon**, it can be reached by easy day trips from Maruba and Orange Walk Town (or longer trips from Belize City and Ambergris).

A rough but easily passable road runs through the finely-named villages of **Dubloon Bank Savannah**, **Bound To Shine** and **Guinea Grass**, into the sugar cane country of the New River. Trucks weighed down with cane lumber by, operated privately by local farmers who are paid by the ton. From the small docks at **Shipyard,** motorboats leave for the hour-long journey along the New River's inky black waters.

The river and surrounding swampland is teaming with wildlife, including a healthy population of Morelet's crocodiles. These gave Lamanai its name – Mayan for "submerged crocodile" – and make the prospect of swimming, while safe, rather nerve-wracking. Apart from pointing out birdlife, most boat drivers will bump up against gutted tree trunks on the shoreline, covered in tiny, sleeping bats, waking them up and sending them in a cloud over passengers' heads.

By the time you reach the ruins, you feel like Indiana Jones, and since you may well have the place to yourself, there's nobody to destroy the illusion.

The last surviving Mayan city: A few thatched-roofed houses have been built

**Preceding pages: boatman on the New River.
Left, the enveloping swamps.**

at the dockside for the ruin's guards, along with an open-air picnic hut and a small museum piled high with Mayan artefacts (nothing too valuable, the best pieces having been removed to Belize City). Several paths run through into the dense jungle, which is now being reinhabited by families of black howler monkeys. Only a small part of the ancient city has been unearthed, and there is a sense that archaeologists are fighting a losing battle to stop the whole site from being reclaimed by nature.

Lamanai was first settled some 3,000 years ago and its most impressive temples were built in the Preclassic period around 100 BC. Several centuries later, in the Classic period, the population had increased from 20,000 to 50,000.

What makes Lamanai unique is that it was still inhabited when the first Spanish conquistadors arrived in search of gold here in the 16th century. The population was about a quarter its Classic number, and its most spectacular temples were untended. How Lamanai survived the cataclysm that devastated the other Mayan cities is unknown. In any case, Spanish missionaries quickly set about building a church to convert the heathens. The Maya rebelled and burned it in the 1640s, but European-imported diseases soon decimated the community. Even so, there were a few Mayan inhabitants here when British settlers arrived in the 1800s; the new colonialists drove them out to Guatemala so the land could be cleared for sugar.

Thomas Gann, a British medical officer and amateur archaeologist made the first modern excavations at Lamanai in 1917, but it wasn't until 1974 that large-scale digging was begun by Canadian David Pendergast of the Royal Ontario Museum.

Exploring the ruins: The Lamanai pyramids are still known by their dry archaeological labels. The first on the path is **P9-56**. While its exterior dates from the 6th century AD, this pyramid was found to have been built over a finely preserved temple from five centuries earlier. The most famous feature is a 13-ft (4-meter) high limestone face

Top speed down the New River.

carved into its side, now protected from the elements by a makeshift roof: its combination of thick lips, bared teeth, dreamy eyes and elongated forehead (created by Mayas flattening their children's skulls) make the image half terrifying, half serene.

A second statue is known to be on the left side of the temple stairs, but archaeologists left it buried to protect it from torrential rains and possible looters.

Lamanai's best-known and most impressive pyramid is **N10-43**, a steep, 112-ft (34-meter) high edifice. It reached its present height by around 100 BC, making it the largest Preclassic structure in the whole of Mesoamerica (although not as tall as the Classic pyramids at Xunantinich and Caracol, it is still considerably higher than any modern Belizean building). Like most Maya structures, it was modified heavily.

The temple's steps are in fair condition and can be climbed for breathtaking views across the jungle canopy and New River, with the cries of birds and occasionally howler monkeys echoing upwards. This makes the perfect vantage point for picturing ancient Mayan rituals (priests would take positions on the temple, with the rest of the population gathered below in the plaza); or imagining Mayan astronomers gathering by night to contemplate the heavens.

Below pyramid N10-43 is the **ball court**, where the violent *pok-ta-pok* was played; archaeologist Pendergast found pottery containing mercury here, the only time the substance has been found at a Maya site. In the makeshift hut nearby is a **stela** carved with hieroglyphics; underneath it was found the bones of six children, assumed to have been sacrificed.

Apart from the Mayan structures, at the nearby village of **Indian church** are the remains of two 16th-century Spanish missions and a ruined sugar mill built by former Confederate soldiers in the 1870s. Despite a recent influx of squatters from neighboring Guatemala and El Salvador, this once-thriving area remains all but uninhabited – and the more mysterious for it.

Emerging at the ruins.

BELMOPAN

Belmopan is the Brazilia of Belize. Founded in 1971, it is an artificial capital that has never quite caught on: in fact, it is still one of the country's smallest towns. Government ministries have their headquarters here, but most politicians would rather commute from Belize City than take up permanent residence; the bulk of the workforce may be employed by the government, but few people are interested in party politics.

The great dream: Belmopan was former Prime Minister George Price's vision of "a modern capital for an emerging nation." The idea of an inland location had first been fielded after Belize City was devastated by Hurricane Hattie in 1961. Price hoped that a planned city would attract Belizeans from all over the country, and eventually replace Belize City as a commercial and cultural center. He also hoped it would centralize the government by bringing each ministry together on the same compound with new, efficient facilities.

The plan sounded promising on paper, but things didn't go quite so smoothly. The new government offices, designed to resemble a Mayan temple and plaza, were much too small, so today many offices are located away from the center of town. Instead of cutting red tape, the move to Belmopan created it. Citizens had to travel all the way to the capital to have documents signed or obtain permits. This proved very time consuming, especially when officials missed appointments or demanded multiple trips: before long, government branch offices in Belize City and other towns were given the same power as the head office in the capital.

But the biggest problem was that Belizeans weren't willing to move to Belmopan – and most still aren't. After more than 20 years, Belmopan has less than 4,000 inhabitants, and most of these are refugees from neighboring countries in Central America. Of the Belizeans who work here, almost all

Preceding pages: high noon before the National Assembly building. Below, government offices designed for the future.

196

SAN IGNACIO AND ITS SURROUNDINGS

When travelers talk about visiting the interior of Belize, they are usually referring to the lush, mountainous rainforests around the town of San Ignacio – heart of the country's booming new "eco-tourism" trade.

The region is a nature-lover's fantasy come true. Spread out across a remote subtropical wilderness are dozens of cabana-style lodges, many of them quite luxurious. Within striking distance – by car, horseback, canoe or foot – are secluded, jungle-rimmed swimming holes, enormous limestone caverns, Belize's most significant Mayan ruins and Central America's highest waterfalls. The constant background music is the shriek of exotic birds, while iguanas, gibnuts and skunks habitually stroll across the well-marked nature trails.

Meanwhile, the dripping rainforests are surprisingly free of Belize's least popular life form, the mosquito – the higher altitude makes days around San Ignacio hot without being overwhelming, while evenings can almost be described as cool.

On the frontier with Guatemala, this is also one of the most Hispanic parts of Belize, populated largely by Spanish-speaking Mestizos and Maya Indians; second in numbers come Creoles, followed by a classically Belizean smattering of East Indians, Chinese and Lebanese. A few British soldiers are still based here to guard the sensitive border, while several large communities of Mennonites farm the rich land and can be seen clattering along the highways in horse-drawn carriages.

Fierce independence: Historically, the region around San Ignacio has always kept to itself. The Maya Indians here put up one of the longest struggles against the Spaniards in the Americas. The Spanish conquest of the 1540s never reached

Preceding pages: morning mist over the Macal River valley; Mayan relics discovered in Cha Chem Ha cave. **Left**, Eva's Restaurant & Bar, social hub of Belize's Wild West.

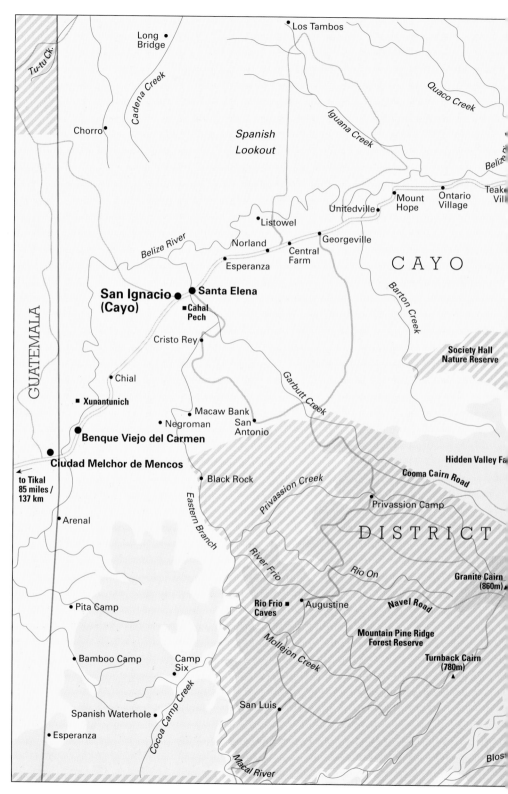

Long
Bridge •

Los Tambos •

Tu-tu Ck.

Cadena Creek

Chorro •

Iguana Creek

Quaco Creek

*Spanish
Lookout*

Belize Ri...

Mount
Hope •

Ontario
Village •

Teak...
Vil...

Unitedville •

Belize River

Listowel •

Norland •

Central
Farm

Georgeville •

C A Y O

Esperanza •

**San Ignacio
(Cayo)** •

•**Santa Elena**

■**Cahal
Pech**

Barton Creek

Society Hall
Nature Reserve

Cristo Rey •

• Chial

■ **Xunantunich**

Macaw Bank •

San
Antonio •

Garbutt Creek

GUATEMALA

• Negroman

• **Benque Viejo del Carmen**

• **Ciudad Melchor de Mencos**

← to Tikal
85 miles /
137 km

Black Rock •

Hidden Valley Fa...

Privassion Creek

Cooma Cairn Road

• Arenal

Privassion Camp ■

Eastern Branch

D I S T R I C T

River Frio

Rio On

**Granite Cairn
(860m)** ▲

• Pita Camp

Rio Frio ■
Caves

• Augustine

Navel Road

**Mountain Pine Ridge
Forest Reserve**

• Bamboo Camp

Camp
Six

Mollejon Creek

**Turnback Cairn
(780m)** ▲

Cocoa Camp Creek

Spanish Waterhole •

San Luis •

• Esperanza

Macal River

Blos...

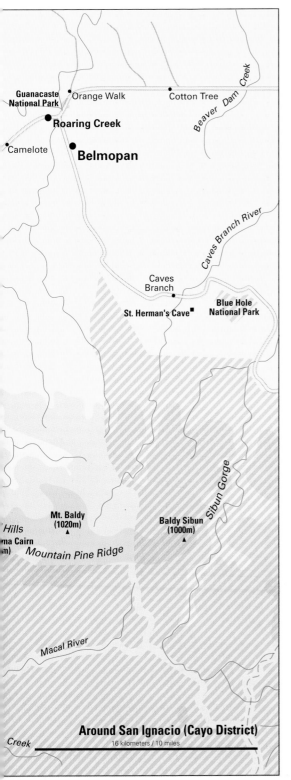

Around San Ignacio (Cayo District)

16 kilometers / 10 miles

this remote region, and later news that the Castilian king expected them to pay taxes, obey Spanish laws and worship the Christian god was poorly received. Newly-built churches were burned in rebellion, and, according to the chronicles, several captured soldiers and missionaries were sacrificed.

The inhabitants of Tipu, a city on the **Macal River** (possibly where the village of Negroman now stands), led the resistance. Two Franciscan friars thought that they had converted them to Christianity in 1618, only to find a year later that the entire population was secretly practicing idolatry. Twenty years later, the same friars were received by pagan priests who performed a mock mass with tortillas as the eucharist. The Maya then smashed the crucifix, roughed up the friars and sent them packing back to the coast.

European diseases like smallpox eventually all but wiped out the Indian population, and by the early 1700s the Spanish were able to assert control and resettle many survivors in Guatemala. British and Creole lumbermen arrived, setting up logging camps and bringing with them the power of the British Crown. They quickly sold off Mayan land and drove the last dispirited natives into easily-manageable towns. San Ignacio started off as the major loading point on the Macal River for mahogany and chicle, growing slowly to its role today as the agricultural center of the region.

Confusingly enough, the district around San Ignacio became known as **Cayo**, after the Spanish word for cayes – coral islands off Belize's coast – while San Ignacio itself is also known as **El Cayo**. The name may be a reflection of the isolation early settlers felt from the rest of the world before a roadway was first pushed through in the 1930s. Until then, boat trips to Belize City took about 10 days, horseback journeys anywhere from two weeks to a month.

Thanks to the country's best paved road, the **Western Highway**, the town of San Ignacio can now be reached in a mere 90 minutes by car from Belize City. En route from Belmopan are the tiny villages of **Teakettle** and **George-**

town, where a large number of Mennonites often gather to sell their wares. The northern turnoff to **Spanish Lookout** leads into the most populous Mennonite area. These Mennonites are by no means traditional, driving around in pick-up trucks, using telephones and mechanical machinery. Pancake-flat and rich brown, the country seems indistinguishable from, say, Ohio.

British colonial outpost: Built in a spectacular valley, on the edge of a ravine above the Macal River, the town of **San Ignacio** is separated from the neighboring village of **Santa Elena** by the **Hawkesworth suspension bridge** – a miniature model of the Brooklyn Bridge. Although it only has one lane, forcing cars to be regulated in each direction by traffic lights, it remains one of the more impressive engineering feats in Belize. San Ignacio was the last frontier in one of the most obscure corners of the British Empire, and several of its buildings retains a faded colonial charm. The **police station**, for example, perched above the bridge, looks like it belongs in

an Indian hill station or a lost provincial outpost in a Somerset Maugham short story. The narrow streets are quiet to the point of somnolescence – although the combined population of San Ignacio and Santa Elena is around 8,000, making this the metropolis of western Belize, hardly any of them are out by day. The exception is Saturday, when farmers from the surrounding countryside flock to the **market** with their produce.

The social hub of San Ignacio (and the official tourist information office) is **Eva's Restaurant** on Burns Avenue, run by wiry Englishman Bob Jones. At lunchtime, when the rest of San Ignacio seems a ghost town, Eva's is hopping: travelers, locals and expats gather here for chile con carne and Belikins every day, and for information on every corner of Cayo district (as well as a two-way radio to contact out-of-town cottages for reservations). Around Eva's are most of the cheap hotels in San Ignacio, and across the street is a **Serendib**, the only Sri Lankan restaurant in Belize (and perhaps all of Central America). Those

Colonial memories at the police station.

seeking more civilized accommodation head up the hillside via the steep Buena Vista Road to the **San Ignacio Hotel** and **Piache Hotel**. Both have good restaurants and views over the Macal River valley.

Just off Buena Vista Road are the **Cahal Pech ruins** – although quite important for Belizean archaeology, the main temple has been "restored" for tourists in a Disneyland style (and unlikely to impress anyone unless it's their first Mayan ruin). Cahal Pech was populated around 1,000 BC until AD 800. The name means "Place of the Ticks," given in the 1950s when the area was used as a cow pasture.

More impressive, in its own way, is the neighbouring **Cahal Pech Tavern**, a large shed that houses San Ignacio's most popular club. The town's dreamy calm breaks after dark on Friday and Saturday nights, when off-duty British soldiers, local prostitutes and Creole citrus workers let loose in a frenzy of live Punta music. Downtown, the disco **Blue Angel** turns into a raucous all-night party with a nod towards Bohemian scenes in larger world cities: amongst the usual crowd in shorts and singlets, you might see a character wearing a purple tuxedo with ruffles. or a blonde woman in slinky black dress, hobbling along the broken streets in high stilettos. (A word of warning: the scene gets increasingly rough as the night goes on, and locals insisted that wire grilles were put over the second-story Blue Angel's windows because too many people were being thrown through them in drunken brawls.)

The easiest hike from town, taking about half an hour, is due north along the Macal River to its meeting with the Mopan at **Branch Mouth** (a good spot for swimming). En route are the fields of **Marathon Tropical Farms**, where Belizean plants and flowers are grown for export. Horses can be hired at **Las Casitas** lodge to visit the village of **Bullet Tree Falls** and the ruins of **Pilar**, dating from the Classical Maya period but little excavated and uninspiring.

Into the wilderness: Although San

Loading up with supplies in San Ignacio.

Ignacio is the urban hub of the region, most travelers check into one of the many mountain lodges that now dot the region. Responding to the surge in eco-tourism, the latest immigrant wave seems to be North American environmentalists and hoteliers, who have colonized the countryside. Comfortable – sometimes very luxurious – cabanas have spread rapidly across the hinterland (tourism authorities say the number leapt in one year from 14 to more than 50). This means that, while having one's own car to explore is an advantage, it is by no means necessary: the various lodges organize tours to every corner of the district (or tours can be aranged through Eva's in San Ignacio).

The most popular excursion in the region is due south of San Ignacio to the **Mountain Pine Ridge Forest Reserve**. The sudden appearance of thick pine forest, looking as if it is straight out of Vermont, is one of Belize's more peculiar geological anomalies. Geologists explain that the unique granite base and nutrient-poor soil content of the area

was either thrust up from below Central America countless millennia ago or was a Caribbean island that was effectively pushed on top of the rest of the isthmus during its formation.

Two access roads run into the ridge from the Western Highway. The first is the Cristo Rey road from Santa Elena, not long before the San Ignacio bridge. This is the same turnoff sign-posted to **Maya Mountain Lodge**, a well-maintained group of cabanas nestled in the forest (billing itself as an Educational Field Station, it is a family-style place run by two American members of the Bahai faith, Bart and Suzi Mickler, who take their eco-tourism seriously).

The Cristo Rey road runs through the one-horse village of **San Antonio**, one of the few places in Belize where Mayan is still widely spoken as a first language (the dialect is Mopan). Just north of town is the house of the five **García sisters**, who sell slate carvings and other Maya handicrafts. Unlike the Maya of neighboring Guatemala, the Belizean Maya have only recently started mar-

Left, welcome sign at the Garcia sisters'. **Right**, a young Mayan artisan.

210

keting such wares to tourists. The sisters were taught by their father, Aureliano, a former *chiclero* (chicle gum base tapper). They have also opened a small museum of Mayan culture in a traditional thatched hut, full of scattered odds and ends. Starting with a small, cottage craft operation, the sisters have built up their small empire with what is, by Belizean standards, hard-nosed business sense.

Two miles (3 km) to the east of San Antonio, on private land, are the ruins of **Pacbitun**, one of the oldest Preclassical Maya sites (it dates from 1,000 BC and flourished as a trading center into the Late Classic period, around AD 900). Local farmers knew about Pacbitun's existence for generations, but it wasn't until 1971 that the first archaeologists made studies here. They found 24 pyramids (the highest is 55 ft/16.5 meters), eight stelae, several raised irrigation causeways and a collection of Mayan musical instruments. The name means "Stones Set in the Earth." Permission to visit must first be obtained from Mr

The Mountain Pine Ridge; Vermont comes to Central America.

Tzul (he's on the turn-off to Pacbitun).

The second access road heads south from Georgeville through the traditional Mennonite community of **Barton Creek**. This is a breakaway group from the modernized community around Spanish Lookout: you feel as if you've wandered into the 19th century as men trundle by with flowing white beards, hats and overalls, while the women wear long black dresses with hats and heavy veils. There is no problem about visiting the Mennonite farms (the elders, who usually speak English, are more than happy to explain their religion), but remember that they are quite serious about not being photographed.

Further south is the ranch **Casa Cielo**, run by **Mountain Equestrian Trails**, which offers horse riding to all levels. MET also arranges trips to the remote **Society Hall Nature Reserve**, lost in the foothills of the Mountain Pine Ridge, between Barton Creek and Roaring Creek. This pristine block of tropical forest, stretching across dramatic limestone karst formations, was given its

heritage listing thanks to the efforts of its German owner, conservationist Svea Dietrich-Ward. It can only be visited by qualified naturalists with prior permission from the Belize Audubon Society.

The two access roads into the Ridge meet 3 miles (5 kms) beyond MET, where another roadside handicrafts store has been set up by Mayan artists hoping to imitate the García sisters' success.

Heart of the ridge: At this point the landscape, with little warning, gives way to pines, mixed in with bromeliads and wildflowers; the birdlife is rich here and the air slowly becomes cooler. A ranger stops traffic at a checkpoint and barrier that marks the beginning of the Mountain Pine Ridge Reserve, registering names and license plates to control illegal camping and logging, as well as to keep a record in case of accidents.

Two miles (3 km) later is the turnoff to **Hidden Valley Falls** (another 4 miles/7 kms along Baldy Beacon Road). These are also known as **Thousand Foot Falls**, although they happen to be 1,600 ft (480 meters) high. From the picnic ground you can watch the thin plume of water stream down a cliffside and disappear into the lush forest below. There are many smaller but arguably more beautiful falls nearby, including perhaps the most charming, **Butterfly Falls**.

Eleven miles (18 km) further south (marked on the left) are the **Río On Pools**, natural rock pools formed by granite boulders. They're in a serene, open setting and ideal for a swim.

Five miles (8 km) south is the turnoff to the **Río Frío Cave**, the largest cave in Belize and the most accessible. During the dry season, it is quite possible to follow the River Frío into the cave's enormous mouth and out the other end (about 870 yards/800 meters). The rocks are a little slippery, but not unmanageable; inside are unusually colored rock formations, stalactites, and the odd colony of bats. There is also a 45-minute outdoor Nature Trail for the energetic.

The road now leads to the only settlement in the reserve, **Augustine**, where camping is permitted and several new tourist accomodations have been set up

Firewood collection.

(including a lodge being built by the Hollywood film director Francis Ford Coppola, whose impressive figure can sometimes be spotted here).

South to Caracol: Call in at the ranger station in Augustine for access further south: passage into the remote **Chiquibul Forest Reserve**, populated only by a few loggers, tree-tappers and archaeologists, is closely monitored.

The main attraction for the average traveler is the ruined Mayan city of **Caracol**. Until 1993, Caracol was only accessible by one of the worst roads in Belize, and archaeologists still tell tales of their four-wheel drives becoming bogged in mud for three days at a time. A new road cuts the driving time from Augustine down to two hours, although the going is still rough and it's usually completely closed when it rains.

The route runs into the **Vaca Plateau**, with a return from pines to the more familiar rainforest foliage and some spectacular views over mountains and river valleys. The only other traffic is likely to be logging trucks and British troop carriers – London still maintains a jungle training camp here, and it's not unusual to run across a few dozen likely lads standing stark naked in a river after a grueling hike.

Beneath the Vaca Plateau are a series of great cave complexes, including the Chiquibul, which may be the largest in the western hemisphere. It was only found by modern spelunkers in the 1970s and remains little explored – although tales of prehistoric fossils being discovered there have caused new interest.

The road becomes progressively more bone-shaking until the ruins suddenly appear – a Mayan pyramid, only recently hacked from the jungle, glimpsed through a gap in the vines. (For a history summary and a walking tour of the ruins, see page 220.)

West towards the border: Before the Western Highway from San Ignacio to the Guatemalan frontier was finally paved in the 1980s, the small towns here were very remote. Their layout and atmosphere – small plaza, bodega with a few shirtless men drinking beer, the

Left, Butterfly Falls. Right, hard work on the Macal River.

inevitable rundown hotel – is distinctively Latino, and if you're asking for directions, many people will only speak Spanish. The remoter forest roads are like scenes from *The Good, the Bad and the Ugly*: lone cowboys in wide-brimmed hats amble past, Indian women might pass loaded down with bundles of sticks, and young boys lead burros under the sweltering sun.

Only 5 miles (8 km) west of San Ignacio is a turnoff that follows a tributary of the Macal River, **Chaa Creek**, to the heart of cabana country. The best known lodge here, **Chaa Creek Cottages**, also has one of the best locations, nestled amongst rainforest-covered hills in the Macal River valley. Strict eco-tourists might object to the manicured, flower-filled grounds, but most visitors allow themselves to be seduced by what might be termed "rustic luxury." Each room is a separate cottage, decorated with Guatemalan handicrafts and using kerosine lamps for light at night. Cool breezes waft through large open windows facing down on the luscious river

valley, and although there are not even mosquito nets, nothing more meddlesome than a flying beetle comes into the room. In this same district are the no less comfortable **DuPlooy's Riverside Cottages**, with their own white sand beach by the River Macal, and a half dozen newer places.

Connected to Chaa Creek Cottages is the **Ix Chel Farm**, a unique facility devoted to researching the healing powers of tropical plants. Ix Chel (the name comes from the Mayan goddess queen, a symbol of healing) was founded by a Chicago-trained herbalist Rosita Arvigo, who convinced a local Mayan shaman, Don Eligio Panti, then in his late 80s, to pass on his learning. Today the farm runs an Ethnobotany Project, funded by the US government's National Cancer Institute, to collect and classify rare tropical plants that may help in the fight against Aids and cancer. In the past, tropical plants have been used in Western medicine against malaria (quinine), for anaesthesia (curare), treating leukemia (vinblastine) and as ingredi-

Chaa Creek Cottages, one of the many lodges in the region.

214

CARACOL

A small sign greeting visitors to Caracol reads, "The Rumors Are True." The ancient Maya city of Caracol was a massive and sophisticated metropolis that remained hidden from the world under a blanket of rainforest for nearly a millennium. Rediscovered half a century ago, it was dismissed as a minor site. But in recent years, archaeologists have realized that Caracol was far more important and powerful than they had guessed: the lost names of Caracol's heroic kings and their legendary battles are now being triumphantly returned to their place in history books.

For over a century in the Classic Period, Caracol controlled the rainforest Petén region (now in Guatemala), including the great – and today much more famous – city of Tikal. Continuing excavations of Caracol's monumental architecture and sculpture are slowly confirming proof of the past glory.

Reemerging from the rainforest: In 1937 a mahogany logger, Rosa Mai, reported the discovery of the ancient city to archaeology officials in what was then British Honduras. The top archaeological official, A.H. Anderson, first visited the site in 1938 and discovered some stelae and the Temple of the Wooden Lintel, the only building then visible.

The world's view of Caracol for the next three decades was formed in three short field seasons in 1950, 1951 and 1953 by the University of Pennsylvania. Several stelae and altar groups were uncovered – and removed. For two seasons Anderson led his own excavation at the site, but in 1961 Hurricane Hattie destroyed most of Anderson's notes and drawings in Belize City.

Archaeologists avoided Caracol, which they considered a medium-size site dominated by Tikal. But in 1983 Paul Healy of Trent University reported that agricultural terracing outside of Caracol's center once supported a much heavier population density than once thought. Today's Caracol Project has

Preceding pages: Mayan carving unearthed at Caracol. Below, four-wheel driving to the ruins.

been run since 1985 by Arlen and Diane Chase of the University of Central Florida. There have been a continuous series of breakthroughs, including the discovery and translation of an altar that describes a military victory over Tikal in the 7th century, as well as one major and 50 lesser tombs.

The site of Caracol was settled by a well-organized Maya group in around 300 BC in the Pre-Classic Period. The city's epicenter was built on a plateau 1,600 ft (490 meters) above sea level, without a natural water source but protected by surrounding hills. The population depended on human-made *aguadas*, or reservoirs, the remains of which can still be seen (one is used by Caracol Project members for reconsolidation of cement and bathing water).

Stelae show a royal lineage entrenched in Caracol by the 5th century AD, reaching its first peak in the year 562, when the ruler Lord Water defeated Tikal. The city subsequently prospered and grew to its ultimate population of about 180,000 people in AD 650. One of Lord

A gardener tends the newly-uncovered site.

Water's sons, Lord Khan II, continued his father's success with a victory over Naranjo in AD 631. A 9th-century renaissance under Lord Makina-hok-kawil brought tremendous construction and expansion to the epicenter and particularly Caana.

Visitors will encounter a rainforest environment nearly identical to Tikal. There are grand ceiba trees, cahoon nut trees (which provided the ancient Maya with nuts) and escoba trees covered with toothpick-sized pricks. Wildlife includes parrots, oscillated turkeys, yellow-billed toucans, red-crowned woodpeckers, a few mot-mots and the occasional howler monkey. Caracol is a designated archaeological and natural reserve, so the beauty of the rainforest and its ruins will not fall to developers.

Exploring the site: Visitors today arrive by road at the epicenter of the ancient city. This is the nexus of Caracol's *sacbe*, or causeway, system from which at least seven raised roads radiated like spokes of a bicycle wheel. With names like **Conchita**, **Pajara-**

Ramonal and **Retiro**, the causeways lead to spectacular architectural groups up to 5 miles (8 km) away, which possibly defined geographic borders of Caracol. Along many of these causeways are agricultural terraces which supplied the city with either food or cash crops – such as cacao and cotton – used in trade.

The **South Acropolis** is an elite residential complex, including an amazingly preserved Late Classic tomb with a corbelled vault. Some tombs at Caracol have the closing dates painted in hematite-red on the bottom-side of the central capstone.

Nearby are the **ballcourts**, where Caracol's athletes played the traditional ballgame. In the center of the main court lies a marker, discovered in 1986, which dates to 9.10.0.0.0. (AD 633) and discusses Lord Water's great victory over Tikal. This defeat helps explain a century-long hiatus in Tikal, when no stone monuments or new architecture were erected. It was a lucky find: for many years the treasure lay underneath a log trucking road.

Plaza A was the city's cultural focus, containing the largest concentration of stelae and altars. The placement of the **Temple of the Wooden Lintel** and its flanking structures are modeled after the astronomical observatory (**Group E** buildings) at **Uaxactun** – where two stelae markers on either side of the plaza would line up with the rising sun during the winter and summer equinoxes. The Temple of the Wooden Lintel's original *zapote*, or sapodilla, wood beams in the back room are carbon-dated to about AD 50. Thorough trenching through the center of the building exposed earlier versions of the temple from before 300 BC, the earliest Pre-Classic days of Caracol.

The well-preserved palaces of **Barrio** were built in the 9th century above earlier buildings. A major drop to the south and east of the plaza indicate how much it was artificially raised.

Altar 24 in **Plaza B** has a fascinating relief depicting two stout men facing each other, their hands bound behind their backs and their hair bound in a knot. Save for a loincloth, these royal figures wear no clothing and are stripped of jewelry (papyrus strips have been placed in their ears instead of jade ear flares). The glyphs explain that the man on the right is a hostage from the site of Ucanal, the man on the left from the unidentified site Q.

Pinnacle of ancient Caracol: The massive **Caana complex**, or "sky place" is counted among the greatest Maya structures of Mesoamerica. It contains palaces, courtyards, pyramids and other buildings whose exact purpose is still unknown. The base of Caana is above a natural limestone hill and measures 330 by 395 ft (100 by 120 meters). Only a narrow strip of the first central staircase has been reconsolidated. The length of rooms on the middle level facing the plaza are all similar, each with a wide front entrance and a large, often U-shaped bench. These rooms were designed for a specific purpose – either as seats to watch the plaza (like luxury boxes at a baseball stadium) or a place to display prisoners or royalty to the peo-

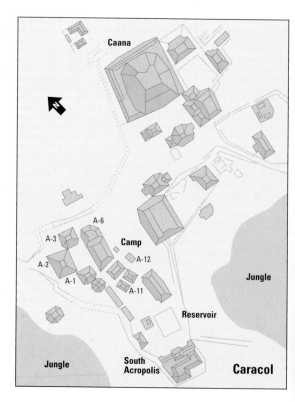

ple gathered in the plaza below. To the west is a special staircase to the next level, which could be ascended and descended hidden from the plaza view.

An open room on the eastern side has special entrances to side rooms – Lilliputian "dwarf" doors that lead to bare rooms with air vents. These rooms might have been used for prisoners, children, animals, storage or any other practical purpose. Soldiers posted at either end possibly guarded access to the second level – which contains magnificent architecture that was surely the pinnacle of ancient Caracol. Visitors enter through a special doorway, with a bench on either side (probably a place to catch one's breath). A central plaza is surrounded by three 40-ft (12-meter) pyramids (they were much taller when complete) and a long rectangular building.

Directly in front of the northern pyramid, **B19,** lie stairs specially built to give access to a tomb buried in an earlier building (**B19-2nd**). The large chamber once contained the body of a very important woman from the 7th century,

but scholars are still determining her identity (she may have been the wife of Lord Water). Between B19 and the eastern pyramid, **B18**, is the entrance to a palatial courtyard surrounded by large rooms. The stucco moulding against the south side of B18 represent a weave design used by the royalty.

Looters found three major tombs in the rear of the western pyramid, **B20**, which can be visited via a trail around Caana. In the second tomb, a painted text on the back wall was destroyed.

An earlier version of this pyramid, **B20-2nd**, began more than 13 ft (4 m) below the current plaza. A 10-ft (3-meter) earth monster mask stood at the base, with an entrance through the mouth (representing the gateway to the Underworld or *Xibalba*). Inside, excavators found a small room with a burned body and graffiti depicting a procession, with a bound prisoner marching ahead of a ruler carried on a litter. The smoke from this room – either from incense or charred corpses – once billowed out through the eyes of the monster mask.

Left, view from the air. **Right**, local worker who helped uncover the site.

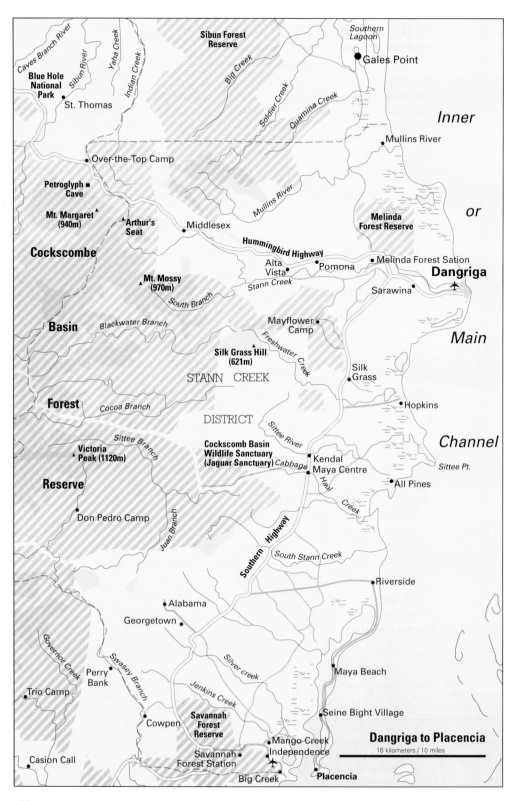

Caves Branch River

Sibun River

Yaha Creek

Indian Creek

Blue Hole
National
Park

St. Thomas

Sibun Forest
Reserve

Big Creek

Soldier Creek

Quamina Creek

Southern
Lagoon

Gales Point

Inner

or

Mullins River

Over-the-Top Camp

Petroglyph
Cave

Mt. Margaret
(940m)

Arthur's
Seat

Middlesex

Mullins River

Melinda
Forest Reserve

Cockscombe

Hummingbird Highway

Alta
Vista

Pomona

Melinda Forest Sation

Dangriga

Mt. Mossy
(970m)

Stann Creek

Sarawina

Basin

Blackwater Branch

South Branch

Mayflower
Camp

Freshwater Creek

Main

Silk Grass Hill
(621m)

STANN   CREEK

Silk
Grass

Forest

Cocoa Branch

DISTRICT

Sittee River

Hopkins

Channel

Sittee Branch

Victoria
Peak (1120m)

Cockscomb Basin
Wildlife Sanctuary
(Jaguar Sanctuary)

Cabbage

Kendal
Maya Centre

Sittee Pt.

Reserve

Don Pedro Camp

Juan Branch

Haul

Creek

All Pines

Southern

Highway

South Stann Creek

Riverside

Governor Creek

Alabama

Georgetown

Silver creek

Maya Beach

Perry
Bank

Swasey Branch

Jenkins Creek

Trio Camp

Cowpen

Seine Bight Village

Casion Call

Savannah
Forest
Reserve

Savannah
Forest Station

Mango Creek
Independence

Big Creek

Placencia

Dangriga to Placencia

16 kilometers / 10 miles

caught the evening sea breeze in this otherwise stiflingly hot location, and saved them from the occasional flood in the rainy season). Fishing dories lie tied up along the banks of the 100-ft (30-meter) wide river, beside canopied ferries loading fruit from Honduras and Guatemala. Vegetable stands and clothing bazaars crowd the narrow streets near the riverside market; newly-arrived Central American refugees wander, bent like old men from the bulging packs on their backs.

Of course, the modern world is creeping in. Instead of pursuing the traditional fishing and farming, many Garifuna have become teachers and civil servants. Cable television has arrived in Dangriga, and a steady flow of cash from large expatriate communities in Chicago, Los Angeles and New York has allowed some wooden houses to be replaced with the cold practicality of concrete. Youngsters sporting $100 tennis shoes and mountain bikes now speed past graying Garifuna women carrying firewood or plastic buckets of water on their heads.

Between the slow pace of traditional subsistence living and the headlong rush for materialism, little attention has been paid to creating a tourist image in Dangriga. The town itself has few obvious attractions, although pleasant to stroll around. It is divided in half by **North Stann Creek**, crossed by a bridge; on the north side are the **town hall** and small **market**, on the south the **post office**. There are a few cheap hotels, restaurants and raunchy bars in the center of town (try the **Kennedy Club** or **Eden Rose**, if you're in the mood for local color). On the northern side of Dangriga is the **Pelican Inn**, which can be used as a base, and a hexagonal disco called the **Round House**. Two miles (3 km) out of town is a toweringly ugly new **monument** to the Garifuna, built by a local politician.

Afro-Caribbean culture: Most people come to Dangriga as a base for exploring the rest of Stann Creek District, including the off-shore cayes, or getting to know the unique Garifuna culture. Despite the changes, it is the devotion of the Garifuna to their roots which sets them apart from other ethnic groups in Belize.

A mystical spiritualism is the glue which holds the culture together: although the Garifuna religion shares similiar West African roots to voodoo practises found in other parts of the Caribbean, it has developed into something quite distinct. Central is the magical practice of *obeah*, whereby forces of good and evil are directed towards individuals through spells. The assistance of a *buyei*, or shaman, is necessary to guide the way through a complex series of rituals and use of talismans that can take many hours. Great care and thought is needed, because the spells can not easily be broken. In fact, if the person placing the spell on someone else dies, it can never be broken.

The basis for the religion is the powerful spiritual bond between past, present and even future members of any family group. In a ritual called *adugurahani* or *duğu*, people communicated with their deceased relatives. The ritual is rarely

observed by outsiders, which contributes to misconceptions and conjecture. Though all *dugus* follow certain broad guidelines, no two are exactly alike. Families go to great expense to secure fresh seafood, pork and fowl, while cassava bread is carefully prepared. Money is collected from family members to pay drummers and the *buyei*, who can commune with the dead.

"A grandmother's interest in her descendants can continue – just as their concern for her continues – after her physical body has passed away," explains a sociologist, Dr Catherine L Macklin. "The family responds to this concern by giving what may in a limited sense be called a combination of party, feast, and family reunion – attended by family members who are deceased, as well as those who are living."

Where the solemnity and secretiveness of the Garifuna religion breeds distrust among outsiders (as recently as the 1960s, some Garifuna were afraid to hold *dugus* in Dangriga for fear of disapproval from local magistrates), this same spiritualism spawns a wealth of creativity among its people in the form of music, dance and art. From radios and cassette players throughout Belize blares the energetic rhythm of Punta Rock, a modern musical interpretation of a cultural dance by Dangrigan Pen Cayetano and his turtle shell band. During the Punta dance, the man attempts to seduce the woman. While turning down these overt advances, the woman displays her sensual powers by making overtures of her own. The seductive movement of pumping hips and the rhythmic beat of the drums make this one of Belize's most popular dances.

Dangriga transformed: Annual festivities also make Dangriga come alive. During Christmas, the popular *wanaragua*, or John Canoe dance, is performed. The dancer wears a mask which resembles an English face with a pencil-thin moustache, topped by a colorful hand-made hat similar to the English naval hats of the 18th century. The entire body of the dancer is covered with white and black clothing and knee rattles made

The thriving metropolis of Dangriga.

of shells. The dance incorporates martial arts movements and was first performed to hone the skills of warrior-slaves. These dances and many more are performed by an internationally renowned group from Dangriga, the Waribagabaga. (Nightly performances can be arranged through Pelican Beach Resort at the north end of town.)

Music, dance and a carnival atmosphere consumes Dangriga during the celebrations commemorating the landing of Garifuna leader Alejo Benji and his followers at the mouth of the North Stann Creek River. This is the most important of local holiday, when the town swells with Garifuna from all over Central America and the United States. The tropical night is alive with drums and the scent of local rum; kaleidoscopic crowds gather around pairs of drummers under stilted clapboard houses and pulse as one with the beat, then disperse to follow the call of other drums to the next house and next bottle of rum. The music continues till sunrise, when everyone gathers riverside for a reenactment

Sunday best.

of the Landing (*see also the chapter "Holidays and Music," pages 85–88*).

The Garifuna are also skilled artists. Primitivism dominates in their painting, with great elaboration of detail, flat colors, and unreal perspective. The lobby at Pelican Beach Resort displays some of the earlier works of Benjamin Nicholas, one of the better known painters. Especially impressive is the mural of the landing. Mr Nicholas' studio (**27 Oak St**) is open to the public and paintings can be commissioned – but be prepared to wait a half year or more for your artwork. Pen Cayetano of Punta Rock fame, is also an accomplished painter, having displayed at many art shows in the United States and Europe. Pen's work is more realistic than other Garifuna painters, but it still retains the attractive aspects of primitivism. Although he now lives in Germany, Pen returns to Dangriga once a year to give street concerts and stock his studio (**5 Moho St**) with art work and crafts such as drums and carvings.

Dangriga teems with crafts. For the

last 30 years, Austin Rodriquez (**32 Tubrose St**) has hollowed out hefty logs of cedar and mahogany – harvested from his own land – to make drums. He cures his own deer and cow hides with lime, salt and sun before working them over the head of drums ranging in size from 6 inches to 2 ft (15 to 60 cm) in diameter. He claims a well-made drum will last 100 years. Throughout the town, skilled craftsmen abound, creating cotton stuffed dolls in traditional Garifuna dress, dried coconut leaf baskets and hats, and maracas made of dried calabash gourds.

Into the Caribbean: Some 12 miles (20 km) off-shore from Dangriga lie a row of tiny coral cayes perched on top of **Tobacco Reef** like gems on a necklace. All are lined with perfect sands and dotted with coconut trees, and can be easily reached in an hour's boat ride from Dangriga.

Of the three inhabited islands, each has a different character that will appeal to different types of visitors. The smallest is **Carrie Bow Caye**, home to the

Smithsonian Institution's Marine Laboratory. Since 1972, scientists from all over the world have come here to study the intricacies of coral reef and mangrove biology. Though much of the work is esoteric – such as measuring flow rates from the openings of sponges or listing obscure animal groups – an invaluable database has been collected.

Since the waters around Carrie Bow Caye are relatively pristine, this database can be used as a measuring device to gauge the health of other sites along the barrier reef. Although drop-in visitors are discouraged, scheduled visits are welcomed (arrangements can be made through Pelican Beach Resort in Dangriga).

Just north of Carrie Bow Caye lies **Southwater Caye**. Sitting on the north end of the island lies **Blue Marlin Lodge**, the only full service scuba resort near Dangriga. **Pelican Beach Resort**, with two large dormitory facilities and a couple of smaller bungalows on the southern end of the island, caters to schools groups and naturalists. Snorkeling is ideal off the southern point; pristine coral reef can be reached without the need of a boat.

Further north, **Tobacco Caye** has been used for centuries as a trading post and fishing camp. Many rustic resorts crowd the island. These are run by local fishermen and their spouses who supplement their incomes by offering tours and modest accommodations. As the only caye advertising camping, Tobacco is a favorite with budget-minded travelers.

Most of the other cayes in Stann Creek District are mangrove covered. One, **Man-O-War Caye**, supports one of the 10 largest colonies of nesting frigate birds in the Caribbean. Other cayes are home to pelicans and cormorants. Some have temporary fishing camps while most are uninhabited. The reefs surrounding many of these remote cayes are spectacular, making this central portion of the Belize Barrier Reef one of the best kept secrets in the country.

Dangriga nightlife: Because Dangriga does not consider tourism a priority, you will find yourself immersed in another culture without the trappings of

Carving Garifuna drums from a cedar stump.

commercialism. If you feel adventurous, spend an evening or two exploring the town's colorful nightlife. Most of the rum shops and dance halls are found along Commerce Street. The **Kennedy Club**, a hangout for the younger generation, features a local "box" (a hired cassette player and music system) and second-floor outdoor patio overlooking the street. Across and down the street is the **Harlem Club**, a ramshackle looking rum shop. The dingy look outside belies the color inside. Graying, bent men will drink to your health between games of dominoes and as many stories as you are willing to listen to. The **Eden Rose**, near the roundabout on the south end of town, is known for music and dancing. A palm-thatched cabana outside is the place to cool off between dances and mix with the locals. If you are looking for more trendy clubs try the **Local Motion** disco on Commerce Street or the **Round House**, a plain hexagonal concrete structure on the beach north of town.

Restaurants/hotels: Though Dangriga isn't a prosperous town, restaurants are as abundant as rum shops, and hotels and guesthouses are available for any budget. For fine dining, listen to the waves roll ashore at Pelican Beach Resort. The dining room is decorated with Belizean tiles and huge photos of local wildlife. The menu includes lobster and shrimp when in season, and year-round fresh fish. Their wonderful Garifuna cooks often include ethnic side dishes.

In the center of town lie a number of establishments catering to neighborhood clientele. **Ritchie's Dinette**, along Commerce Street, serves Spanish and Creole dishes of rice and beans. **Shipmate's**, to the south of the footbridge across the North Stann Creek River, serves seafood and fried chicken. The dining room at **Sunrise**, one of many Chinese restaurants in town, is clean and neat. The menu includes curries, chop suey and more than 10 soups.

On your way out of town along the Stann Creek Valley Road, the **White Castle** is a well-lit third-floor restaurant serving rice and beans plus fresh sea-

Morning journey to the cayes.

food. During the evening, children ply the streets with baskets of *panades* (fish or bean filled ground corn patties served with vinegary onions) and *garnaches* (fried tortillas topped by beans, onions and cabbage), great appetizers.

Though limited, accommodations in Dangriga are safe, clean and varied. On the beach at the north end of town, the Pelican Beach Resort is the favorite of most travelers to Dangriga. The two-story colonial-style building looks like something out of the past – hardwood floors, ocean view porches, full length bath tubs and ceiling fans. As the only full service hotel in Dangriga, the Pelican Beach Resort is friendly, clean, and maintains the character of the family-run operation that it is.

In the middle of town next to the post office is the **Bonefish Hotel** with air-conditioned rooms and television. On the less expensive side is **Pal's** guest-house, a favorite of the budget minded traveler. Clean, friendly and safe, Pal's sits 50 ft (15 meters) from the beach near the Havana Bridge. The Hub Guest-house is a gathering place for back-packers and locals, sipping a cool drink on the outdoor patio.

Up the North Stann Creek, near the bridge, **Jungle Huts Hotel** has private cabanas on the river bank.

South of Dangriga: While Dangriga is the largest Garifuna settlement in Belize, smaller colonies lie scattered along the southern Belizean coast. Eight miles (13 km) south of Dangriga lies the sleepy village of **Hopkins**. It can be reached by sea from Dangriga across the **Commerce Bight Lagoon**, or from the west along a 4-mile (7-km) road linked to the **Southern Highway**. The entrance road crosses over a wide, marshy area rich with coastal birds such as tiger herons and great egrets.

The seashore at Hopkins is lined by scores of tall coconut trees sprouting from mountains of soft sand. Nets, draped over palmetto poles, lie drying in the sun beside fishing dories pulled up on the beach. Clumps of Mayan-style homes – palmetto walls and palm-frond roofs – sit perched on stilts with magnificent views of the azure Caribbean to the east and jungle covered mountains to the west. The village is less than a generation old, and relies heavily on harvesting seafood from the reef that lies 5 miles (8 km) offshore. But thanks to its strategic location, tourism is becoming more important: the village makes a great stop for a swim after a visit to the Cockscomb Wildlife Sanctuary, followed by a nap in a hammock along the secluded beach.

For those wishing to catch the early morning light as fishing nets are loaded into dories, overnight accommodations have begun to appear in Hopkins. **Sandy Beach Lodge**, located at the southern end of the village, offers small rooms in thatched cabins a scant 50 yards (45 meters) from the sea. The lodge is managed and operated by a cooperative of local women who take pleasure in discussing their community and culture over a meal of local Garifuna foods, based on coconut milk, garlic, basil and black pepper. Banana and plantain (a larger, starchier banana which must be cooked) are grated, mashed, boiled or

Garifuna matron.

234

baked. Fish boiled in coconut milk, called *serre*, served with beat plantain called *hudut*, is a deliciously rich meal.

Most meals in Stann Creek are accompanied by one form or another of the endless varieties of cassava – an integral part of the Garifuna heritage (some writers even translate the word Garifuna as "cassava-eating people"). Cassava, or manioc, is a woody shrub or herb which, like potatoes, has tuberous roots. But unlike potatoes, the juice which lies between the fibers of the manioc root is poisonous. The secret of extracting the root, passed down through the Caribbean, involves a two-day process. First, the root is dug out before daybreak. The skin is peeled off, and the root is grated into a mash on stone studded boards. This mash is placed into a *wala*, a long, narrow, loosely woven tube made of palm fronds. When stretched, the *wala* compresses the mash, squeezing out the poisonous fluid.

The resulting dehydrated cassava mash is then sun dried and made into flour, which can be sifted and baked into flat round loaves. The coarse "trash" left from the sifting is baked black and simmered with ginger, sugar and sweet potatoes into a favorite drink called Hiu. Like a fevergrass tea called bachati, and citrus juice, all with copious quantities of sugar, Hiu is one of the typical drinks of the Garifuna.

Ruins of the sugar industry: A coastal road heading south out of Hopkins leads to the village of **Sittee**, perched on the high but eroding banks of the Sittee River. During the 18th century, the river was a major artery for the flow of sugar and timber from the interior. An old **sugar mill**, discovered in 1990 as bulldozers cleared land for citrus, lies one mile east of the Southern Highway on the Sittee road. Vines and trees hide towering smokestacks and huge rusted gears. One of the first steam railway engines in Belize sits in a jungle clearing, a tree growing from its boiler. Parts of an old sawmill lie strewn about the banks of the river, often found by farmers chopping bush from the citrus groves.

Today, instead of the whine of saw-

mills and the clank of steam engines, toucans and parrots squawk above the river-banks, feeding on the wealth of mangoes, figs and other natural fruit trees which thrive in the rich alluvial soils. Three-ft (1-meter) long iguanas bake in the sun on towering fig trees. Manatee frequent the lower reaches of the river and jaguar have been spotted swimming across the river from bamboo forests on one side to dense mangrove swamps on the other. A boat trip up the river is a perfect introduction to the biological wealth of tropical watersheds, for the Sittee River drains a huge region fringing the north border of the Cockscomb Basin.

North of Dangriga lie the spectacular wildlife habitats of the **Southern** and **Northern Lagoons**. Surrounded by limestone hills, mangrove forest and savanna marshland, they provide breeding and calving grounds for one of the highest concentrations of manatee in the Caribbean. Two islands in Northern Lagoon support tremendous nesting colonies of white ibis, great egrets and other small herons, while the coastline opposite Southern Lagoon is the largest nesting concentration of loggerhead and hawksbill turtles in Belize. The government of Belize has recognized the lagoons' significance by declaring them part of a Special Development Area, requiring special planning procedure before development.

A narrow, 2-mile (3-km) long spit of land called **Gales Point** juts into the middle of Southern Lagoon. A small Creole community of the same name is one more subsistence fishing and farming community that has turned to tourism for its future – tourists are especially fascinated by the manatees here. The village is building a hotel to be run and staffed by residents, while local figure Raymond Gentil rents four rooms and offers basic meals. Mr Gentil is true to his name – he is a friendly, gentle man who can arrange tours to view manatee, the bird islands, or the spectacular **Ben Loman's Cave** (bring your own flashlight). Gales Point also makes a perfect day trip from Dangriga.

Diving with manatee at Gales Point.

GARIFUNA ODYSSEY

The Garifuna are relatively recent immigrants to Belize, settling near Dangriga only after an epic two-century journey across the Atlantic and around the Caribbean (note: technically, the people are called the Garinagu and the culture and language are Garifuna, but the people are commonly referred to as Garifuna).

They are a unique racial blend of escaped African slaves and Caribbean island Indians. Their story begins on the island of St Vincent, where, before the arrival of Europeans, Carib Indians arrived from South America to subdue the Arawak people and absorb their culture. Historians often depict the Caribs, a disciplined, war-like people, as ferocious cannibals – a view probably conjured up by people fleeing from their superior armies, and encouraged by Europeans when they arrived to colonize the Caribbean islands themselves.

The English and French first ventured into the Caribbean in 1625, beginning 35 years of warfare against the Caribs. In 1660, a British peace treaty guaranteed the "perpetual possession" of the islands of St Vincent and Dominica to the Carib people. But eight years later the British broke the treaty and took possession of the islands.

Meanwhile, in 1635, two Spanish ships carrying captured Nigerian slaves were shipwrecked off the St Vincent coast. Some of the African captives managed to swim ashore and found shelter in the Carib settlements. The relationship between the indigenous Caribs and marooned Africans followed a stormy course over the next century and a half, from reluctant acceptance to intermittent warfare and, finally, wholesale fusion of the two cultures.

By 1773, this hybrid people, now known as the Garifuna, was the dominant population of St Vincent. Unfortunately, Europeans were now ready to take over the Caribbean entirely. More and more British settlers landed on St Vincent, until there was no question of Britain's design: the colonial forces would never tolerate a free black community at the very heart of their own slave plantations. In 1796, following repeated raids to remove the British settlers, the Black Caribs attempted one all-out attack. It was a bloody defeat. Five thousand Black Caribs were captured and the great Carib chief and statesman Joseph Chatoyer (Satuye) was killed.

Less than a year later, fearful of a resurgence of the Black Caribs' power, Britain deported some 2,000 to the island of Roatan off the northern coast of Honduras. Many died of disease on the journey, and the rest were abandoned with supplies for only three months. Even so, the marooned Garifuna not only survived but flourished.

An abortive takeover by royalists against the republican government of Honduras in 1823 found the Garifuna siding with the losing faction and facing continued persecution. Again, it was time for the community to move on, this time to another British colony – British Honduras (now Belize).

In 1832, under the leadership of Alejo Benji, a large group of Garifuna landed on the coast of Stann Creek, followed by many more. They've been there ever since. November 19, Garifuna Settlement Day, is a national holiday in Belize, commemorating the landing of Alejo Benji and his followers and the end of the 200-year exodus. ∎

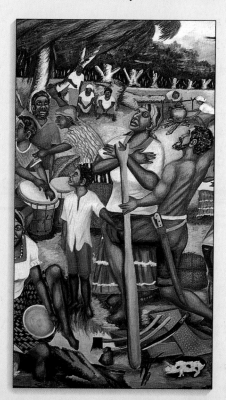

Artist's impression of the landing at Dangriga.

livestock. If Belize could set aside enough territory to protect a "viable population," the cats would leave the cattle alone.

Armed with Rabinowitz's hard scientific data, conservation groups within Belize successfully lobbied the government to award full protection status to the Cockscomb. In 1984, the Cockscomb Basin became a forest reserve and no-hunting zone, and in 1986, 3,600 acres (1,460 hectares) around Rabinowitz's research camp were set aside as the world's first jaguar reserve. Finally, in 1990, the entire 100,000 acres (40,500 hectares) of the Cockscomb Basin was declared a Wildlife Sanctuary.

Return of the rainforest: Today, the Cockscomb Basin Wildlife Sanctuary stands as the flagship protected area for Belize and an important refuge for the jaguar. The small Mayan village which once existed within the basin has been relocated to the entrance road to the sanctuary, allowing the jungle to re-grow and animals to roam at will. The entire staff of the sanctuary, all Mayan

Indians, come from this new community, called **Maya Center**, while other villagers derive indirect income from the sanctuary as naturalist guides or by selling crafts to the ever-increasing number of tourists.

The sanctuary is about an hour's drive south of Dangriga on the Southern Highway, with a 5-mile (8-km) entrance road beginning at Maya Center. Numerous trails – all carefully mapped, well maintained and safe – can provide days of rainforest exploration, while a new **visitors' center** explains the geological, anthropological and natural history.

To cool down after a morning hike, try inner-tubing down the **South Stann Creek River** or swimming in crystal-clear pools beneath refreshing mountain waterfalls. For the best views of the basin, follow the difficult **Ben's Bluff Trail** to the top of a commanding ridge; the truly hardy can even hike to **Victoria Peak**, Belize's second-highest mountain and possibly its most spectacular. At 3,675 ft (1,120 meters), it is considered part of Central America's

Teaching a group of visiting Belizeans, Cockscomb Park.

PLACENCIA AND ITS SURROUNDINGS

In the seaside bars of **Placencia**, patrons can indulge in mild dispute about what their village's name actually means. Some insist it is French for "pleasant point," others say "peaceful point," while still others believe it means "patience." The exact meaning doesn't really matter, as Placencia is both pleasant and peaceful – and a good dose of patience doesn't hurt if you're going to enjoy it.

But see Placencia while you can. As gateway to the longest sand beaches in Belize, the village is poised on the pinnacle of discovery. Less than 10 years ago, it could only be reached by fishing boat; in 10 years, you won't recognize the sleepy, seaside resort it is now.

French heritage: Placencia's name, shared by the village and its peninsula, was given by Huguenots. Members of this strict Protestant sect fled religious persecution in Europe, tried out Nova Scotia in Canada, then immigrated to Belize in 1740. They chose this remote point, which the ancient Maya had once used as a fishing camp (as excavated pottery shards and house mounds indicate).

The Huguenots were eventually beaten by the tropical heat and diseases from the nearby swamps, abandoning the settlement in 1820. But they did have occasional good times: dozens of 17th-century bottles and clay pipes have been dug up at the appropriately-named **Rum Point**, a couple of miles north of town, where it is thought that Huguenot men came here to smoke and drink out of sight of their womenfolk and away from religious restrictions.

Though little concrete evidence exists, local legend has it that buccaneers often used the excellent protection of the Placencia Peninsula as a harbor. They too probably put Rum Point to good use. Today the site is occupied by the **Rum Point Inn**, a luxurious beachside resort of futuristic design.

Placencia was restarted as a fishing camp in the mid-1800s, and with the wealth of marine life and proximity of the Barrier Reef, prospered. Though many of the fishermen have given up their lines and spearguns for binoculars and dive gear, cashing in on their local knowledge to guide tourists around, the village still celebrates June 29 as Fishermen's Day. A Catholic Mass, boat parade and the blessing of the fishing fleet precedes a town-wide party where visitors are welcomed.

The dirt road running 26 miles (42 km) along the peninsula's spine was only built in 1986, connecting Placencia to the **Southern Highway**. If you're driving here, take special care: during dry spells, clouds of dust can block your vision, and oncoming vehicles materialize out of nowhere; watch out for buses driven at breakneck speeds and narrow wooden bridges. Dangriga may be only 51 miles (82 km) north, but the drive can be exhausting. In 1993, a new airstrip was opened a few miles north of town, and most people prefer to fly.

Tropical calm: Placencia must be one of the most laid-back places in Belize – which is saying a lot. **Main Street** is

Preceding pages: two views of the cayes off Placencia. **Left**, rasta at rest. **Right**, small cayes give Placencia its character.

actually a single concrete sidewalk running through the village, built 30 years ago as a means of wheel-barrowing fish around without fighting the sand. It still serves as the main artery of life in town. Clapboard houses on stilts are randomly clustered along the walkway, with locals hiding beneath shaded porches during the heat of the day. Near sunset, children appear selling hot *panades* (fish- or bean-filled ground corn patties) and beach volleyball games start on both sides of the walkway.

The north end of the sidewalk starts at the beach designated for campers and tents. To the south, it ribbons its way past numerous local businesses. Along this "busy" 100-ft (30-meter) section, you can browse through original T-shirt designs and other local crafts at the **Seashell Gift Shop** (but don't buy any black coral on display, it is protected under international agreement and you may not be able to bring it through customs). Stroll across the walkway toward the beach and sample local Belizean dishes or fresh seafood at the

Kingfisher Restaurant. Back across the walkway, **Daisy's** scoops out homemade icecream and pastries for dessert. Then take in the volleyball next to one of Placencia's oldest structures, the octagonal **Anglican Church**.

The walkway ends near the **police station**, **fishermen's co-op** and what could be termed the heart of town – the open-air **Post Office**. Here Jamie Leslie will sell you stamps, airline tickets or a cold beer while providing any advice or directions you may need.

Behind the Post Office starts a sandy path with another string of resorts, restaurants and rental businesses. **Brenda's Cafe**, the **Dockside Bar** and **Tentacles Restaurant** are relaxing places for a sunset drink and meal. Just offshore are many foreign yachts tugging at their anchors and local fishing skiffs bringing in their daily catch.

Opposite the Post Office, along the dusty road leading out of town sits a warehouse called **Wallen's Market** – the place to buy meats, produce, cold drinks or any other odds and ends. Next

The hubbub of "Main Street."

door is the **Orange Peel Gift Shop**, one of many in Placencia selling hand-painted T-shirts and fine woodwork. Opposite Wallen's market is the **ball field**. Here, on most Saturdays, games of cricket – with teams in spotless white uniforms – begin around 10am.

Belize's finest coastline: Placencia is one of the few places in Belize where you can walk for miles along a sandy beach. It is possible to stroll 7 miles (11 km) north to the village of **Seine Bight** without interruption. Despite the many upscale resorts lining this coast, there are still many secluded beaches to call your own for the afternoon.

Swimming is best at the points of land where sand builds up. Snorkelers will find meadows of grass beds bordering the coastline, dotted by clusters of small coral patch reefs. Beware of boats while swimming. Tourist and fishing boats continually ply the coastal waters of Belize. In Placencia village, the town council has placed buoys along the shore to mark an idle zone – for all boats – to help protect swimmers. Belizeans have

always known that the diving is also better in the southern half of the country. The problem has always been a lack of infrastructure, pushing up travel costs. Before the airstrip, visitors had to fly into **Big Creek** across the bay, and catch a water taxi to Placencia. Today there are three major dive operators – **Placencia Dive Shop** at **Kitty's Place**, **Rum Point Divers** and the **Turtle Inn** – offering complete dive packages. Several scuba shops offer everything from equipment rental to instruction, while smaller operations such as the **Paradise Hotel** offer snorkeling trips to nearby cayes.

What makes the diving so interesting off Placencia is that it marks the change in the Barrier Reef's structure from northern Belize to the south. North of **Columbus Caye**, the area behind the reef is mainly flat, with extensive grass beds and patch reefs. As you move south toward Placencia, the reef structure transforms into a region of sink holes, pinnacles and extraordinary formations called "faroes" – atoll-like structures which support a vast array of ma-

Boats at bay.

rine habitats (an example is **Laughing Bird Caye**, one of Belize's newest national parks). South of Columbus Caye, the Barrier Reef drop-off becomes a near-vertical wall beginning in only 35 ft (10 meters) of water.

Around the cayes: A typical diving excursion might include a morning dive outside the Barrier Reef on the drop-off amongst marine life such as spotted eagle rays, hawksbill or loggerhead turtles. Lunch can be taken on one of the picturesque islands inside the reef, such as the **Silk Cayes**, followed by snorkeling around the rich waters. The final dive for the day could be at any of the hundreds of possible sites inside the inner reef. On the way home, if you pass by **Long Coco Caye**, chances are that a pod of dolphins will chase your boat's bow wake. If you are lucky, you can slip quietly into the water and observe from a distance the graceful underwater ballet of these marine mammals.

Even if you can't dive, snorkeling can offer you more than a glimpse of the wonders of the Belize marine waters.

Coral gardens abound in 10 to 15 ft (3 to 5 meters) of water around the **Scipio** and **Colson Cayes**. Frigate birds, brown boobies and pelicans nest on a trio of small islands around what is known as **Bird Caye**. The rich birdlife above the water fuels an explosion of marine life below, including tremendous schools of small herrings and anchovies. The bottom is alternately carpeted by seagrass, colonial anemones and corals, and sink holes and drop-offs are accessible even to beginner snorkelers.

As mentioned above, both Laughing Bird Caye and the Silk Caye group (sometimes called the Queen Cayes) offer spectacular underwater scenery, in deep water as well as snorkeling depth. Mixing snorkelers and divers on the same trip is no problem.

The rich variety of marine habitats also makes Placencia an excellent place for sportfishing. Grassy shallows around many of the islands are home to schools of bonefish, tarpon and permit. Trolling along drop-offs and channels nearly always lands barracuda and jacks, and **The faces of Placencia.**

occasionally the mighty kingfish. Outside the Barrier Reef, the catch includes grouper and snapper. **Kingfisher Sports** specializes in fly fishing, while **Seahorse Guides** is run by the three Young brothers, who know the southern Belize reefs as well as anyone in the country. Even so, new sites are discovered frequently and there is enough sea to keep divers visiting new sites year after year.

The mangrove habitat is one of the most important ecosystems in Belize. Kayaking and canoeing in the **Placencia Lagoon** is one way of silently viewing the tremendous amount of wildlife here. Though unpredictable, manatee feed in the extensive grass beds and calve in the secluded bays and rivers emptying into the lagoon. White ibis, snowy egrets, and pelicans feed, roost and nest around and on many of the small islands. Most of the larger resorts along the peninsula road provide access, guides and water-craft for a quiet afternoon's exploring.

Excursions from Placencia: The Garifuna people of Seine Bight are some of the friendliest in Belize – it is, or was, home to most of the workers in the resorts up and down the peninsula, so they more than welcome tourists. With 600 inhabitants, it is often referred to as a "grandmother village" because many younger people have left to find jobs, sending money back to the grandparents who take care of the children.

The town is pure Garifuna. Ask for Mr Nick (Nicholas), the self-appointed town tour guide. He can take you through sandy yards below stilted planked houses; introduce you to graying men playing dominos in the shade of a laden breadfruit tree; or let you watch a medicine woman mixing a herbal brew for the common cold. But mainly he likes to visit the few pubs in town to take some "bitters". His colorful tour is the perfect way to experience the culture, not just observe it.

Seine Bight is struggling to open up the village to tourism and still protect the Garifuna culture. A few small tourist establishments have sprung up to explore the possibilities. The **Kulcha**

Rum Point Inn, north of the township.

Shackas serves Garifuna dishes and has four modest rooms with an outside bath. At least once a week, a cultural night is celebrated with turtle shell bands, dancing and discussions about the Garifuna culture. **Aunty Chigi's Place** has three rooms with a shared bath. On the north end of town is a new and more upscale lodging called the **Nautical Inn**.

Nestled together across the lagoon from Placencia, the small towns of **Big Creek, Independence** and **Mango Creek** owe their existence to the revived banana industry in Belize. Bananas were virtually wiped out in the 1940s by disease. A slow recovery is still underway, but a new deep water port has been dredged at Big Creek allowing huge container ships to take bulk loads of the fruit. Environmentalists aren't so enthusiastic. While providing employment and foreign exchange for Belize, the heavy use of fertilizers and pesticides on nearby plantations is affecting the delicate offshore ecosystems, while acres of tropical forests are being levelled to plant bananas.

Prior to the 1940s blight, bananas where loaded on railroad cars and shipped to the coast at **Monkey River Town** to be loaded on shallow drafted barges. This Creole and Garifuna outpost has never recovered from the industry's crash. Again, tourism is the *deus ex machina* for keeping the young people at home. Much of the surrounding forest along the Monkey River has been declared a Special Conservation Area and a few small, communal guest houses have appeared.

Located 10 miles (16 km) south of Placencia, the town is accessible only by boat. On the way is **Rocky Point**, a manatee hangout. A slow ride up the jungle-lined river is a chance to view iguana, howler monkeys, crocodiles and a variety of tropical birds. About 5 miles (8 km) upstream is a clear, cool swimming hole (don't worry about the crocodiles, they are very shy and non-aggressive) and a sandbar where you can eat a picnic lunch before drifting quietly back down the river.

<u>**Right**</u>, **red mangroves on the Monkey River.**

256

a guide from Santa Cruz can still be hired if you want to tour the site, almost everything is overgrown by tall grass and thorny scrub. Eroding stelae lie exposed to wind and rain.

Better maintained is **Lubaantun** (Place of Fallen Stones), the largest site in Toledo, which lies high on a ridge above a valley cut by the Columbia River, 1½ miles (2 km) from the village of **San Pedro Columbia**. Lubaantun was built completely without the use of mortar; each stone was precisely cut to fit snugly against its neighbor. Those lucky enough to visit Lubaantun will find local caretaker Mr Santiago Coc an enthusiastic tour guide with a wealth of information (he assisted with the 1970 Cambridge excavations of the site). Uphill from nearby **Indian Creek** village is the ceremonial center of **Nim Li Punit** (Big Hat), with splendid views and 25 stelae, eight of them carved.

Some 1½ miles (2 km) from the entrance road to Lubaantun ruins is **Fallen Stones Butterfly Ranch**, which produces 600 butterfly pupae a week for export to Europe and the United States. For a small fee, you can tour the farm or stay overnight in Kekchi houses built on the side of the hill (be prepared to climb hills). There is an outdoor restaurant with the finest views possible of the Columbia River Forest Reserve. Four wheel drive is necessary during the rainy season (and recommended any time).

Another curiosity outside of San Pedro Columbia is the **Dem Dats Doin Farm**, which is trying to replace the Mayans' environmentally destructive way of life – the slash-and-burn traditions of milpa farming – with a more sustainable system. Described as an "Integrated, Energy Self-Sufficient, Low Input, Organic Mini-Biosphere," it is run by a couple of transplanted Americans. Between a biogas digester and photovoltaics, they have reached 95 percent energy self-sufficiency. For a small fee, the owners will give you a personal tour complete with flow charts and illustrations to help you understand the operation. They also run a small bed and breakfast operation on the farm.

At work at the village water pump.

COROZAL DISTRICT

Tucked up in the northern limit of Belize, Corozal District looks like it has changed little since colonial days – or, by a further stretch of the imagination, the days of the Maya. The district is still only sparsely populated and scattered with small, sleepy villages. Its entire eastern half is swampy savannah, accessible only by a rough road which roughly traces the New River and Freshwater Creek; the western coast is dominated by sugar-cane, and is one of the most intensely cultivated agricultural areas in the country.

Corozal District's population has been largely Spanish-speaking for many generations, thanks to violence across the Mexican border. In the mid-1800s, Mexico's Yucatán Peninsula was wracked by the murderous Caste Wars, waged between enslaved Maya Indians, Mestizos and whites. After the battle of Bacalar in 1849, thousands of refugees, both Indian and Mestizo, fled south to the relative safety of British Honduras. While Corozal District shares the mixed ethnicity that so characterizes Belize, many of its people still bear Maya surnames such as Ek, Uck and Tzul.

Local British settlers were delighted to discover that the refugees were competent farmers (a trade that Creoles have traditionally disdained). With mahogany and logwood exports declining, they set about exporting sugar back to England. By the mid 1860s, sugar production had risen to 1 million lbs (450,000 kg) a year and was being turned into 50,000 gallons (230,000 liters) of rum.

Sugar cane has shaped the social history of northern Belize. By the 1930s the enormous Libertad factory was built here; in the 1960s it was purchased by the British firm Tate & Lyle, which set about increasing sugar production to the maximum. Even small landowners, formerly subsistence farmers, began to grow the undemanding cane, known as

Preceding pages: the Town Hall, Corozal. **Left**, Crank Bridge, San Estevan.

"the lazy man's crop." Sadly, US demand for sugar collapsed in the 1970s; although 75 percent of local land was devoted to sugar cane, the Libertad refinery closed in 1986. Having abandoned maize growing and other milpa crops, many small farmers began relying upon relatives abroad or turned to growing the more lucrative marijuana.

While raw sugar-cane is still grown everywhere, it is now processed in Orange Walk district.

Dreamy urban center: Only 20 minutes' drive from the Mexican border is the district's urban hub, **Corozal Town**. The name Corozal comes from the cohune, a large, graceful feather-duster palm that likes fertile soil and was a symbol of fecundity to the Maya. Founded in 1849 by refugees from the massacre at Bacalar, the town today is neat and clean, designed on a classically Hispanic grid pattern with three parks and friendly, mostly Spanish-speaking people. Until 1955, its homes and buildings were thatch and adobe. But that year, Hurricane Janet tore the town to shreds; rebuilding brought the structures of concrete and wood that characterize the town today.

Corozal faces the sea but has no real beaches, while a sea-wall separates the polluted **Chetumal Bay** from the town. There are the remains of a small **fort** near the main plaza, from the days of the Caste Wars when Mexican bandits regularly crossed into Belize; the **town hall** has a mural depicting local history, by painter Manuel Villamor Reyes (which includes a scene of the Indian massacre at Bacalar, Mexico).

With 10,000 people, Corozal Town one of Belize's largest settlements, but it retains the sleepy look of an undiscovered outpost. Oddly, research indicates that the place has been more or less continuously occupied from 1200 BC.

Occasionally protruding from the ground in the northern parts of the city are a series of line-of-stone foundations, the remnants of a Maya settlement called **Santa Rita Corozal**. While most Maya structures were elevated, those of Santa Rita were only slightly

Waterfront, Corozal Town.

raised, so subsequent building was made on top of ancient tombs and residential structures. When excavation began in the 1980s by a husband-and-wife archaeological team, the Chases, it was found that more than 50 percent of Santa Rita's structures had been paved over by present-day Corozal Town. Some had even been ground up for road fill. Today only one (not terribly impressive) structure can readily be seen, near Corozal's Coca-Cola and Belikin beer distribution center.

Interesting finds at Santa Rita included a few gold objects – which suggest possible trade with Mexican civilizations like the Aztecs, since Belize is not a gold producer and gold is not normally associated with other Maya sites in Belize. A skeleton inlaid with jade and mica was another unique find at the site.

Not far from Corozal Town is the region's best known Mayan ruin, **Cerros**, which means "hills." It is pleasantly situated on the peninsula between Corozal Bay and **Lowry's Bight**, the gateway at the river mouth into the interior of Belize and northeastern Petén. Evidence of intensive Pre-Hispanic agriculture has been identified along these rivers. Cerros was occupied primarily during the late Preclassic period, roughly from 300 BC to the beginning of the Christian era, with a peak population of about 2,000.

Cerros can be reached by boat from Corozal Town or by land along a rough dirt road (passable only in the dry season). Three acropolises and plazas can be seen, although the structures are covered by vegetation and the tall masks, depicting people and animals, were plastered over by archaeologists to protect them from the elements. Cerros' largest structure, Number Four, is little more than 70 ft (21 meters) tall with a massive base, roughly 175 by 200 ft (53 by 60 meters) and offers a panoramic vista of the coast from its peak. It was possibly abandoned when the Maya started relying on overland trading routes instead of the waterways for which Cerros was strategically located.

Other excursions can be taken north

Left, taxi drivers on a domino break, Corozal Town. **Right**, sugar-cane workers of Mexican descent.

to **Four Mile Lagoon** or further to the fishing village of **Consejo**, which has holiday homes and the **Adventure Inn**, a popular resort for fishermen.

Sugar and swamps: The paved **Northern Highway** runs south of Corozal Town, through the western half of the district towards Orange Walk Town. The route passes through lands devoted to sugar-cane. Five miles (8 km) south is the ruin of the **Aventura Sugar Mill**, one of the oldest in the district. Only a single chimney remains standing. Villages along this route are still geared to producing cane, although its value is much reduced and it has to be sent south to Orange Walk for processing.

Different topography wrote a different history in the eastern half of Corozal District. Although the Maya normally did not find swampy land to their liking for settlement, there is evidence that they lived here.

This is one of the least developed parts of Belize, and until very recently was difficult to reach by car (a better road has been put through, although still dodgy in the wet season – four wheel drive is advised). Small villages like **Little Belize** and **Chunox** dot the way, and at the end of the road is the fishing village of **Sarteneja**. The name means "hole in a flat rock," referring to a *cenote* or well. This certainly must have been an attraction to the ancient Maya in this low rainfall district, with levels of precipitation well below the rest of Belize.

Sarteneja is a pleasant enough place to pass an afternoon. The buildings' pastel colors are drained by the fierce sun, and you can go swimming right off the main pier in waters that range from milky to clear. Often local builders can be seen repairing or building boats in dry dock while fishermen cruise in with their catch of lobster, conch or fish. With only one bus service each day, many Sartenejans find crossing the bay by boat to Chetumal in Mexico cheaper and more convenient than traveling to Belize City for shopping.

Just outside Sarteneja – and the main reason for coming to this remote corner – is the **Shipstern Nature Reserve**, **Cane heads for the refinery.**

284

founded in 1988. It was originally a self-sustaining business devoted to exporting butterflies to Europe and the US; the profits were used to finance the nature reserve and preserve 22,000 acres (8,800 hectares) of coastal savannah.

The reserve features an extensive, shallow, brackish water lagoon system, home to breeding colonies of many varieties of birds like the Reddish Egret and the Wood Stork. The latter is rapidly disappearing in both North America and Belize – near Shipstern, one of the last remaining breeding colonies of Wood Storks was almost destroyed by Mexican poachers, who like to barbecue the fledgling young. Today a watchman is stationed in a remote camp in Shipstern to stand guard over a nesting colony of these stately birds, and numbers of successfully fledged young are rapidly increasing.

The fishing village of Sarteneja.

Shipstern Nature Reserve headquarters feature a few neat stuccoed buildings. Although butterflies are no longer exported, flight cages filled with colorful species are still on view; visitors are treated to a pleasant tour and a visit to the botanical collection. In 1990, the Reserve's Chiclero Botanical Trail opened and one can take a pleasant stroll through dense forest and find labeled trees common to this coastal forest type.

The reserve produces a newsletter, *Paces*, which discusses local environmental concerns and is distributed throughout Sarteneja village. Sunny days are probably the best time to visit the reserve as the butterflies are most active then (on overcast days, they tend to hide amidst the foliage).

Onwards to Mexico: The border crossing into Mexico is just north of Corozal Town, at **Santa Elena** on the Río Hondo. Regular buses run to the Mexican town of **Chetumal** (passengers disembark for border formalities and walk across the small bridge, where the bus is waiting for them on the other side). Many Belizeans make the trip in a day for a taste of the distinctly different atmosphere of Mexico and to take advantage of Chetumal's many duty-free stores.

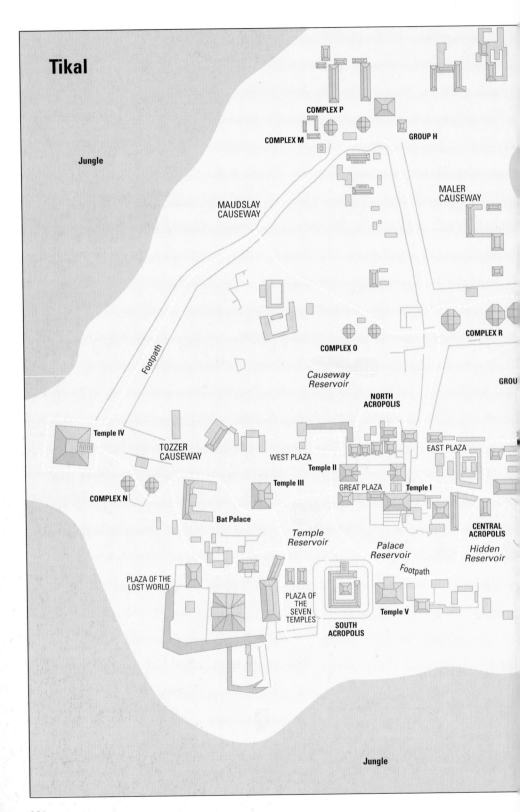

Tikal

Jungle

COMPLEX P

COMPLEX M

GROUP H

MALER
CAUSEWAY

MAUDSLAY
CAUSEWAY

Footpath

COMPLEX O

COMPLEX R

*Causeway
Reservoir*

GROU

NORTH
ACROPOLIS

Temple IV

TOZZER
CAUSEWAY

WEST PLAZA

EAST PLAZA

Temple II

Temple III

GREAT PLAZA

Temple I

COMPLEX N

CENTRAL
ACROPOLIS

Bat Palace

*Temple
Reservoir*

*Palace
Reservoir*

*Hidden
Reservoir*

PLAZA OF THE
LOST WORLD

Footpath

PLAZA OF
THE
SEVEN
TEMPLES

SOUTH
ACROPOLIS

Temple V

Jungle

banana growing region, it's better known now for beaches.

In northern Guatemala, around Tikal, the mountains drop off to the low grasslands and dense, hardwood rain forests of the Petén, a sparsely populated region that constitutes one-third of the country's territory. The rainforest around Tikal is rich in the flora and fauna already familiar to visitors to Belize – the classic menagerie of deer, fox, jaguars and howler monkeys.

About 55 percent of Guatemalans are *indígenas*, descendants of those remarkable people, the ancient Maya. The other 45 percent are *ladinos*, a cultural rather than racial term. A person becomes *ladino* by adopting Euro-American style dress rather than wearing *traje* (traditional dress), by speaking Spanish rather than one of the more than 20 different Mayan languages and by adopting other non-indigenous cultural traits. Most *indígenas* live in the highlands and in Alta Verapaz, farming ridiculously small *milpas* (fields) of maize and beans. But in order to understand their present lives,

Cotton candy sold by young Mayan.

we need to go back in time (*see "The Ancient Maya", pages 25–31*).

Tikal at its zenith: Before starting a walk through the site, imagine the city in its original glory, around AD 705. At its height, Tikal was home to 55,000 to 100,000 people, all living within an area of 23 sq. miles (60 sq. km). The great city's many temples were constructed of limestone rubble; limestone also provided lime for stucco and plaster to cover the temples' surfaces, which gleamed white above the jungle. Flashes of red and touches of other colors glinted off the roof combs. The colors were symbolic: green represented the young maize plant (considered sacred), as well as the quetzal feathers worn by royalty, water, fertility, and the ceiba tree at the center of the world (hence the value placed on jade, which was worn by royalty). Certain colors were associated with the four directions: white was linked with north, yellow with south, red with east and black with west.

Picture the city alive with activity. Smoke drifts from thousands of cook-

ing fires in outlying residences and from copal incense lit by priests on the temple steps, mingling with low, scudding clouds. Nobles and other upper-class citizens wager on games in the ball court just south of where laborers are working on the construction of Temple I. This pyramid represents a sacred mountain, considered to be the source of maize.

According to Mayan cosmology, in the center of the world stands a giant ceiba tree, whose roots extend through the nine layers of the underworld, ruled by the Nine Lords of the Night, and whose branches reach to the top of the thirteen layers of the upper world, also ruled by deities. These gods were all considered manifestations of the creator god, called Hunab Kun or Itzamná. (If this is confusing compare it to the Christian Trinity.) It is no accident that the ruler of Tikal in AD 705, Ahau Cacau, constructed the pyramid-tomb with nine levels, each slightly smaller than the one below, like the tiers of a wedding cake, since nine is the number of the Lords of the Night. The top of the temple was capped by a roof comb with a large carved portrait of Ahau Cacau himself.

Nearby, in the East Plaza, the market activity would be at its height. Men, and women with babies tied on their backs, sit behind piles of maize, squash, breadnuts, chili peppers, beans, tomatoes, yucca, sweet potatoes, cacao (these chocolate beans also functioned as currency throughout Mesoamerica), salt, honey, mats, flowers, dyes, tobacco leaves, cotton textiles and pottery. A few women sold hot tortillas and beans to hungry clients. At one end of the market there might be a boy with a tame parrot or monkey, and a row of vendors with fish, venison and a few tethered rabbits, turkeys, turtles and ducks.

At the other end of the market, specialty trade items might include stingray spines from the Caribbean for ritual self-mutilation; obsidian cores for tools; volcanic rocks from the Guatemalan highlands, used for grinding stones; and Spondylus shell beads from Ecuador.

Necklace vendors at the Guatemalan border.

Clients pause, bargain, and trade, then load their goods in net bags, slinging their tumplines across their foreheads and heading home along the paved causeways (*sacbes*), followed by their children carrying tiny bundles.

The divine ruler of Tikal, Ahau (also spelled Aw) Cacau, is a striking figure sporting a quetzal feather headdress, jade necklace, ear ornaments, wristlets and pectoral jewelry, a jaguar skin over a kilt and underskirt, belt, cotton loincloth, elaborate loin ornaments, anklets, deerskin sandals and miscellaneous ritual paraphernalia. He reposes on a small hassock in the Great Plaza surrounded by retainers waving away mosquitoes. Like all Mayan rulers, Ahau Cacau is somewhat strange looking by our standards. His forehead slopes back sharply, a mark of beauty among the Maya, who practiced cranial deformation – when Ahau Cacau was a baby his mother would have tied a board over his forehead to elongate his skull.

Ahau Cacau halts his inspection of the construction of Temple I, which will commemorate his reign and serve as his tomb, to receive a delegation from Kaminaljuyú in the highlands. Their arrival is heralded by six musicians playing trumpets, drums, flutes and rattles. Related by blood to the rulers of Kaminaljuyú, Ahau Cacau is involved in secret talks with them concerning an alliance against other Mayan city-states. Like the city-states of ancient Greece, the Mayan polities are a fractious lot and fight among themselves.

Inside Temple II, constructed earlier by Ahau Cacau, his mother pierces her tongue and pulls a thorn-embedded cord through it. She collects her blood on bark paper, which she will offer to the gods for the success of her son's venture, along with the blood-soaked cord. Both ritual blood-letting and the sacrifice of humans captured in war are carried out at Tikal to propitiate the gods before important ventures and to commemorate such events as the end of a time period and the ascension or death of a ruler. Later, Ahau Cacau will use a stingray spine to pierce his cheeks, ears

Ancient Mayan carving at the Tikal Museum.

and penis, for the gods demand blood.

Walking tour of the ruins: Much of what we know about Tikal has resulted from recent archaeological research. The University of Pennsylvania's Museum conducted extensive excavations between 1956 and 1969, when the Guatemalan Institute of Anthropology and History took over the excavation and restoration work. Other scholars have made considerable progress in deciphering the Mayas' written language, providing us with an understanding of the meaning of the glyphs on the stelae and buildings throughout the site.

The best place to start a tour of the ruins is the **Morley Museum** located just outside the ruins in Tikal village, at the western end of the airstrip. Among the displays is a reconstruction of Ahau Cacau's tomb, including ceramics, incised bone artefacts, and jade jewelry – necklaces, ear ornaments, wristlets and head-dress decorations. (Other artefacts from Tikal are housed at the National Museum of Archaeology and Ethnology in Guatemala City.) The museum also sells maps of the ruins and books on archaeology and natural history.

The road from the museum to the ruins ends in a trail with a three-way fork. The path to your right leads to **Complexes P, Q** and **R** and the **North Zone**; the left fork takes you to the **Temple of the Inscriptions (Temple VI)**; and the branch straight ahead leads to the heart of the site: the **Great Plaza, Temples I** through **V**, the **North, Central**, and **South Acropolis**, the **Ball Court**, and other important buildings.

Tikal, like Rome, was not built in a day. In fact, the occupation of the site spans 1,650 years, from 750 BC (the Middle Preclassic) to AD 900. The city, consisting of at least 3,000 buildings, was situated near great swamps where raised fields were constructed for agriculture, with higher paved causeways along the canals serving as main roads. Ecologists agree that slash-and-burn agriculture as practiced by modern Maya could not have supported the populations of the ancient large cities: aerial surveys have revealed the grids of fields and

The Great Plaza.

canals covered 965 sq. miles (2,500 sq. km) in Belize and Petén. A fish nibbling on a water lily is often found on royal Maya dress, symbolizing abundance and wealth, and there is good evidence that Classic Maya society was organized on a feudal model with the nobility controlling the land.

The best place to start is at the reconstructed **Great Plaza** area, which is today the center of Tikal ruins (in the Classic era, however, the heart of the city was the East Plaza, where the main market was located). The Maya frequently built new constructions over old; in the Great Plaza, four different plaster floors were laid one on top of the other between 150 BC and AD 700. Seventy stelae and altars, originally painted red, are located in and around the plaza. The stelae, each of which originally had an altar beside it, commemorate the rulers of Tikal. Many of these rulers are carved in bas relief in profile on one side of the stela, although some are shown full face. The other sides contain glyphs giving dates and genealogies (sometimes including a god and the Tikal emblem glyph).

Ahau Cacau's tomb, **Temple I**, is also called the **Temple of the Giant Jaguar**, because of the jaguars carved on the lintels inside it. The temples represent one of the main architectural styles at Tikal, a squared-off wedding-cake pyramid topped by a temple with a roof comb in a two-thirds to one-third ratio. The pyramid is approximately 100 ft (30 meters) high, and the temple rises another 50 ft (15 meters). If you are energetic and not acrophobic you can climb the stairs to the top – using the chain that has been installed as a handhold – and enter the temple.

What surprises many people is the small interior size of these buildings. The Maya had not developed the true arch in their architecture, but used instead the corbeled vault. Stones on each wall are progressively set inward until they almost meet and are topped by a row of capstones, resulting in long, narrow rooms, usually with carved wooden lintels over the doors. The temples were

The Central Acropolis.

not designed to hold large numbers of worshippers, however, but to impress the great mass of people standing in the plaza below.

Opposite Temple I, to the west, is **Temple II,** also called the **Temple of the Masks** after two huge masks, now barely visible, that were carved on each side of the stairway just below the temple door. A giant face once adorned the roof comb. This temple was also constructed by Ahau Cacau and may have been dedicated to his wife or mother; the portrait of a woman is carved on a lintel of the temple.

Temple III, the **Temple of the Jaguar Priest**, is situated behind Temple II. This building has not been reconstructed and is probably the last pyramid and temple built at Tikal, since the stela in front carries the date AD 810. It is well worth climbing Temple III for a look at its carved wooden lintel, which depicts a human with a distended stomach – interpreted as either a pregnant woman or a portly ruler. The lintel dates from between AD 790 and 810, which

means it has survived 1,200 years of tropical weather.

Temple IV is located farther to the west. This enormous edifice stands 212 ft (65 meters) high, making it the tallest structure at Tikal and one of the tallest pre-Hispanic buildings still standing. It was built during the reign of Ahau Cacau's son, Ruler B (also called Half-darkened Sun), around AD 741, but there is considerable debate as to whether he is buried under it.

Dismantled pyramids: On the north side of the Great Plaza is the **North Acropolis**, a group of buildings which were begun around 200 BC as monuments to the ancestors of various rulers. Such early classic kings as Jaguar Paw, Stormy Sky and Curl Nose are buried beneath pyramids in this group. Like the Great Plaza floor, the pyramids have been built over several times by later rulers. How do we know what's inside? The University of Pennsylvania dismantled the pyramid and temple called structure 5D-33, revealing successive onion-like layers. This edifice is in the first row

On the prowl: a grey fox in the ruins.

(the third from the left as you face the North Acropolis). What you see now are two earlier cores and part of the last pyramid, which was originally more than 100 ft (30 meters) high and which hid the rest of the North Acropolis.

To the south is the **Central Acropolis**, also known at the Palace Group. Archaeologist William Coe calls it "an incomparable architectural achievement in ancient America." The 42 palace structures span 4 acres (1.6 hectares) and housed rulers, priests and administrators. They represent a second major architectural style at Tikal: elegant, rectangular buildings, one to five stories high, with narrow, windowless, corbel-vaulted rooms, all grouped around a courtyard to form an enclosed area.

At the time of their occupation, these palaces were stuccoed and painted inside and out and richly furnished with mats, ceramics, and textiles. Some have built-in platforms that may have served as beds and benches. The buildings were probably used primarily for sleeping and storage, as Tikal's climate allowed most activities, including teaching, to be carried on outside.

Southeast of the Central Acropolis is **Group G**, another palace and administrative complex. Group G is also called the **Palace of Vertical Grooves** because of the unusual vertical stone facings on the exteriors. These structures, too, were built over earlier buildings; the walls of one room covered entirely by the last construction were embellished with graffiti.

Ancient games: The **Ball Court** is between Temple I and the Central Acropolis. The ball game was a quintessential Mayan activity – almost every Mayan site has a court. We know something of the game because it was portrayed on ceramics and mentioned in the Mayan epic the *Popol Vuh (see pages 25–31).*

There are also ball courts in the **East Plaza** and three courts, side by side in the **Plaza of the Seven Temples** – which, situated southwest of the Central Acropolis, received its name from seven unexcavated temples that line the east side of the complex. Preliminary work

Plaza of the Lost World.

indicated that the plaza was plastered over a number of times, beginning in the Preclassic era.

The third main architectural style found at Tikal is the truncated pyramid – in other words, a layered pyramid without a temple on top. A good example of this style is the **Lost World Pyramid**, located to the southwest of the Central Acropolis. Originally this structure was 100 ft (30 meters) high, with four stairways flanked by giant masks. Its core may date to as early as 500 BC; it was rebuilt in its final form some time before AD 300.

The pyramid's main function was calendrical or astronomical. Mayanists insist that the word "observatory" should not be used to describe these temples because many were not used to follow the movements of the planets and stars, but were used in such ceremonies as those marking the end of a solar year or the beginning of a 52-year cycle.

The trail leading southeast past Group G is actually a causeway. It leads to the **Temple of the Inscriptions (Temple**

VI), as does the left fork of the trail at the entrance to the ruins. This pyramid and temple were completed around AD 736 to mark the inauguration of Ruler B. Later the roof comb was added; its glyphs give a different date, AD 766.

The entire east side of the roof comb contains glyphs listing the genealogies of Tikal rulers over a period of nearly 2,000 years. The stela and altar on the west side of the temple commemorate Ruler B, who must have been a bellicose sort: the altar shows a bound, face-down captive, perhaps someone who was sacrificed at Ruler B's accession to the throne or captured by him in warfare and sacrificed on some other occasion.

At the opposite end of the ruins is the **North Zone** and **Complexes P, Q**, and **R**, reached by the right-hand trail at the entrance or by a causeway leading north behind Temple I. **Complexes Q** and **R** both have twin pyramids with stairways on all four sides, which face each other on the east and west sides of a plaza. The north side was occupied by a stela and altar marking the *katun* ending, while a single-story palace-type building anchored the south.

Twin pyramids were constructed for public commemorations of the end of a *katun*, a period of 7,200 days or almost 20 years. The pyramids were used for one *katun,* after which another set of twin pyramids was built. There are nine twin pyramid complexes at Tikal. **Complex P** is unexcavated, but also contains twin pyramids and a stela and altar erected by Ruler B.

Guatemalan crafts: In the village near the museum you will see people selling crafts, most of them from the highlands. Ixchel, the ancient Mayan goddess of the moon, childbirth, and weaving, must continue to smile on the Maya because the highland Guatemalan (and Mexican) Maya are geniuses at the loom.

Among the finer textiles for sale are belts, wall hangings, and the beautiful cotton blouses (*huipiles*) worn by the women, which are woven on the stick or backstrap loom. The cotton for these textiles was once hand-spun, but is now factory-made. The backstrap loom, composed of a series of sticks or poles, gets

The long climb down.

its name from the manner in which tension is applied. One end is fastened to a post in the weaver's house, the other is tied to a strap which passes around her hips. Little girls, as young as three years old, can be seen kneeling at the backstrap loom in the highlands, learning to weave. The beautiful motifs are not embroidered (as many people suppose) but are woven, a technique called supplementary weft or weft brocading. The different colors and motifs indicate the weaver's community, a kind of code which allows anyone who has learned it to identify immediately a woman's home locale. Textiles woven on the backstrap loom are incredibly labor-intensive, and many such pieces are true works of art. Consequently, most of these items will be higher priced than others.

You will also see the cotton cloth used for the women's wrap skirts (*cortes*). This is made on the European-introduced treadle loom, as are the women's shawls (*rebozos*). These fabrics are tie-dyed before they are woven: the technique is called ikat in English and *jaspe*

in Spanish (meaning speckled or mottled) because of its feathered or mottled appearance, an essential part of its appeal. In the highlands you can sometimes see hundreds of feet of wrap stretched out along the roadside in preparation for tying and dyeing. Usually white cotton yarn, this is wrapped with a "resist", such as string or plastic, then dyed. The dye doesn't penetrate the wrapped part, which remains white when the resist material is removed. *Jaspe* is also labor-intensive, although the actual weaving on the treadle loom goes fairly fast.

In response to travelers' interest in more practical items, the artisans are making wallets, day-packs, purses, shirts, pants and skirts from *jaspe* fabric and weaving placemats, tablecloths and napkins. They are also combining the old and the new: leather belts with pieces of handweaving and hair wraps, shirts made from a patchwork of denim and old *huipiles*. You may also see woollen blankets from Momostenango and silver or silver-wash jewelry.

A Maya and her tapestries.

Magnum Belize, 718 Washington Avenue, Detroit Lakes, Minnesota, 56501. Tel: (218) 847 3012/ (800) 825 0825.

Ocean Connection, 211 East Parkwood, Suite 108, Friendswood, Texas 77546. Tel: (713) 996 7800/ (800) 365 6232.

Capricorn Leisure, 2 Haven Avenue, Port Washington, New York 11050. Tel: (516) 944 8383/(800) 426 6544.

Tropical Adventures Travel, 111 Second North, Seattle, Washington 98109. Tel: (206) 441 3483/ (800) 247 3483.

Canada

Belize High Commission to Canada, 112 Kent Street Suite 2005, Place de Ville, Tower B, Ottawa, Ontario, Canada K1P 5P2. Tel: (613) 232 7389/ 7453; fax: (613) 232 5804.

United Kingdom

Belize High Commission, 10 Harcourt House, 19a Cavendish Square, London W1M 9AD. Tel: 0171-499 9728; fax: 071-491 4139.

Cox & Kings, St James's Court, 45 Buckingham Gate, London SW1E 6AF. Tel: 0171-834 7472; fax: 0171-630 6038.

Explore Worldwide Ltd., 1 Fredrick Street, Aldershot, Hants, GU11 1LQ. Tel: 01252 319448.

Journey Latin America Ltd., 16 Devonshire Road, London W4 2HD. Tel: 0181 747 8315/747 3108; fax: 0181 742 1312.

Trips Worldwide Ltd., 9 Byron Place, Bristol BS8 1JT. Tel: 01272- 292 199; fax: 01272 292 545.

Toucan Adventure Tours, Exodus Expeditions, 9 Weir Road, London SW12 OLT. Tel: 0181-675 5550; fax: 0181- 673 0779.

South American Experience, 47 Causton Street, London SW1P. Tel: 0171-976 5511.

Germany

Wolf Kahles, Honorary Consul, Lindenstrasse 46-48, 7120 Bietigheim, Bissingen. Tel: (071) 42 39 25; fax: (071) 42 332 25

PRACTICAL TIPS

EMERGENCIES

Police – Tel: 911
To report a crime – Tel: 02-44646 (Belize City).
Ambulance/Fire – Tel: 90.

Security and Crime
Almost every corner of Belize is extremely safe, with almost no crime against tourists ever reported. The big exception is Belize City and Orange Walk, where caution is required. Don't walk the streets at night. Hold-ups and petty theft are regular after dark, so everyone telephones for a taxi, even to travel short distances (make sure you confirm the price with the driver before you get in the car).

The city is quite safe by day, although keep an eye out for pickpockets. Also, loitering around the Swing Bridge are a number of panhandlers, hustlers, dealers and "tour operators" who can be quite persistent. When you cross the Swing Bridge during the day, avoid conversation and don't hang around taking photos with expensive camera equipment.

Most tourists avoid Belize City altogether, which is a pity because it holds a great deal of dilapidated colonial charm and the situation is no worse than most Central (or, for that matter, North) American cities. The so-called "crime wave", attributed to young Belizeans returning from Los Angeles, began only a few years ago and the locals are confident that with new police measures it is nearly over.

Loss of Belongings
In the unlikely event of a theft, it should be reported immediately to the police. The main benefit of this is to get a copy of the police report in order to claim from your travel insurance company. Travel insurance is always recommended.

Medical Services
Considering the high quality of food and its preparation as well as the potable tap water in most tourist areas it is uncommon for visitors to contract stomach problems. Should you require the services of a physician, your hotel can recommend one nearby.

PUBLIC HOSPITALS
Medical Associates, Belize City, tel: 02-30303.
Belize City Hospital, tel: 02-77251.
Corozal Hospital, tel: 04-22076.
Belmopan Public Hospital, tel: 08-22263.
Orange Walk Hospital, tel: 03-22143.
Punta Gorda Hospital, tel: 07-22026.
San Ignacio Hospital, tel: 09-22066.
Doctors' Quarters, Dangriga, tel: 05-22085.

WEIGHTS AND MEASURES

The English imperial system of measures is generally used, with speed and road signs in miles, not kilometers. Exceptions to this are fuel, which is sold by the American gallon, and some of the large number of imported goods, which are weighed using the metric system.

BUSINESS HOURS

Most stores and offices are open from Monday–Friday 8am–noon and 1–5pm. Some stores are open in the morning only on Wednesday and Saturday, or in the evening from 7–9pm. Banks are open Monday–Thursday 8am–1pm; Friday 8am–1pm and 3–6pm.

TIPPING

You will become aware that many in the service industry depend almost entirely on tips, although there are no definite rules about what to do or how much to give. Baggage handlers and hotel porters expect a couple of dollars. Many hotels add 10 percent service to the final bill, to be divided among the unseen employees. If you enjoyed your guided day trip, it is customary to tip the guide a few dollars.

Tipping in restaurants depends slightly more on the tone of the establishment and the customer's satisfaction. Tips are not obligatory, but if you're happy with the service (rather rare in a country where waiters tend to be slow and sullen) you can either round up the total or add 10 percent. It is not necessary to tip the taxi driver since a price should be firmly established before entering the car.

MEDIA

Newspapers
Apart from the weekly independent, *Amandala*, most newspapers are owned by political parties and thus dwell on bad-mouthing the opposition. The main mastheads are the *Belize Times* (run by the PUP) and the *People's Pulse & Beacon* (UDP). The *Reporter*, although owned by a UDP member, is a fairly independent business-oriented newspaper.

While in San Pedro, try the small *San Pedro Sun* or the *Coconut Wireless*, edited from Lily's Hotel.

Radio and Television
Belizeans prefer the radio to most other forms of media. Strolling around Belize City at lunchtime, you will hear its crackling cadences rise and fall from popular eateries and open doorways. Radio Belize at 834 AM has English and Spanish programming – tune in for local and BBC World News, official announcements and continual weather information interspersed with the usual rock and reggae selection.

POSTAL SERVICES

Belize City post office is based in a rambling old colonial building on the north side of the Swing Bridge (intersection Queen and North Front streets – you can't miss it from the bridge). Belizean stamps are some of the most beautiful in the world with their depictions of native flora and fauna, and are highly prized by collectors. Allow up to 10 days for mail to arrive in the United States and at least two weeks to Europe, Asia or Australia. The post office is open from 8am–noon and 1–5pm (4.30pm on Friday).

TELECOMS

The international dialing code for Belize is 501.
Although there are few public telephones in Belize, your hotel will have fixed rates for local and international calls. Check the rate before you make the call. The more expensive hotels also have fax and telex services available.

Telephone, telegraph and telex services are also available at Belizean Telecommunications Ltd on Church Street, just off Central Park, 8am–9pm weekdays, 8am–noon on Sunday. International Direct Dialing is available from most parts of Belize. International calls, tel: 115.
Belize Directory Assistance, tel: 113.

TOURIST OFFICES

The Belize Tourist Office has recently moved (although some maps haven't caught up). The current address is:
Belize Tourist Board, 83 North Front St, PO Box 325, Belize City, Belize. Tel: 02-77213/73255/33041; fax: 02-77490. The office is open from 8am–noon and 1–5pm.

For information on conservation issues and Belize's ecology generally:
Belize Audubon Society, 29 Regent St, PO Box 1001, Belize City. Tel: 02-77369.
Belize Center For Environmental Studies, 55 Eve Street, Box 666, Belize City. Tel: 02-45739.
Rainforest Research Institute, 40 1/2 Miles Old Northern Highway, Maskall Village. Tel: 03-22199.
Program for Belize, 2 South Park Street, Belize City. Tel: 02-75616/75617. Postal address: PO Box 749, Belize City, Belize, Central America.

For information about Mayan archeological sites or permission to visit certain sites contact:
Belize Department of Archaeology, Belmopan. Tel: 08-22106.

EMBASSIES & CONSULATES

Belgium Consular Representative, Marelco Ltd, Queen Street, Belize City. Tel: 02-45769/45773.
Brazil, Honorary Consul, 8 Miles Northern Highway, Ladyville. Tel: 02-52178.
British High Commission, 34/36 Halfmoon Avenue, Belmopan. Tel: 08-22146.
British High Commission, (Residence), Roseapple Street, Belmopan. Tel: 08-22147.
Canadian Consulate/Consulat du Canada, 83 North Front Street, Belize City. Tel: 02-31060.
Chile, Honorary Consul, 6/8 Trinity Boulevard, Belmopan. Tel: 08-22134.
Commission of European Communities, 1 Eyre Street, Belize City. Tel: 02-72785/32070.
Cuban Consul General, 6048 Manatee Drive, Belize City. Tel: 02-31105.
Royal Danish Consulate, 13 Southern Foreshore, Belize City. Tel: 02-72172.

Embassy of the Republic of China, 7 Cork Street, Belize City. Tel: 02-78744/31862.

France, Honorary Consul, 9 Barrack Road, Belize City. Tel: 02-32708.

Germany, Honorary Consul, 123 Albert Street, Belize City. Tel: 02-73343.

Guatemala, Ambassador, 6 Miles Northern Highway, Ladyville. Tel: 02-52634/2612.

Honduran Consulate, 91 North Front Street, Belize City. Tel: 02-45889.

Israel, Honorary Consul, 4 Albert Street, Belize City. Tel: 02-73991/73150.

Italian Consular Representative, 18 Albert Street, Belize City. Tel: 02-73086.

Jamaican Consulate General, 99 Freetown Road, Belize City. Tel: 02-45926.

Lebanese Consul General, 2 Miles Western Highway, Belize City. Tel: 02-73103/44146.

Mexican Embassy, 20 North Park Street, Belize City. Tel: 02-30193/30194.

Netherlands, Honorary Consul, 14 Central American Boulevard, Belize City. Tel: 02-73612/32748.

Nicaragua, Honorary Consul, 2 1/2 Miles Northern Highway, Belize City. Tel: 02-44232.

Royal Norwegian Consulate General, 1 King Street, Belize City. Tel: 02-77031.

Panamanian Consulate, 5481 Princess Margaret Drive, Belize City. Tel: 02-44941.

Sweden, Honorary Consul, 11 Princess Margaret Drive, Belize City. Tel: 02-44117.

UNICEF, 6 Eyre Street, Belize City. Tel: 02-78795.

United States Embassy, 29 Gabourel Lane, PO Box 286, Belize City. Tel: 02-77161; fax: 02-30802.

Venezuelan Embassy, 18/20 Unity Boulevard, Belmopan. Tel: 08-22384.

GETTING AROUND

ON ARRIVAL

Most travelers' first vision of Belize is the quaint Phillip Goldson International Airport. Immigration can be cleared quickly, although Belizean customs officials inexplicably insist on checking every tourist's luggage. There is a currency exchange window near the exit (if this is closed, you can get by on US$ without problems), as well as a tourist information booth (that provides very little information).

Many tour operators put travelers straight on to connecting flights or mini-van service s to hotels and jungle lodges.

Independent travelers will find a taxi rank outside the airport doors. Rates into Belize City are fixed by a cartel and are fairly hefty for the 20–25 minute ride; rates to other parts of Belize can be negotiated (get into the habit of confirming the price before you get in). On arrival, although tipping is not mandatory you could round up the amount or add something if there is baggage handling involved. Belizeans know how to receive tips graciously.

There is also an airport shuttle bus that only departs three times a day and strangely does not connect with incoming flights.

PUBLIC TRANSPORT

Bus

Buses run hourly between Belize City and the major towns to the north and west, less frequently to the south. Contact one of the following bus companies for schedule information:

Batty Brothers Bus Service, 15 Mosul Street, Belize City, tel: 02-72025/74037.

Corozal, tel: 04-23034.

Orange Walk, tel: 03-22858.

Venus Bus Lines, Magazine Road, Belize City, tel: 02-73354.

Novelo's Bus Service, West Collet Canal, Belize City, tel: 02-77372.

PRIVATE TRANSPORT

Taxis

Downtown Belize City is small enough to handle on foot and during the cool of the day this is the way to get around. At night, you should travel by private car or taxi, even for short distances, because of the prevalence of street crime. Hotels and restaurants are used to calling for taxis, which arrive almost immediately. Again, confirm the price with the driver. In Belize City, the number is tel: 02-32916.

Some resorts will hire taxis to transfer small groups from the airport. In San Pedro, you might use a taxi to get from your hotel into town at night, unless the resort has a shuttle service. (Many resorts have complementary bicycles for this purpose, or motorized golf carts to hire from the more luxurious establishments.)

Taxis can also be hired to get between towns or to explore the countryside (in San Ignacio, for example, the taxi cartel has fixed rates to various jungle lodges and ruins).

Car Rental

An exhilarating way to start your trip is to pick up a hire car or jeep from the airport and simply drive off. In the interior, your own transport comes in very handy: you are free to visit wildlife reserves and archaeological sites at your own pace or make trips from your lodge (which is often in the middle of nowhere) to town.

Drive on the right hand side of the road. Speeds

and distances are measured in miles and although there isn't always great signposting, you usually don't get lost.

Unfortunately, there are some drawbacks. Renting a car in Belize is expensive, especially in comparison to the United States, and a hefty damage deposit is demanded (you pay for the first US$1,000 in any crash). A meticulous inventory of current scratches or dings is the car company's way of telling you to take it easy. Fuel is also very expensive.

The other drawback is the poor condition of many roads and some hire car companies will only hire out 4WD vehicles if you're traveling in the south. The route out to San Ignacio is quite good, although conditions worsen dramatically as soon as you turn off. Driving south is not recommended: despite their charming names, Hummingbird Highway and Manatee Road have dangerously large potholes that reduce your speed to a snail's pace, so the driver won't be seeing much of the scenery. Visitors to Dangriga and Placencia, therefore, might consider taking a 15-minute flight instead.

Two-wheel drive cars are fine on most roads if it doesn't rain. If you can afford it, 4WD vehicles are preferable, especially on mountain tracks leading to ruins and during the rainy season. Remember that sudden rainstorms can render these dirt roads impassable, so inquire as to their condition before setting out.

There is a wide choice of car rental companies in Belize City, with the following the most recognized:
Avis, Radisson Fort George Hotel, Belize City. Tel: 02-31987; fax: 02-30225.
Budget, 771 Bella Vista, Belize City. Tel: 02-32435/33986; fax: 02-30237.
International Airport, tel: 02-52385.
Crystal Auto Rental (the "rent-a-wreck" of Belize), 1 1/2 Miles Northern Road, Belize City. Tel: 02-31600; fax: 02-31900.
Hertz, 2 1/2 Miles Northern Highway, Belize City. Tel: 02-32710/32981; fax: 02-32053. (This is generally regarded as the most reliable place in Belize to rent cars; they offer the cheapest weekly rates, have an office on the north side of Belize City and have the best record for helping out if you have mechanical problems.)
Hope & Sons Co., Ltd (specializes in jeep rental), Auto Rentals, Tours & Variety Store, 82 New Road, Belize City. Tel: 02-31941/31335.

By Plane

With roads so terrible, small propeller plane services have been set up to cover most of Belize. This is by far the most common and convenient form of getting around for travelers.

Stiff competition between the four main domestic airlines has created a high level of efficiency. The tiny aircraft arrive on time; the pilot quickly arranges the passengers into a seating plan and you're away. Few flights take more than half an hour. The most common are from Belize International Airport to San Pedro – 20 minutes, with spectacular views of the coral reef – and south to Placencia and Dangriga. If leaving from Belize City, make sure you know whether the flight you are taking will be departing from the International Airport or the smaller, but more commonly used Municipal Airport on Barracks Road.

With airstrips now on Ambergris and Caulker Cayes, many visitors are avoiding Belize City altogether and flying direct to their jungle resorts and Mayan ruins inland. There are also light airplane tours to the ruins of Tikal in neighboring Guatemala.

SCHEDULED AIR SERVICES
Island Air (Ambergris Caye; Caye Caulker; Caye Chapel; Flores, Guatemala), General Delivery, San Pedro, Ambergris Caye. Tel: 02-31140.
Maya Airways (cayes; southern Belize), Box 458, 6 Fort St, Belize City. Tel: 02-7215. US reservations: tel: (800) 552 3419.
Tropic Air (cayes; western and northern Belize; Flores, Guatemala; Cancun, Mexico), PO Box 20, San Pedro, Ambergris Caye. Tel: 02-45671. US reservations: tel: (800) 422 3435/(713) 449 5230.

CHARTER SERVICES IN BELIZE CITY
Caribee Air Service, tel: 02-44253.
Javier's Flying Service, tel: 02-45332.
Su-Bec Air Service, tel: 02-44027.

By Boat

The alternative to flying from Belize City to the cayes is to take one of the scheduled and unscheduled boat services.

From Belize City, next to the Swing Bridge, the powerful *Thunderbolt* and *Hustler* depart promptly every morning for San Pedro via Caye Caulker with room for around 20 passengers each. The trip to San Pedro takes around one hour and 15 minutes, enough time to burn light-skinned passengers to a crisp if they're not protected from the sun. The *Andrea* leaves from the dock outside the Bellevue Hotel in late afternoon, Monday–Friday, earlier on Saturday. Both the *Soledad* and the *Pegasus* make unscheduled trips of around 45 minutes to Caye Caulker, leaving from the docks behind the Shell Gas Station on North Front Street.

It's easy to take the same services for the 15-minute ride between San Pedro and Caye Caulker, or hop onto any number of other boats plying the route. Keep in mind you can always find a boat that will take you privately for a price. For fishing and snorkeling, there are many independent (and cheap) boat operators competing with the resorts and large tour operators. The arrangements are flexible: meet them at the docks in town or arrange a pick-up from your resort; you can also choose where you want to snorkel or fish.

More structured activities, such as scuba-diving, sailing or waterskiing can easily be arranged through your hotel or with one of the many operators lining the main street of San Pedro, which is the commercial center of the cayes.

Transport to and from other cayes by boat is most easily achieved by arrangement with hotels. Alternatively, book your own boat at the docks.
(*See* Activities, page 248 for lists of dive and fishing operators, cruise lines, etc.)

ON DEPARTURE

For those leaving Belize by land there is no departure tax, although drivers must pay a small exit fee of US$2.50 and surrender their Belize driving permit. A departure tax is levied at the International Airport.

WHERE TO STAY

Belize can offer tourists a great array of accommodation ranging from comfortable budget hotels to luxurious beach resorts and jungle lodges with vast tracts of pristine wilderness as their grounds.

Alternatives include small private guest houses, huge, internationally-owned hotel chains, diver-oriented resorts on the outer cayes, lodges that cater to the eco-tourist with bird-watching lists and evening discussions, and health resorts providing herbal body wraps.

The style or specialty of each hotel or lodge can be radically different, and is often created by the environment. Although staying in urban centers might give a traveler more insight into the local Belizean character and culture, the majority of visitors come to taste nature.

For accommodation in lodges and on some cayes, it is difficult to give price guides as they usually offer deals which include diving or fishing trips, or rainforest treks, etc. They are mostly quite expensive, but very convenient and usually worthwhile.

Categories are as follows, for a double room:
Expensive = US$95–$175
Moderate = US$45–$90
Budget = under US$45

There is usually an additional 10 or 15 percent service charge plus 5 percent room tax unless otherwise stated.

BELIZE CITY

Belize City has hotels on both sides of Haulover Creek, connected by the Swing Bridge. Although the commercial center is on the south side, most of the better hotels are located on the northern side, which is also a more attractive neighborhood.

Expensive

Bellevue Hotel, 5 Southern Foreshore, Belize City. Tel: 02-77051/77052; fax: 02-73253. Located on the southern shoreline, with lovely views from the front rooms only, this old expanded house begins with a small dim lobby and ends in dank narrow hallways. Only a few of the rooms are passable but the management is professional and the over-air-conditioned restaurant serves reasonable food. The saving grace is the upstairs lounge bar, one of the best in the city, with divine breezes and views over the bay.

Belize Biltmore Plaza, Mile 3, Northern Highway, Belize City. Tel: 02-32302; fax: 02-32301. Large, sophisticated hotel 3 miles (5 km) from downtown Belize City. Swimming pool, private bathrooms and tropical garden.

Radisson Fort George Hotel, 2 Marine Parade, PO Box 321, Belize City. Tel: 02-77400; fax: 02-73820. US reservations: tel: (800) 633 4734. The Radisson Group recently took over the Holiday Villa Belize Inn and it has now become the Executive Club wing of the Fort George Hotel. All the facilities expected of a luxury hotel with emphasis on business travelers – meeting and conference rooms, fax, copier, courier, secretarial services, as well as pool, cable TV, duty-free shop and travel agent. Located in the Fort George area.

Ramada Royal Reef Resort and Marina, Barrack Road, Belize City. Tel: 02-32670; fax: 02-32660. US reservations: tel: (800) 228 9898. The largest of the luxury hotels. A sprawling Miami-style edifice facing out to sea, situated on the northern shoreline. The Ramada boasts a private marina from which to transport guests on day trips to the cayes, as well as large, glassed-in, air-conditioned public areas and huge pool with swim-up bar. There is nightly live entertainment in the Blue Hole Bar, Orchid Cafe and Wave Salon. Tours available.

Moderate

Bakadeer Inn, 74 Cleghorn Street (off Douglas Jones St), Belize City. Tel: 02-31400/31286; fax: 02-31963. For those who prefer US motel-style accommodation. All mod-cons including safe parking and full American breakfast included in the rate.

Chateau Caribbean, 6 Marine Parade, PO Box 947, Belize City. Tel: 02-72813/30800; fax: 02-30900. Old-style mansion and seafood restaurant facing out to sea with an atmosphere of Caribbean days gone by. Some rooms in original building very nice although renovation is needed throughout.

Colton House Guest House, 9 Cork Street, Belize

City. Tel: 02-44666. Only a few rooms available in this grand old home quietly nestled in the Fort George area. Popular amongst discerning Belizeans, the house has a large cool veranda where guests seem to spend most of the day.

Fort Street Guest House, 4 Fort Street, PO Box 3, Belize City. Tel: 02-30116; fax: 02-78808. US reservations: tel: (800) 538 6802/(303) 674 9615. A cosily renovated doctor's residence, this is one of the few hotels in Belize City with some local charm.

The wooden veranda is cooled by bay breezes and is probably the nicest spot in town in which to enjoy an afternoon cocktail. The upstairs rooms are large and airy with mosquito netting over big canopy beds. Shared bath, but there are plans for some rooms to have en-suite bathrooms. Main floor restaurant with antique furniture, fresh flowers and good fare. The only criticism is that service deteriorates when the management is not present. No service charge.

Glenthorne Manor, 27 Barrack Road, Belize City. Tel: 02-44212. Another old mansion, this one a conglomeration of styles. Each room with its own interior design concept. Eccentric management provides solid Belizean breakfast. Guests may use kitchen. Laundry facilities available.

Orchidia Guest House, 56 Regent Street, Belize City. Tel: 02-74266; fax: 02-77600. On the southern side of of the river, an old house with front porches decorated with wrought iron, hanging orchids and bromeliads. A bright cheery place, some rooms with air-conditioning, clean and secure.

Budget

Eyre St Guest House, 7 Eyre Street, Belize City. Tel: 02-77724. A good value guest house in an elegant but run-down building. Quiet and clean with good ventilation, most of the rooms have shared baths. Inexpensive vegetarian meals are available.

Mom's Triangle Inn, 11 Handyside Street, PO Box 332, Belize City. Tel: 02-45523/45073; fax: 02-31975. Most popular with young and adventure travelers, Mom's also has one of the city's best restaurants for Belizean food. All rooms have private bathtubs and fans or air-conditioning, in colorful old-fashioned settings. Located between the Swing Bridge and the Fort George area.

North Front St Guest House, 124 North Front Street, Belize City. Tel: 02-77595. Run by North Americans, rooms are basic although very reasonably priced. Breakfast and fixed-price dinner is available as well as laundry service and safe parking.

Sea Side Guest House, 3 Prince Street, Belize City. Tel: 02-78339. Very popular with seasoned travelers. Big sitting area and breakfast available.

BELIZE DISTRICT

Chaux Hiix Lodge, Crooked Tree Village. US Reservations: Tel: (800) 765 2611 or write to: Box 185, Flatwood, Wyoming, WV 26621. For the serious bird or nature lover. Isolated lodge surrounded by a variety of wildlife; located near the Chau Hiix archaeological site. Prices include meals, transfers, horseback riding, tours etc. Access by boat in the wet season or via Baboon Sanctuary in the dry.

Community Baboon Sanctuary Bed and Breakfasts, via Belize Audubon Society. Tel: 02-77369/78562. Stay with a Creole family within the area of the sanctuary to see black howler monkeys as well as learn about the lifestyle of rural Creoles. For room, board and guide fees contact the Audubon Society, or the Sanctuary Manager. Budget.

Crooked Tree Resort, Crooked Tree Village, PO Box 1453, Belize City. Tel: 02-77745. Reserve well in advance. Catering to visitors of the Crooked Tree Wildlife Sanctuary operated by the Belize Audubon Society. Idyllic lakeside setting of seven cabanas. Tours should be arranged in advance through Native Guide Systems, 1 Water Lane, Belize City. Tel: 02-25819. Moderate.

Maruba Resort and Jungle Spa, 40½ miles, Old Northern Highway, Maskall Village. Tel: 03-22199. US reservations: tel: (800) 627 8227/(713) 799 2031; fax: (713) 795 8573. Thirty miles (50 km) north of Belize International Airport. A unique and eccentric lodge, with cabins designed by the owner along different themes. Luxurious health and beauty services such as Japanese spa, massage and herbal body wraps available, as well as an excellent restaurant (Californian-Belize, with gibnut sometimes turning up on the menu). The sculpted jungle grounds, with various artworks and waterfall swimming pool are designed for peace and tranquility. Recommended for the visitor who wants to relax and be pampered. Tours are conducted to Lamanai and Altun Ha. Meal plans available. Airport pickup is $45 extra.

River Haven, ABM Limited, PO Box 78, Belize City, Central America. Tel: 02-300063; fax: 02-32742. Houseboats for hire. Boats sleep four. Cruise along inland tropical waters of the Siburn River and see jungle-life from a different angle.

AMBERGRIS CAYE/SAN PEDRO

San Pedro is the sandy township on Ambergris Caye where you can find plenty of inexpensive places to stay, each with its own relaxed beachy quality. The larger resorts can be found along the shoreline at varying distances out of San Pedro.

Expensive

Belize Yacht Club Ltd, PO Box 1, San Pedro. Tel: 02-62777; fax: 02-62768. Luxury suites complete with kitchens and verandas are ensconced within a formidable enclosure just a short walk south of San Pedro. Marina facilities available. Appropriate for longer stays.

Captain Morgan's Retreat, 3 Miles North of San Pedro, tel: 02-62567; fax: 02-62616. US reservations: Tel: (800) 447 2931. Attractive thatched cabanas on palm-shaded beach. One transfer each way from the airport is included in the price. The usual fishing, snorkelling and diving can be arranged.

Journey's End Caribbean Club, 4½ miles North of San Pedro, Box 13, San Pedro Town. Tel: 02-62173; fax: 02-62028. US reservations: tel: (800) 447 0474. Massive, slightly run-down complex of cabins and hotel blocks isolated at the northern end of the Caye. All the usual activities are provided from the resort's marina and a large pool is located at the back. The resort has floodlit tennis courts, basketball court, two restaurants and three bars, one with wall-to-wall slot machines and complimentary use of sailboards and canoes. Best suited for large groups or the swinging singles scene. Free scheduled boat transfers into town. Restaurant could be better. Meal plan available.

Ramon's Village Reef Resort, San Pedro Post Office, San Pedro. Tel: 02-62071/2229; fax: 02-62214. US reservations: tel: (601) 649 1990; fax: (601) 649 1996. Just outside San Pedro on one of the better sections of beach, Ramon's is a well-managed system of furnished cane cabanas, each with fan and private bath. The grounds include a salt-water swimming pool, the famed Purple Parrot Bar and a dining pavilion that serves excellent food. Some suites with kitchenettes.

Victoria House, 2 Miles South of San Pedro, Box 22, San Pedro Town. Tel: 02-62067/2240/2304; fax: 02-62429. US reservations: tel: (800) 247 5159. Extremely comfortable and elegant resort where Harrison Ford stayed during the filming of the *Mosquito Coast*. Choice of spacious suites with air-conditioning and balconies or private cabanas, all with perfect Caribbean Sea views. Watersport activities available from private marina, including open-water dive certification program. To get into town, rent a golf cart, take the scheduled shuttle bus or use the complimentary bicycles. The restaurant is good, and they'll cook your day's fishing catch. Rooms, cottages and deluxe suites available.

Moderate

Barrier Reef Hotel, Old Blake House, General Delivery, San Pedro. Tel: 02-62075; fax: 02-62191. One of the oldest houses in San Pedro. Popular for the veranda rooms in the original building, which overlook the center of the town's life, as well as the sea. Can be noisy due to the disco opposite.

Coral Beach Hotel and Dive Club, Box 614, San Pedro. Tel: 02-62013; fax: 02-62001. Just a hotel on the main street of San Pedro, no fancy facilities, where the emphasis is on diving. Packages including diving and meals are available.

Paradise Resort Hotel, Box 888, Belize City. Tel: 02-62083/2021/2230; fax: 02-62232. Another tasteful compound of South Pacific-style bamboo and thatch cabins, this time with the convenience of being on the northern edge of the township. Paradise has its own sandy beach, bar and gift shop, diving, fishing and travel services.

Royal Palm Villas, Box 18, San Pedro. Tel: 02-62148; fax: 02-62329. About 1½ miles (2 km) south of San Pedro; spacious rooms with wood floors and ceiling fans or more expensive apartments. Tranquil atmosphere on a wide beach and friendly management. Meal plans available.

San Pedro Holiday Hotel, Box 1140, Belize City. Tel: 02-62014; fax: 02-62295. This quaint old hotel lobby opens onto the main street of San Pedro, a hive of activity with its tour desk, swimwear boutique and friendly bar. Walk through the lobby and you're suddenly on the beach once again. Rooms with fans or air-conditioning. Apartments with air-conditioning.

Spindrift Hotel, San Pedro. Tel: 02-62174/2018; fax: 02-62251. Carpeted, air-conditioned suites or less expensive rooms with fans in the center of San Pedro. Surprisingly good Italian restaurant downstairs and lively cocktail lounge popular with divers. No service charge.

Sun Breeze Beach Resort, PO Box 14, San Pedro. Tel: 02-621919; fax: 02-62346. US reservations: Tel: (800) 327 3573; telex: 6714153 LARCHOT. Yet another hotel compound on the beachfront only minutes from town, with all rooms air-conditioned (which successfully blocks the occasional noise from the nearby airstrip). The dive shop can arrange lessons and certification. New pool is under way.

Budget

There are plenty of no-frills hotels in the heart of San Pedro. Try **Lily's Caribena**, tel: 02-62059; **Conch Shell Inn**, tel: 02-62962; or **Hotel San Pedrano**, tel: 02-62054.

CAYE CAULKER

There are no luxurious hotels on Caye Caulker and this is part of the attraction for many visitors. There are, however, many relaxing places to stay. Just stroll around and take your pick.

Shirley's Guest House, tel: 02-22145. Last hotel on the south end of the island. Shirley is a great hostess and the quiet, comfortable rooms open straight onto the beach.

Tropical Paradise Hotel, tel: 02-22142; fax: 02-22225. The most up-market offering. Towards the south end of the village near the old island cemetery, a tidy compound encompassing light rooms with fans and private bath. Some newer luxury cabanas with air-conditioning, TV and fridge. Has the most organized restaurant.

All other accommodation is budget level, although some offer private baths, such as the **Rainbow Hotel** and next door, the **Reef Hotel**. The **Split** is a collection of shady thatched cottages at the northern end with sand and water on three sides.

CAYE CHAPEL

Pyramid Island Resort, Box 192, Belize City. tel: 02-44409; fax: 02-31104/32405. US reservations: Tel: (800) 325 3401/(606) 329 2660. The only resort, run by the owner of the caye. All the usual watersport facilities (check availability before booking), dive shop, full-service marina, fresh-water pool, bar, tennis, air-conditioned basic rooms. No service charge. Meal plan available.

ST GEORGE'S CAYE

Cottage Colony, c/o Bellevue Hotel, Belize City. Tel: 02-77051/77052. Cottages and watersport services managed by the mainland hotel. Inquire at hotel lobby in Belize City.

St George's Lodge, Box 625, Belize City. Tel: 02-44190; fax: 02-30461. US reservations: tel: (800) 678 6871. Catering mainly for divers, this is a highly rated resort. With four diving guides (including two instructors), four dive boats and three compressors, this is a good choice for certification. Cottages with thatched roofs and sea breezes. Reduction for non-divers and children.

GALLOWS POINT CAYE

The Wave Resort, c/o Hotel Belcove, 9 Regent Street, Belize City. Tel: 02-73054; fax: 02-77600. Second-floor hotel rooms facing out to sea. Cold showers, fishing, snorkeling, diving, etc.

BLUEFIELD RANGE

Ricardo's Beach Huts, c/o Anna Lara, Mira Rio Hotel, 59 North Front Street, PO Box 55, Belize City. Tel: 02-44970. Accommodation in "over-water" cabanas. Learn about the lives of the fishermen who manage a commercial fishing/lobster venture within these small cayes. Room prices include transportation to the caye and all meals.

TURNEFFE ISLANDS

Blackbird Caye Resort, 81 W Canal Street, Belize City. Tel: 02-77670; fax: 02-73092. US reservations: tel: (800) 537 1431/(713) 658 1142; fax: (713) 658 0739. An environmentally sensitive ecotourism resort popular with divers and conservationists due to the beauty of its natural surroundings. Swim with dolphins in a protected lagoon.

Calabash Cay, contact: Coral Cay Conservation Ltd., 154 Clapham Park Road, London SW4 7DE: tel 0171-498-6248, fax; 0171 498 6248. For people wanting to work hard, help preserve the Belize barrier reef and learn about marine ecology. Coral Cay Conservation runs a series of marine survey expeditions to assist the Coastal Management Unit of Belize.

Volunteers must have some basic diving qualifica-

tions and be able to join the expeditions for at least 28 days.

Turneffe Flats, PO Box 36, Deadwood, South Dakota, SD 57732. US reservations: tel: (605) 578 1304; fax: (605) 578 3447. Package deals for fishermen include accommodation at the **Fort George Hotel** in Belize City, boat trip to the island, meals, fishing, and accommodation at the camp. Deep-sea fishing day trips.

LIGHTHOUSE REEF

Lighthouse Reef Resort, Northern Two Caye, PO Box 26, Belize City. Tel: 02-31205. US reservations: tel: (800) 423 3114/(813) 439 1436. Handy base for diving expeditions. Luxury accommodation including air-conditioning, private bath, restaurant, bar and shop. Fishing and other sightseeing arranged.

GLOVER'S REEF

Glover's Reef Atoll Resort, Long Caye, PO Box 563, Belize City. Tel: 08-23505/22505. Bring your own food, or catch it. Rustic cabins, well-water, outhouse, gravity shower, etc. Very inexpensive deals including the boat trip.

Manta Reef Resort, Southwest Caye, PO Box 215, Belize City. Tel: 02-31895/45606. US reservations: Tel: (800) 342 0053/(305) 226 2029. Seven-night package deals from arrival at Belize International Airport. "Over-water" bar/restaurant.

SOUTH WATER CAYE

Blue Marlin Lodge, PO Box 21, Dangriga. Tel: 05-22243; fax: 05-22296. US reservations: tel: (800) 798 1558. Real diving resort atmosphere. Certification course available. Also billiards, windsurfing and more. Hot water showers, fans, "over-water" dining. Diving packages available.

Pelican Inn; Osprey's Inn; Frangipani House, c/o The Pelican Beach Resort, PO Box 14, Dangriga. Tel: 05-22044/22004/22541; fax: 05-22570. A choice of basic a but comfortable dormitories, apartments or separate wooden vacation houses, all run by the Pelican Beach Resort in Dangriga. Pelican's beach provides heavenly Caribbean relaxation and snorkeling and the resort will send over a resident cook for groups. Owners Therese Bowman Rath and Tony Rath are authorities on local environmental issues and can arrange visits to nearby Carrie Bow Caye for the Smithsonian Research Center. A comprehensive list of tours is also available.

TOBACCO CAYE

A range of modest accommodation, usually run by the families of local fishermen. A good contact is Mr Elwood Fairweather. Contact him at the **Rio Mar Hotel** in Dangriga, tel: 05-22201.

DANGRIGA

Pelican Beach Resort, PO Box 14, Dangriga. Tel: 05-22044/22004/22541; fax: 05-22570. Very pleasant and efficiently run hotel just outside Dangriga. Breezy rooms facing out to sea with private bath. A great base for visiting the southern cayes. (The owners, Therese Bowman Rath and Tony Rath, also run various establishments on South Water Caye, listed above.) Tours can be taken from here to the Cockscomb Basin Wildlife Sanctuary, Gales Point and other local points of interest including the town itself. Visits can also be arranged to the Smithsonian Research Center on Carrie Bow Caye.

Soffie's, Chatuye Street, Dangriga. Tel: 05-22789. New hotel with great balcony views over sea and river. Wonderful Belizean hostess, good Creole and Garifuna food. Fun place to be.

Hotels in Dangriga township are basic. Try the **Hub Guest House**, tel: 05-22397; **The Riverside**, tel: 05-22168; or **Rio Mar Inn**, tel: 05-22201. Some also offer boat excursions or accommodation on the cayes.

PLACENCIA

Ranguana Resort, Placencia. Tel: 06-23112. Five cabins on water's edge all with fridge and free coffee-making facilities. One double and one single bed in each. Three front cabins have wonderful views.

Rum Point Inn, Tel/fax: 06-22017. US reservations: tel: (504) 465 0769; fax: (504) 465 0325. A luxury complex, facing the sea about 2 miles (3½ km) north of Placencia township, including five uniquely designed cabanas. Individual stained-glass patterns set into the rounded, whitewashed concrete walls allow for delicate light patterns, creating a soothing environment. Very good dining and small library in an attractive communal house facing out to sea.

Kitty's Place, Tel: 06-22017/22027. Laid-back beachfront units popular with ex-pats for long stays (many guests come for two weeks and barely make it into the nearby township). Good food in the upstairs restaurant is accompanied by North American jazz and blues on the music system. Rickety old bicycles for the short cycle into town. Some apartments with kitchenettes.

Turtle Inn, tel: 06-22017. Picturesque little thatched cottages make up a classic vision of a Caribbean hideaway, set in their own sandy beachfront compound. Solar electricity so there's no generator noise (almost unique in Belize). American owners can provide assortment of boating and inland trips including rainforest treks.

Sonny's Resort, tel: 06-23203. Twelve seafront rooms and some wonderful new beach cabanas. Very comfortable but the most expensive hotel in the village.

BIG CREEK

Toucan Inn/Bill Bird Lodge, PO Box 1137, Belize City. Tel: 06-22092; fax: 06-22037. Welcome retreat from the heat of the township. Shady porch with plants and wicker chairs and a swimming pool.

PUNTA GORDA

Fallen Stones Butterfly Ranch and Jungle Lodge, San Pedro Columbia, Toledo. This innovative, conservation ranch is situated about a mile (1½ km) from Lubaantum and 40 minutes from Punta Gorda in the Maya Mountains. Accommodation in small thatched cabanas. Two restaurants serving good local Kekchi food. Fascinating butterfly farm and jungle animal visitors.

Nature's Way Guest House/Belize Adventure Travel, 65 Front Street, PO Box 75, Punta Gorda. Tel: 07-22119. Run by an American/Belizean couple, Nature's Way boasts a small library with material on local Belizean culture and the Toledo district. An unusual wooden house of eight rooms, most with shared bath.

Miramar Hotel, PO Box 2, Punta Gorda. Tel: 07-22033. Air-conditioning, cable television and private bath in the most expensive rooms. Located near center of town.

Safe Haven Lodge, c/o 2 Prince Street, Punta Gorda. Tel: 07-22113. Fishing or diving packages are the speciality at this cabana-style lodge located on the Rio Grande a few miles north of Punta Gorda. Meals, lodging, fishing or diving packages. Discounts for non-sportspeople.

Toledo Ecotourism Association, 65 Front Street, Punta Gorda. Contact Trips in the UK for information, Tel: 01272 292199. Innovative new project designed to open up village homes and culture to tourists and help fund the preservation of traditional Mayan life. Guests stay at the Village Guest House which is clean and comfortable and lit by kerosene lamps. They are shown local farms, forests, rivers and waterfalls, and join village families for meals. Contributions to conservation, village health and education programs are very welcome. There is also the chance to watch or help in the cocoa harvesting for Maya Gold Chocolate. Relatively expensive.

BELMOPAN

The Belmopan Convention Hotel, 2 Bliss Parade, Box 237, Belmopan. Tel: 08-22130/22340; fax: 08-23066. US motel-style. Comfortable, air-conditioned, good for business travelers. Within walking distance of government offices.

Bull Frog Inn, 25 Half Moon Avenue, PO Box 28, Belmopan. Tel: 08-22111; fax: 08-23155. Another straightforward, motel-style place, except that its restaurant is the best place to eat in Belmopan.

TEAKETTLE (6 miles from Belmopan)

Warrie Head Ranch & Lodge, c/o Belize Global Travel Services, 41 Albert Street, PO Box 244, Belize City. Tel: 02-77185/77363; fax: 02-75213. An old logging camp converted into a working citrus and vegetable ranch, popular with groups of tourists. 500 acres (200 hectares) of protected forest with howler monkeys, river swimming, walking trails.

SAN IGNACIO & SURROUNDS

Almost everyone who comes to this region stays not in the San Ignacio township but in the lodges that dot the surrounding countryside. Most hotels in San Ignacio itself are budget places, with one exception: **San Ignacio Hotel**, 18 Buena Vista Road, PO Box 23, San Ignacio. Tel: 09-22034; fax: 09-22034. A basic concrete building but well situated, with pleasant terraces facing across the Macal River. The breezy dining room is popular at lunchtime, especially with visiting archaeologists, and it seems to have its own typically Belizean character. No service charge.

Among the other hotels in town, try the **Venus Hotel**, tel: 09-22186; **Piache Hotel**, tel: 09-22032; **Central Hotel**, tel: 09-22253 and **The New Belmoral Hotel**, tel: 09-22024.

JUNGLE LODGES

The following are isolated cottage-style resorts in the region around San Ignacio:
Blancaneaux Lodge, Central Farm, PO Box B, Cayo District. Tel: 09-23878. Francis Coppola's new venture. An incredible lodge in exquisite surrounds, real luxury in the jungle. Wonderful views from all the cabanas. Best wood-burning pizza oven in the area and lot of activities available.
Casa Cielo Cabanas and Mountain Equestrian Trails (MET), Mile 8, Mountain Pine Ridge Road, Central Farm, Cayo District. Tel: 08-23180; fax: 08-23235. The best place for horseback riding enthusiasts. Trips throughout Mountain Pine Ridge and surrounding terrain. Also nature treks, horse-drawn wagons, tours to Tikal and swimming.
Chaa Creek Cottages, PO Box 53, San Ignacio, Cayo. Tel: 09-22037; fax: 09-22501. Probably the most comfortable place in the San Ignacio region, set with spectacular views of the Macal River valley. The elegant private bungalows are decorated with Mayan tapestries; there are no locks, all windows open onto the river, and each room uses kerosene lamps (there is no electricity). Impressive landscaping and manicured tropical grounds. About 20 minutes' drive from San Ignacio, or you can get there by traveling an hour down river by canoe. Good restaurant, pleasant open-air bar; highly recommended. The Panti Medicinal Trail is also just next door, and

tours are offered to Mountain Pine Ridge, Xunantanich, Chumpiate Maya Cave and more. Canoeing, rafting, horseback riding.
Maya Mountain Lodge and Educational Field Station, Box 46, San Ignacio. Tel: 09-22164; fax: 09-22029. US reservations: tel: (800) 344 MAYA. Nestled in the foothills of Mountain Pine Ridge, about one mile (1½ km) above San Ignacio, this lodge/classroom/reference library is run like a tight ship by the environmentally zealous Bart and Suzi Mickler. Meet them and their young family for an after-dinner discussion. They are proud of their unspoilt surroundings and you will be urged to take one of their own chartered trails, which are marked with botanical points of interest. Cabins are nicely decorated, some with hammocks outside on porches. There is an exhaustive list of local tour options as well as the usual activities such as horse riding and canoeing. Real home-style dinners. Bart and Suzie enjoy accommodating study groups and tourists wishing to learn about ecotourism issues.
Mt Pleasant Hidden Valley Inn, 4 Miles Coona Cairn Road, Mountain Pine Ridge Forest Reserve, Box 170, Belmopan. Tel: 08-23320/3321; fax: 08-23334. US reservations: tel: (800) 334 7942; fax: (904) 222 1992. One of the more luxurious choices in the Mountain Pine Ridge area. Access to waterfalls and river swimming, mountain trails, etc. Meals included. Advance reservations required.
Pine Ridge Lodge, 17 Miles Mountain Pine Ridge Forest Reserve. Tel: 09-23310/2215. More modest establishment of Belizean-owned cabins near Thousand Foot Falls. Hiking and swimming, etc.
Windy Hill Cottages, Graceland Ranch, San Ignacio. Tel: 09-22055; fax: 09-23080. Self-contained cottages with color TVs and stocked refrigerators. Activities include canoeing to Spanish Lookout, horseback riding along the Mopan River and swimming in the resort pool.

ORANGE WALK DISTRICT

ORANGE WALK TOWN

Hotel Barons, 40 Belize-Corozal Road, Orange Walk Town. Tel: 03-22518/22847; fax: 03-23472. Not many visitors stay in Orange Walk Town itself, but this is the best hotel if you do. Plain, air-conditioned rooms and private showers. Hotel has pool and enclosed parking.

RAINFOREST

Chan Chich Lodge, (Rio Bravo Conservation Area), 2 South Park Street, Belize City. Tel: 02-75616/ 75617; fax: 02-76961. US reservations: PO Box 1088, Vineyard Haven, Massachusetts, MA 02568. Tel: (800) 343 8009; fax: (508) 693 6311. Currently rated as the best of Belize's jungle resorts, Chan Chich has the rare privilege of being located within the plaza of a Classic Mayan ruin. Very tasteful cabanas, constructed of local woods with surrounding porches, receive rave reviews. Pristine forest surroundings afford glimpses of tropical birds, monkeys, and (possibly) jaguars. Possible to get here by road if you're hardy; most people fly.

Program for Belize, Rio Bravo Research Station, *see* address in previous entry. New venture into tourism right in the heart of the rainforest. Accommodation in a basic dormitory or spacious cabana. Talks given by experts and working demonstrations of jungle conservation and *chicle* production. Well-organized trails into the forest, notably to the famous Mayan La Milpa site. Good library and shop, friendly hosts. A unique holiday experience.

COROZAL DISTRICT

Adventure Inn, PO Box 35, Corozal Town (hotel located in Consejo Shores). Tel: 04-22187; fax: 04-22243. Relaxing cottages overlooking the Caribbean. Constant light breeze good for sailing and windsurfing. Tours to Mayan ruins.

Tony's Inn & Resort, South End, Corozal Town. Tel: 04-22055; fax: 04-22829. Tours are conducted throughout the Corozal district. Friendly, helpful management.

EATING OUT

WHAT TO EAT

Belize's national dish may be rice and beans, but that doesn't mean that local cuisine stops there. The tropical reef fish, lobster and conch, available in season on the cayes and transported across Belize, are luxurious ingredients for a national cuisine. (Conch should not be eaten during the out-of-season months of July, August and September.) Belize can also offer an exotic range of tropical fruits, especially in the interior. Try a "sour-sap" milkshake for a start, then ask for whatever other bizarre produce is the local favorite.

The latest jungle resorts boast gourmet dining using local meats such as gibnut (*paca*) and brocket deer, usually throwing in a range of vegetarian dishes (beyond rice and beans, that is). The Gariganu Belizeans of the south coast enjoy their traditional *cassava* or coconut bread while the Creoles will make fry jacks or Johnny cakes.

All Belizeans, however, are loyal to the national brew — Belikin beer — with the cheaper domestic version more highly regarded than the export label. Remember that tap water should not be drunk in the cayes or in the south.

Many tourists find themselves eating regularly at the resorts, either out of convenience or because they are included in their package deal. Even so, try to experience some of the smaller Belizean restaurants. Since many of the resorts have a standard international style, this is another way to meet some Belizeans and begin to appreciate their friendliness. The following choices include some to help you get out of the hotel complex.

WHERE TO EAT

BELIZE CITY

Fort Street Guest House, 4 Fort Street. Tel: 02-30116. Antique decor, candlelit tables and fresh flowers make for a romantic Caribbean setting. Gourmet Belizean concoctions with high success rate, and vast cocktails. Service can be sullen, but the food is good and overall can be highly recommended. Expensive.

GG's Cafe & Patio, 2B King Street. Tel: 02-74378. The romantic patio atmosphere makes this a good place for lunch or dinner.

The Grill, 164 Newtown Barrack Road. Tel: 02-45020. Easier to get to by car, since it's a little out of the way. The Grill is a fairly pricey, British-run establishment popular with locals for dinner or special occasions. The decor is plain and modern but there is great variety on the menu and the kitchen seems to manage it all fairly well. Try the cold shrimp salad or Jamaican-style.

Macy's Cafe, 18 Bishop Street. Tel: 02-73419. A lunchtime hive for Belizean business people enjoying what may be the best Creole cooking in the city. Don't be intimidated by the close quarters or shared tables: you'll be welcome to join any table. The food is cheap and plentiful. Try the fish balls if they're on the menu. Most main dishes include rice and beans or beans over white rice.

Mom's Triangle Inn, 11 Handyside Street. Tel: 02-45523/45073. Legendary, especially among young budget travelers. Wholesome Belizean and American cooking. Packed on Sunday mornings.

Scoop's, Corner of Eve Street and Goal Lane. Tel: 02-44699. The Ben and Jerry's ice cream joint of Belize. It's also available at the supermarket.

SAN PEDRO (Ambergris Caye)

The hotels listed in *Where To Stay* all have their own restaurants. Any stroll along the beachfront or sandy streets of San Pedro takes you past an endless string of blackboards advertising the daily dining specials — in other words, the competition is high. New places are opening (and closing) every week, mostly quite decent, but the following are known successes:

Celi's Restaurant, adjacent to Holiday Hotel. Daily

fish specials are very good and desserts are excellent. Casual setting and moderate prices.

Elvi's Kitchen, Pescador Drive. Tel: 02-62176/62359. Large thatched roof enclosure supported by a growing tree, this is a trendy place to hang out as the sun goes down. Food ranges from hamburgers and club sandwiches to fish in wine sauce and sauteed lobster.

Mary Ellen's Little Italy Restaurant, at the Spindrift Hotel. Tel: 02-62866. Attractive Italian restaurant with surprisingly authentic pasta dishes and delicious pizzas. The waiters are young but very professional and Mary Ellen is eager to satisfy her customers. Definitely worth a visit. There's even a good wine list. Prices are slightly less than at the resorts.

Ramon's Village, on the Beach, San Pedro. Tel: 02-62071. Serving international-style dishes, this restaurant can also be recommended to prepare the fish you caught out fishing that afternoon.

PLACENCIA

Most Placencia eateries are open from 8am–2pm and 7–11pm.

BJ's Restaurant, on the main road. Tel: 06-23108/23202. A popular place serving local dishes, specializing in seafood (try the conch fritters) and wonderful juices.

Dora's on the main sand walkway (opposite the spot where fishermen hang out – you can't miss it). Dora, a feisty woman who has grown huge on her own cooking, whips up some astonishingly spicy, huge meals; the colorful restaurant, full of candles and lights, really starts hopping after dark. The ideal place to try some Caribbean cuisine.

The Galley, across the playing field (ask anyone for directions). May serve the best sour-sap milkshake in Belize. You might wait up to 45 minutes for it, but the result is pure heaven. Other lovingly made cakes and desserts on display.

Two tourist-style restaurants, **The Kingfisher** and **Tentacles Bar & Steakhouse** are located at the southern end of Placencia and are popular with expats. Expensive.

The best choices among the resort restaurants are **Kitty's Place**, which charges about $15 for a set three-course meal, and **Rum Point Inn**, where the dining room is rather fancier.

AROUND SAN IGNACIO (CAYO DISTRICT)

The best restaurant in Belmopan is in the **Bullfrog Inn** (see Where to Stay). If you are passing through by bus, the **Caladium Restaurant** at the bus station is a clean bright place that has decent food and great people-watching.

In San Ignacio township, you can't go past **Eva's Bar and Restaurant** – which doubles as a gift shop, tour desk and tourist information office – located in the heart of town on Burns Avenue. Eva's has come to be the place where everyone meets, maybe due to the loquacious and happy nature of the English owner and barman, Bob. The food is cheap and hearty. Belizeans rub shoulders with tourists at the checked vinyl tablecloths, cooled (barely) by overhead fans. For atmosphere it can't be beaten, so try and escape your lodge for at least a drink.

The hilltop **San Ignacio Hotel** is a lively lunchtime scene with wonderful breezes through the open windows from across the Macal River. Dishes range from rice and beans to kebabs and lobster for between $4 and $10. If you love curries, Belize's only Sri Lankan restaurant, **Serendib**, is across the street from Eva's.

ATTRACTIONS

CULTURAL

Belizeans are a culturally diverse bunch, but there is not a lot to do in the way of formal musical concerts, performances or the like (there isn't even a cinema in the entire country). The main way of getting to understand Creole culture is by meeting people informally in bars, restaurants and on the beach; even such Creole celebrations as Settlement Day every September offers little more to the outsider than a chance to get drunk with everyone else.

Spanish-speaking Belizeans in the north and west have a few more Hispanic rituals and holidays, although they are based around the church and family, as in the rest of Latin America. Mexican-style fiestas are held in Corozal at Carnival time (the period before Lent begins, a shifting date every year), Colombus Day and Christmas, when colorful posadas re-enact the search of Mary and Joseph for shelter.

The Garifuna population in Southern Belize feel very strongly about their heritage and they come together with great enthusiasm from November 19 to the end of the year in celebration of the anniversary of their ancestors arrival in Dangriga in 1823. If you are visiting Dangriga at this time you might see masked Joncunu dancers, drumming and impromptu music concerts or hear the conch shells blown on Christmas Eve (although, once again, the main manifestation at all these times is bouts of public drinking). Other Garifuna religious ceremonies are regularly performed, but rarely in view of outsiders. You could ask around, but generally visitors aren't really welcome.

There are pockets of Mennonite communities in the north Cayo District, each following tradition to varying degrees (some refuse to use machines more developed than horse-drawn buggies, others use full-scale harvesters). While most tourists don't feel inclined to approach the Mennonites, apart from stealing a photograph (which Mennonites actually object to very strongly), it is interesting to talk to a family and find out how they live. Since it would be inappropriate to conduct scheduled tours, you must visit by private transport.

ARCHAEOLOGICAL SITES

For most tourists, the prime cultural attraction in Belize is its wealth of Mayan archaeological sites (there are an estimated 600 sites in the jungle, the highest concentration in Central America, and four important Maya towns were discovered in 1993 in the Maya Mountains). Tourists can visit a number of these sites by themselves or contact a local operator for a guided tour. It is also convenient to make a day trip to the famous site of Tikal in Guatemala from Belize. Here is a brief summary of the most visited sites.

Cerros: Located on a peninsula across from Corozal Town, Cerros was once important as a coastal trading center that embraced new forms of art and architecture. Tallest temple is 72 ft (22 meters). Can be reached by boat from Corozal or by road during the dry period from January–April.

Santa Rita: Corozal itself is built over the Maya center of Santa Rita – the largest building has now been excavated and is open to the public. Important during the Late Post Classic Period and occupied right up until the Spanish arrival in the 1500s.

Cuello: Recent discovery, important for establishing the start of the Mayan culture at around 2,600 BC, much earlier than previously thought. Ruins are mostly covered by vegetation on private land accessible by permission only from the Cuello Rum Distillery during business hours. Tel: 03-22141.

Altun Ha: Famous for the discovery of the Jade Head, the largest carved jade object found in the Mayan area, which represents the Sun God Kinich Ahau. Located 31 miles (50 km) north of Belize City, the main plaza consists of 13 temples and residences. Local tour operators run daily trips.

Lamanai: Impressive ceremonial center which was occupied from 1500 BC until the 19th century. Can be reached either by road from San Felipe during the dry season or by scenic boat ride taken from Guinea Grass, Orange Walk Town and Shipyard. If you only have time for one ruin in Belize, this would be a good choice.

Xunantunich: The largest pyramid, El Castillo, is located across the river from the town of San José Succotz, near the western border with Guatemala. Interesting for three clearly discernible *stelae* on display. Private and tour vehicles take the old-fashioned car ferry.

Cahal Pech: Situated on the hill overlooking San Ignacio, Cahal Pech consists of 34 structures, as well as ball courts, temples and *stelae*. Occupied from 1000 BC to AD 800. A short steep walk up from the township, the site is open to the public.

Caracol: Permission is required from the Department of Archaeology to visit this newly excavated site, the largest Mayan city found in Belize. Located about 30 miles (48 km) south of Augustine within the beautiful Chiquibul wilderness, the dirt access road is only open and passable when it's dry (otherwise don't attempt it).

Lubantuun: Known for its unusual style of construction. Pyramids and terraces are made of dressed stone blocks with no mortar. Situated one mile (1½ km) past the village of San Pedro Colombia. Accessible on foot, 20 minutes from the roadway. Accommodation in Punta Gorda Town or San Anonio.

Tikal (Gutatemala): World-famous as the probably the most impressive of all Mayan archaeological sites. One- or two-day trips are offered by many Belizean tour operators, by plane from Belize City or San Pedro, or you could take the bumpy overland trip from San Ignacio. The ruin can certainly be visited in a day, but many people recommend an overnight stay to really appreciate the place once the tourist buses have left. Double-check visa requirements for visiting Guatemala before arriving at the border.

ENVIRONMENTAL

For information pertaining to many of Belize's wildlife reserves contact:

Belize Audubon Society, 29 Regent St, PO Box 1001, Belize City. Tel. 02-77369. Check on the seasonal conditions of the Community Baboon Sanctuary, the Cockscomb Basin Sanctuary, the Crooked Tree Sanctuary and the Half Moon Caye Natural Monument if you're planning to visit. The society also manages Guanacaste Park and the Blue Hole National Park. A bird checklist is available.

The following is a summary of wildlife reserves and natural attractions for visitors:

Belize Zoo and Tropical Education Center: Founded by American Sharon Matola, the zoo has the widest range of Belize's animals housed in famously natural enclosures. Make your visit early before the day gets too hot and the animals disappear to sleep. Thirty miles (50 km) west of Belize City, 14 miles (23 km) east of Belmopan. Most Belize City hotels offer tours to the zoo, and a taxi ride is not exorbitant. Also check Venus Bus Lines (tel: 02-73354) or Batty Brothers (tel: 02-72025).

Bermudian Landing Community Baboon Sanctuary: Black howler monkeys (called baboons by Belizeans) now number around 1,200 in this reserve located in north-central Belize, an easy day trip from Belize City or Maruba resort. Contact the Belize Audubon Society about staying with a family in the area, guide fees, group tours. Tel: 02-77369.

Blue Hole National Park and St Herman's Cave: Surprisingly blue swimming hole 12 miles (19 km) southeast of Belmopan on the Hummingbird Highway; nearby are subterranean streams, sinkholes and limestone cave systems. St Herman's Cave is a 45-minute hike from the Blue Hole or a 10-minute hike from a trailhead located one mile (½ km) north along the Hummingbird Highway. Take a flashlight and waterproof boots.

Cockscomb Basin Wildlife Sanctuary: Prime attraction is the jaguar, however elusive. Also home to many birds, including macaws, toucans and vultures. Located in the Stann Creek District, with access by road from the Southern Highway at the Mopan village of Maya Center, 25 miles (40 km) south of Dangriga or somewhat further from Placencia. Register first at the visitor's booth in Maya Center.

Crooked Tree Wildlife Preserve: Prime attraction is the bird life. Network of inland lagoons, swamps and waterways located 33 miles (53 km) northwest of Belize City. Arrange your visit in advance with the Belize Audubon Society. Access by boat. Possible to stay in family homes at Crooked Tree Village or at more up-market accommodation nearby in Crooked Tree Resort or Maruba Resort. (*See* Where to Stay.)

Gales Point Manatee Preserve: Tours are conducted from Dangriga to the waterways near the isolated Creole fishing community of Gale's Point. The walrus-like manatee surface for air at key breathing holes where tourists can observe them.

Guanacaste Park: Approximately 50 acres (20 hectares) of tropical forest in the Cayo District, approximately 2 miles (1 km) north of Belmopan, established by the Belizean government on Earth Day (April 22) 1990. Giant guanacaste trees over 100 feet (30 meters) tall as well as exotic wildlife such as jaguarundi, kinkajou, paca, agouti, bats and opossum. Accessible by bus, taxi, private car or package tour.

Half Moon Caye Natural Monument: 45-acre (18-hectare) sanctuary managed by the Belize Audubon Society. Part of Lighthouse Reef, the furthest offshore atoll. The reserve protects a large colony of red-footed boobies as well as other rare sea birds.

Hol Chan Marine Reserve: If you only snorkel in one location on the Barrier Reef, it probably should be here. A natural channel lures an abundance of fish and allows a dazzling variety of coral. Included as part of most snorkeling tours conducted from San Pedro on Ambergris Caye. Removing, touching or disturbing anything is prohibited and you must alight very carefully from the boat onto the seabed.

Monkey Bay Wildlife Sanctuary: A few miles west of the Belize Zoo along the Western Highway. It consists of 1,070 acres (432 hectares) of pine, palm savanna, freshwater wetlands and lagoons. Secluded bathing beach along the Sibun River. Ideal for birdwatching. Camping is allowed for a small fee, as well as canoeing, hiking, etc. Enquiries to: Monkey Bay Wildlife Sanctuary, PO Box 187, Belmopan, Belize.

Mountain Pine Ridge and Hidden Valley Falls: Located in the Cayo District foothills, southeast of San Ignacio. Unusual natural phenomenon (for Central America, at least) of 300 sq. miles (777 sq. km) of pine forest, looking straight out of Vermont. Birds and butterflies, limestone caves and white water rivers. Many operators in San Ignacio have day tours. Hidden Valley Falls is the prime attraction within Mountain Pine Ridge, being the highest waterfall in Central America, as well as having the delightful Río On swimming holes. Attractions within the reserve are well marked.

Río Bravo Conservation and Management Area: 202,000 acres (82,000 hectares) of sub-tropical forest in the northwest corner of Belize managed by the non-profit group, Program for Belize. Wildlife includes, howler and spider monkeys, king vulture, jaguar, puma and ocelot, 400 species of birds, 250 species of orchids and much more. Visitors should stay at Chan Chich lodge or at the Rio Bravo Research Station. (*See* Where to Stay.)

Río Frío Cave and Chiquibul National Forest Reserve: South of Mountain Pine Ridge is a 45-minute nature trail to Río Frío, the largest river cave in Belize. Further into the Chiquibul wilderness is pristine forest and more cave systems, one of which contains ancient Mayan pots. Tours are available from Chaa Creek Cottages and Mayan Mountain Lodge.

Shipstern Nature Reserve and Butterfly Breeding Center: Some 22,000 acres (8,900 hectares) of seasonal hardwood forest, mangrove shoreline and saline lagoon systems located 3 miles (5 km) from Sarteneja. Unique environments nurturing wading and fish-eating birds, Baird's tapir, deer and 200 species of butterflies. (Definitely worth visiting on a sunny day.)

ARCHAEOLOGICAL AND WILDLIFE TOURS

Eco Tours, 99 Freetown Road, Belize City. Tel: 02-33507; fax 02-32182. Multilingual guides, daily tours to archeological sites including Tikal. Transfers to Cancun and Merida. Car/4WD hire.

Far Horizons, PO Box 1529, 16 Fern Lane, San Anselmo, California, CA 94960. Tel: (415) 457 4575; fax: (415) 457 4608. Archaeologist run cultural discovery tours and custom itineraries for individuals and groups.

International Expeditions, 1 Environs Park, Helena, Alabama, AL 35080. Tel: (800) 633 4734/(205) 428 1700. Ten-day tours of Mayan ruins with optional extensions to Copan in Honduras and the Barrier Reef.

Native Guide Systems, 1 Water Lane, Belize City. Tel: 02-75819; fax: 02-74007. Guide services agency covering all Belize attractions. Custom designed tours for photography, bird-watching, nature study and general touring. Also sailing, diving, fishing, boat charter, etc.

S & L Travel Services, 91 North Front Street, PO Box 700, Belize City. Tel: 02-75145/77593; fax: 02-77594. Tours to wildlife reserves and Mayan sites, Belize Zoo, Mountain Pine Ridge, Tikal by road. **Trips**, 9 Byron Place, Bristol, BS8 1JT, UK. Tel: 01272 292199; fax: 01272 292545. Can organize tailor-made wildlife and adventure trips to form all, or part, of a holiday. Good contact for special interest trips.

ECOTOURISM

Belize is a world leader in environmentally conscious tourism strategies. Conservation groups and the government have recently launched a number of new ecotourism projects to help fund conservation initiatives. (*See* Where to Stay for information regarding accommodation offered by conservation projects.)
Coral Cay Conservation Ltd (CCC), 154 Clapham Park Road, London SW4 7DE, UK. Tel: 0171 4986248; fax: 0171 4988447. CCC has been working with the government on a coastal zone management initiative along the Belize barrier reef since 1986. It is now working with the University of Belize to construct a marine research center on Calabash Cay, Turneffe Atoll.
Program for Belize, 2 South Park Street, Belize City. Tel: 02-75616/75617. A new venture invites travelers to visit the Rio Bravo Research Station to increase funding and provide information about rainforest preservation.
Toledo Ecotourism Association, for information in the UK contact: Trips, 9 Byron Place, Bristol BS8 1JT, England. Tel: 01272 292199; fax: 01272 292545. Revenue from the association's guest house is directed back into local communities.

NIGHTLIFE

Nobody comes to Belize for the nightlife. There is nothing remotely like the party scene common in other parts of the Caribbean, even in San Pedro.

Nevertheless, there is no shortage of bars in any Belizean town, usually with live music (no matter how appalling); nearly every town has a dance or two on weekends, where you can try to do the punta – a difficult pelvic gyration and foot stomp that relates to the equally frenetic punta music (a beat that makes rap seem effete). Bars and dances really don't get going until midnight so reserve your strength.

In Belize City, try the bar at the **Belleview Hotel** for a chance to meet bizarre characters (it was likened in the 1980s to Rick's Bar in *Casablanca*, although these days you're much less likely to be asked to run guns to El Salvador or a drug shipment to Texas). A good late-night place to meet Belizeans is **Lindbergh's**, an open-air hut on Newtown Barracks Road (next to the Grill Restaurant). The action starts late, even on weekdays.

San Pedro is packed with bars, in every resort (try the **Purple Parrot** at Ramon's) and all around the town – just walk along the docks and pick one that seems lively. Many have different theme nights, providing certain drinks for free; in some places, a game is played where patrons bet on a chicken strutting over a large board, trying to guess where it is going to shit.

In smaller places like Placencia, the nightlife scene is based on the hotels and resorts; **Tentacle's Bar** at the tip of the peninsula is very popular with expats, though it can get fairly degenerate. A sign on the bar (Men and Ships Rot in Port) says it all.

In San Ignacio, try out the **Cahal Pech Tavern** near the ruins above the town – another giant hut where you can punta till dawn. The **Blue Angel** disco is an amazing scene on weekend nights, patronized by an enormous crowd that includes what may be Belize's lone transvestite. Again, beer and punta until dawn, but you should leave long before then – the place has a reputation for brawls.

SHOPPING

Unlike Guatemala and Mexico, Belize has not developed a souvenir industry or nurtured Indian crafts. However, a couple of small operations around San Ignacio are beginning to teach old skills such as Mayan pottery and slate carving. Leading the way are the García sisters, who run a shop in San Antonio (refer to the main text for a description). They also sell jewellery made from ziricote (a hardwood) or the occasional mahogany carving.

Considered superior by many is the lesser-known carver David Magnano, who runs a tiny shop in San José Succotz by the Guatemalan border. Ask in town for directions to his house. More stalls are being set up by hopeful Mayan artists every month in the region around San Ignacio.

Many hotels near San Ignacio stock Guatemalan Indian handicrafts. Note that they are many times cheaper when bought in Guatemala, if you are heading on a day trip to Tikal.

In Belize City, the upper level of the central marketplace houses a number of small souvenir shops. There are also a few tacky places in San Pedro worth glancing at. Anyone truly desperate for a Belizean souvenir should check out the huge selection of T-shirts and straw hats available on San Pedro.

More practically, consider a bottle of Marie Sharp's Habanero Salsa, a chili sauce that comes in three different strengths; many tourists become addicted to the taste, especially on their morning scrambled eggs.

Don't buy black coral or turtle shell souvenirs, as this encourages their depletion, and is illegal.

Most major hotels and resorts have their own tour desk which provides day tours to the local attractions. (For contacts, *see* Where to Stay*).* There are numerous tour operators in the United States, Canada and the United Kingdom offering all-inclusive package deals to Belize.

The following operators can organize coastal activities (diving, fishing, sailing), inland activities (horseback riding, trekking, birdwatching, canoeing) as well as trips to wildlife reserves and archaeological sites.

Diving

Indigo Belize, PO Box 450987, Sunrise, Florida, FL 33345. Tel: (800) 468 0123/(305) 473 1956; fax: (305) 473 6011. Also specializing in live-aboard dive trips on the *Manta IV.*

Joe Miller Photography, Fido's Courtyard, San Pedro. Tel: 02-62577. Underwater camera rental, advanced instruction, slide processing and emergency Nikon repair.

Out Island Divers, San Pedro, Ambergris Caye. Tel: 02-62151; fax: 02-62810. US reservations: PO Box 3455, Estes Park, Colorado, CO 80517. Tel: (800) BLUE HOLE/(303) 586 6020. Well established diving specialists offering live-aboard on the *Reef Roamer II* and *M.V. Celestial.* One-, two- and three-day dive trips including Lighthouse Reef, Turneffe Islands and Glover's Reef.

Peter Hughes Diving, 1390 S Dixie Highway, Ste. 2213, Coral Gables, Florida, FL 33146. Tel: (800) 932 6237/(305) 669 9391. Luxury dive vessel the *Wave Dancer* cruises the offshore atolls with gourmet meals and unlimited free drinks.

Tortuga Dive Shop, San Pedro. Tel: 02-62018; fax: 02-62251. Specializing in single day dive trips.

Fishing

Blackline Marine Service, Box 332, Mile 2.5 Northern Highway, Belize City. Tel: 02-44155; fax: 02-31975. Fishing and sightseeing charters, marina, hull and engine repairs, complete dive shop.

Kingfisher Sports Ltd, Placencia Village. Tel: 06-23104. US reservations: tel: (512) 826 0469. Boat rental, flycast/spincast, inshore, offshore, bungalows, camping.

Triton Tours, 1111 Veterans Blvd. Ste. 5, Kenner, Louisiana, LA 70062. Tel: (800) 426 0226/(504) 464 7964. Deep-sea fishing aboard the *Jenny Rose '28.*

Turneffe Flats, Blackbird Caye, Turneffe Islands, 56 Eve Street, Belize City. Tel: 02-45634. US reservations: tel: (605) 578 1304; fax: (605) 578 7540. Sportfishing specialists.

Cruises

American Canadian Caribbean Line, PO Box 368, Warren, Rhode Island, RI 02885. Tel: (800) 556 7450/(401) 247 0955. Twelve-day trips departing from Radisson Fort George Hotel dock including cayes and Mayan ruins.

Sailing

Heritage Navigation, San Pedro. Tel: 02-62394. The island trading vessel *Winnie Estelle* goes on one-day charters through the cayes.

Sailing Fantasy, Ramon's Reef Resort, San Pedro. Tel: 02-62439. Catamaran trips and rental.

Sea Kayaking And River Trips

Eco-Summer Expeditions, 1516 Duranleau Street, Vancouver, BC V6H 3S4, Canada. Tel: (604) 669 7741; fax: (604) 669 3244. Also includes river running, rainforest exploration and horseback riding on one-, two- or three-week trips.

Jungle River Tours, 20 Lovers Lane, Orange Walk Town. Tel: 03-22293; fax: 03-22201.

River Haven, ABM Ltd, Po Box 78, Belize City, Tel: 02-31221; fax 02-32742. Inland tropical water-trips on houseboats. One day to several weeks. Captain's training course inclusive.

Mountain Biking

Mountain Bike and Raft Tours, Red Rooster Bar & Grill, 2 Far West Street, San Ignacio. Tel: 09-23016; fax: 09-22057. Mountain bikes (21-speed) can be rented at Mountain Pine Ridge biking. Rafting in Class 1 and 2 rapids. Land tours to Tikal.

Horseback riding

Mountain Equestrian Trails, 8 Mi. Mountain Pine Ridge Ridge Road, Central Farm Post Office. Tel: 08-23180; fax: 08-23235. Reservations are required for the multitude of horseback riding trips and trail rides on offer .

FURTHER READING

General Information

Belize: A Natural Destination, by R. Mahle and S. Wotkyns. John Muir Publications, New Mexico, 1993. A good introduction to Belizean wildlife and natural history.

Inside Belize, by T. Barry. The Inter-Hemispheric Education Resource Center, 1992. A good run-down of society and politics.

Profile of Belize 1990, by Society for the Promotion of Education and Research, Belize City. Cubola Publications/Spear Press. Good for facts and figures.

History

The Baymen of Belize, by S. Forbes (compiled by S. Fairweather). The classic account of the Battle of St George's Caye by a participant, not a bad read. Gives a good idea of life at the end of the 18th century.

The Baymen's Legacy: A Portrait of Belize City, by Byron Foster. Cubola Publications, 1987. A vivid, if scattered, account of the troubled city.

Environmental Concerns

Advances in Environmental and Biogeographical Research in Belize, by P. Furley. University of Edinburgh, 1989. Heavy going for the uninitiated, but a gold mine if you're serious.

A Belize Rainforest: The Community Baboon Sanctuary, by Horwich and Lyon. Orang-utan Press. Everything you wanted to know about howler monkeys and much, much more.

Ecology and Environment in Belize, by D.M. Munroe. Occasional Publication No. 12, University of Edinburgh, 1989. A rundown of the scientific facts and figures.

Mayan Heritage

The Invisible Maya: Population History and Archaeology at Santa Rita Corozal Precolumbian Population History in the Maya Lowlands, by D.Z. Chase. University of New Mexico Press, 1990. For the serious student.

The Maya, by Michael D. Coe. Thames and Hudson, London, 1980.

Tikal, A Handbook of the Ancient Maya Ruins, by William R. Coe. University Museum of the University of Pennsylvania, Philadelphia, 1967.

The Popul Vuh (various translations available). The Mayans' sacred text.

Maya Ruins in Central America in Color: Tikal, Copán and Quiriguá, by William M. Ferguson. University of New Mexico Press, Albuquerque, 1984.

Warlords and Maize Men, by B. Foster. Cubola Publications, 1989. An easy-to-read introduction to the major Mayan sites in Belize.

Archaeology at Cerros, Belize, Central America, by V. Scarborough. Southern Methodist Press, 1991. The latest on Cerros.

The Blood of Kings: Ritual and Dynasty in Maya Art, by Linda Schele and Mary Ellen Miller. George Braziller Inc., New York, 1986.

Chapter 3: Mesoamerica in The Ancient Americas: Art from Sacred Landscapes, Edited by Richard F. Townsend. The Art Institute of Chicago, Chicago, 1992.

Time Among the Maya, by Ronald Wright. Weidenfeld & Nicholson, 1989. An entertaining and informative account of the author's journeys around Central America, with insights into the Mayan cultures and history.

Wildlife

Birds of North America, National Geographic

Fishwatchers' Guide to West Atlantic Coral Reefs by C.C.G. Chaplin. Harrowood Books, Valley Forge, Pennsylvania, USA. Comprehensive guide to the fish of the Caribbean.

Birds of Central America and Mexico, by Irby L Davis.

Jungle Walk, by Kate Stevens. Comprehensive listings and illustrations of all the birds and animals of Belize. Available in shops and hotels in Belize.

Checklist of the Birds of Belize, by Wood, Leberman and Weyer. Pittsburgh: Carnegie Museum of Natural History Special Publication. Essential reading for the bird-watcher.

Coral Reef

Guide to the Coral and Fishes of Florida, the Bahamas and the Caribbean by J. Greenberg. Seahawk Press, Miami, USA.

Peterson Guide to Coral Reefs by Eugene Kaplan. Overview of coral, fish and underwater animals.

The Field Guide to Ambergris Caye, Belize by R.L. Woods, S.T. Reid and A.M. Reid. A thorough exploration of the coast and coral.

Plants

Orchids of Guatemala and Belize by O. Ames and D.S. Correll. Dover Publications, New York, 1985.

Fruits and Vegetables of the Caribbean by M.J. Bourne, G.W. Lennox and S.A. Seddon. Macmillan, 1988.

Tropical Trees Found in the Caribbean, South America, Central America and Mexico by Dorothy and Bon Hargreaves.

Collins Guide to Tropical Plants by Wilhelm Loetschert and Gerhard Beese. Collins, 1981. A well-illustrated guide to tropical plants.

Language

Creole Proverbs of Belize. Cubola Publications, 1987. The often hilarious and poetic everyday sayings of Creole Belizeans, gathered by Dr Colville Young.

OTHER INSIGHT GUIDES

Among the 185 titles in the *Insight Guides* series, the books which highlight destinations in this region include: *Insight Guides* to *Costa Rica, The Caribbean, Jamaica,* and *Trinidad and Tobago.*

In the *Insight Pocket Guide* series, *Yucatán* provides carefully timed itineraries designed to appeal to the short-stay visitor.

ART/PHOTO CREDITS

INDEX

T

U–V

W–Y